TEACH FOR CLIMATE JUSTICE

TEACH FOR CLIMATE JUSTICE

A VISION FOR TRANSFORMING EDUCATION

Tom Roderick

HARVARD EDUCATION PRESS
CAMBRIDGE, MA

Paperback ISBN 978-1-68253-807-4

Library of Congress Cataloging-in-Publication Data is on file.

Published by Harvard Education Press,
an imprint of the Harvard Education Publishing Group

Harvard Education Press
8 Story Street
Cambridge, MA 02138

Cover Design: Ciano Design
Cover Image: Alistair Berg/DigitalVision via Getty Images
The typefaces in this book are Latienne and Agenda.

For Magdalena and Simeon

CONTENTS

INTRODUCTION

JASMINE LOCKE TEACHES literature and composition with ninth and eleventh graders at Westview High School in Beaverton, Oregon. She begins her classes with a check-in: How is your heart today? What do you need from the community today? "The climate crisis comes up when there's been a climate disaster, or they hear some bad news about climate on the news," she says. "They want to talk about it. It's weighing on them. What concerns me most is that they're increasingly expressing a lack of trust in adults—not just government officials but all adults. They seem to be saying, 'It's our future. Does anybody care?' "

Jasmine cares. The teachers featured in this book care. The great majority of teachers across the country care—and care deeply—despite the challenging conditions in schools that make it hard to express our caring as fully as we would like to.

Teach for Climate Justice is a call to action—an urgent plea for educators everywhere to rise up and demand the time and resources needed to express our caring by addressing our students' true needs, which include radical, transformative education for climate justice.

The book highlights the work of outstanding climate justice educators and invites all educators to join them in the adventure they have undertaken. They are participating in a global movement to save the environment for future generations, to usher in a new era of climate justice, and to transform the dominant mind-set that sees our fragile environment as a field for unlimited exploitation into one based on humility and respectful reciprocity with nature. Writer, philosopher, and longtime environmental activist Joanna Macy calls this the "Great Turning."[1]

These educators are contributing to the Great Turning by doing what their profession calls them to do: They are providing great education attuned to their students' needs and the needs of humanity during this time of environmental crisis. Global warming, species extinction, and their impacts on human life and civilization will be the primary factors shaping the lives of the children and young people in school now and in the future. Our students will, in turn, be called to shape the world they are growing into: It has fallen to their generation to shoulder a major share of the responsibility for turning things around before it's too late. Yet, schools in general are paying little attention to this reality. When climate education is offered it is generally *about* climate change rather than *for* a habitable planet, *for* the transition from fossil fuels to sustainable sources of energy, and *for* climate justice.

No easy path lies ahead. The vision I propose asks educators to shoulder a big responsibility, while acknowledging that we are already pedaling as fast as we can, often uphill, to handle the responsibilities we already have. We can't pedal faster or add one more thing to an already overflowing basket on our bikes. Rather, we must reimagine the purpose of education and organize to demand the time and resources needed to focus on what's most important. This book does that reimagining and describes trailblazing work by outstanding educators who show the way. If you are already educating your students for climate justice, or if you aspire to do so, this book is for you.

Why climate *justice*? Because low-income people of color and Indigenous people across the globe have paid the highest price for a world economy based on fossil fuels. Although they are least responsible for the environmental crisis, they stand first in line to suffer the catastrophic consequences of global warming and environmental degradation. Rich nations, which have amassed wealth from extracting and depleting resources from colonized countries, have a moral obligation to share the wealth they have stolen to help those countries mitigate and adapt to the climate emergencies they are facing.

Why climate *justice*? Because in the United States, a disproportionately high number of low-income Black and brown people live in places where they breathe polluted air and drink contaminated water. "I can't breathe!" cried George Floyd twenty times before he died on May 25, 2020, on a Minneapolis, Minnesota, street. Too many Black and brown people in our country are having trouble breathing, even if they don't have a police officer's knee on their neck. All of us deserve to live in places where we can breathe clean air and drink clean water.

Why climate *justice*? Because large numbers of all races are suffering inequality in the richest country in the world.[2] Half of the people in the United States live paycheck to paycheck; forty million live in poverty; eighty-seven million have no health insurance or are underinsured; and half a million are homeless. Meanwhile, a 2017 *Forbes* magazine article noted that three people (Warren Buffett, Bill Gates, and Jeff Bezos) own more wealth than that owned by the entire bottom half of the nation.[3]

The voices of people of color in the United States and around the world must help shape the movement to sustain all life. The real needs of people of all races who are hurting must be acknowledged and addressed as we make the transition from fossil fuels to sustainable sources of energy. Only a broad-based, inclusive, and unified movement can bring about the transformational changes required to turn things around. The fight for the environment and the fight for justice are one.

Now and in the years ahead, our students need skills in understanding and managing the strong feelings the crisis evokes. They need what Parker Palmer calls "trustworthy relationships and tenacious communities of support" to weather hard times.[4] To make intelligent choices as participants in a democratic society, they need to know and appreciate nature. They need to understand that humans are part of nature and completely dependent on natural systems for survival. They will need to learn that an ever-expanding economy—a goal unthinkingly embraced by people across the political spectrum—is not compatible with a healthy environment. And they need to comprehend the implications of that reality.

They must understand the causes of the crisis (not only the science but the history, economics, and politics) so that they can think intelligently about solutions. They must understand the power of civil resistance: how large numbers of so-called ordinary people working together have achieved transformative changes to advance the cause of justice in the past—and can do so again. They must have adults whom they can look up to and who will take their concerns about the future seriously.

Above all, our students need to experience and practice *active hope*. Joanna Macy and Chris Johnstone envision active hope not as something we have, but as something we do.[5] During their time in school, students need opportunities to envision the world they *hope for* and work to create that world as their contribution to the Great Turning. They need to understand that at this critical moment in human history, we are all called to participate in a great adventure that will imbue our lives with meaning and purpose. They need to experience the joy of linking arms with others to achieve something *huge*. They need tools to take good care of themselves so that they can thrive and sustain their work for the long haul.

We can foster these strengths in the children and young people in our care. These exciting and perilous times call for an expansive vision of education—an education worthy of our students' dreams and of the opportunities and responsibilities that have been thrust upon them.

Teach for Climate Justice is the first book to offer a comprehensive vision of what preK–12 education needs to be at this critical inflection point in human history. It is not a curriculum. It presents a vision to guide teaching, learning, and curriculum development. Grounded in great teaching and interdisciplinary learning from classrooms around the country, the book describes teaching strategies and examples of best practice and provides a bibliography and links to resources for the classroom and school. This book invites educators to undertake a risky and exciting journey to make this vision their own and unleash their creative energies, offering their gifts of active hope while creating the conditions for students to offer theirs.

The vision has eight dimensions, each described in a chapter of the book, as follows:

- Build the Beloved Community: Strong Hearts United for Climate Justice
- Cultivate Love and Understanding of Nature
- Educate for Deep Understanding of the Climate Crisis
- Practice Active Hope: Envision a Just and Sustainable Future
- Teach for Civil Resistance: The Power of Grassroots Movements to Effect Transformational Change
- Support Students to Act for Climate Justice
- Engage the Whole School—and Beyond
- Go Forth with Heart, Joy, and a Fighting Spirit

Where does this vision come from? What is the basis for it?

I came to education through the civil rights movement in the sixties. I have a master's in education from Bank Street College of Education, and I taught elementary school for nine years—two years teaching third grade at Public School 92 in Harlem and seven years as teacher-director of a parent-controlled storefront school in East Harlem. For thirty-six years I served as executive director of Morningside Center for Teaching Social Responsibility, founded in 1982 as Educators for Social Responsibility Metropolitan Area by educators concerned about the danger of nuclear war. Over the years, I led Morningside Center to become a national leader in partnering with schools to develop high-quality, research-based programs in social and emotional learning (SEL), restorative practices, and racial equity. My expertise also includes community building, program and curriculum development, professional development of educators, and leadership support for school transformation.

Notice that I do not include climate activism or climate education in the areas of expertise I developed while at Morningside Center. The climate crisis was not a major focus of our work during my tenure. I've done my best to fill that gap during the past three years.

When I retired from Morningside Center at the end of 2018, I had two thoughts about how I might spend my time (in addition to playing with the grandchildren). I would join the climate movement, and I would consider whether to write a book to share what I had learned from my work of educating for racial equity and social responsibility.

An admirer of our work at Morningside Center introduced me to Nancy Walser, then acquisitions editor at Harvard Education Press. We had a conversation or two and I realized that the two goals were compatible. I could write a book to share my thinking about what education should be in a time of climate crisis and draw on my past work as it seemed relevant. Nancy liked the idea. So began the process of writing this book. A year and three months of that time was a back and forth between Nancy and me, as she helped me shape the book and clarify its purpose as an argument book, not a how-to. A shout-out to Nancy for believing in me and the book and for being so patient!

Writing the book has been an adventure, much more about looking forward and learning than about drawing from the past. Witness the books in the resource section of the appendix, nearly all of which I read and studied. Every chapter addresses a huge topic that required a good amount of reading, research, thinking, and interviewing. Shaping all that into a relatively short chapter was daunting—and without exception, this process drew me into a wrestling match. That's the best image I can think of to describe it. Fortunately, it was as rewarding as it was challenging. I hope you have as much fun reading these chapters as I've had in wrestling with them.

I acknowledge the audacity of this project. I'm arguing that the primary purpose of education at this turning point in human history must be to nurture a generation of courageous, intelligent, and wise nonviolent fighters for climate justice.

In discussing the dimensions of the vision, I specify the skills, understanding, and values our students need to develop during their fourteen years in school to become fighters for climate justice. The outstanding educators featured in this book ground the vision by sharing stories of how they nurture those strengths in their students.

My hope is that this book expands your sense of what is necessary and what is possible and that it provides ideas, tools, and inspiration to help you live the vision in a spirit of adventure, gratitude, and celebration.

Adventure, gratitude, and celebration? How are they possible with so much suffering going on in the world and so many heart-breaking and infuriating things occurring daily? A key message of this book is that we must face these realities, feel our heartbreak, grieve our losses, acknowledge our anger—and still say *Yes!* to life.

Sophie Schwadron, one of the teachers featured in this book, says that she takes strength every day from her work to make her kindergarten classroom a microcosm of the world she hopes for. Creating the world we hope for in our classrooms and schools can be grounds for gratitude and celebration on a daily basis. To prevent us from burning out as we offer our gifts of active hope, we also need social and emotional skills and support from family, friends, colleagues, and teachers. That's why fostering SEL and building equitable school and classroom communities are the foundations for my vision of effective climate justice education and the topic of the first chapter of this book.

Read on and enjoy!

Please wrestle with this book, as I have wrestled with the knowledge, ideas, strategies, and stories in writing it. Here are some questions you might ask yourself during and after each chapter:

PAUSE AND REFLECT

- What are the points here that you agree with?
- What would you like to argue with?
- What, if anything, inspires you to take some kind of action?
- What questions come up for you? What would you like to ponder or learn more about?

GO DEEPER

- Engage a friend or colleague as a listening partner for sharing thoughts and feelings.
- Start a study group based on the book.
- Try strategies and activities the book suggests and discuss your experience with a partner.
- Begin a journal, if you don't do journaling already, to note thoughts and feelings that arise as you read the book and develop your work as a climate educator.
- Ask yourself: What do I most hope *for* the world? In your journal, jot down your first thoughts, whatever comes to mind. Do this often and see what develops.

CHAPTER 1

Build the Beloved Community: Strong Hearts United for Climate Justice

DR. MARTIN LUTHER KING JR. dreamed of a beloved community in which all people are valued, respected, and treated with dignity. In "Paul Robeson," by Gwendolyn Brooks, the poet has the great African-American singer and activist "Warning in music-words/ devout and large,/that we are each other's/harvest; we are each other's/business;/we are each other's magnitude and bond." A beloved community is a place where people take responsibility for each other's thriving; live the truth that "we are each other's harvest"; and do their best to create rich harvests all around.

The climate crisis calls on educators to embrace this lofty and inspiring dream. What better foundation for climate justice education than the experience of living and working in a community engaged in restoring connections among people of different racial, class, and cultural backgrounds; in ending racism and all forms of oppression; and in living the truth that we are each other's harvest!

School can be a microcosm of what we hope for the world. As educators, we are privileged to have the opportunity to create and live such a gift daily in our work. But how?

The first meeting of the Student Climate Club at the Math and Science Exploratory School, a public middle school in Brooklyn, drew some twenty-five students, a much greater turnout than expected.

Teacher Cheryl Grau opened the meeting by asking, "Why did you come?"

The students' replies, echoed around the circle, were "I want to live."

"I want you to live, too," Cheryl told them. "I hope we can turn this situation around, and I'm going work with you and support you so that we can do our part to make that happen."

Increasingly, climate anxiety and despair are affecting our young people. A 2022 Ed Week Research Center Survey found that 37 percent of teenagers feel anxious when they think about climate change and its effects and more than a third feel afraid. Many also said they feel helpless and overwhelmed.[1] As climate activist Greta Thunberg has said, her generation is grieving over the threat to their future and is enraged at adults for standing by while the house burns.

The climate crisis affects the mental health of adults as well, especially those charged with parenting and educating the young. Reflects Cheryl:

> I have a big sense of urgency about the climate crisis. If you're informed and you stay informed, you're going to be overwhelmed by anxiety. Or you put your head in the sand, you put on blinders and go about your business. But when you have children sitting in front of you and you understand what condition we're in, you have to take action. These kids know. They know, and it feels like a real betrayal not to join them in every way we can. To have them look you in the eyes and say, "We want to live," and they know it's the truth and I know it's the truth, it's a staggering responsibility.

As educators, we are all too aware of the challenges many of our students face. We see young people who are living in poverty; who have been separated from parents by death, incarceration, and opioid addiction; who have witnessed or experienced racism and violence; who are suffering from abuse; who are considering suicide; and who are under stress from trying to keep up with their peers on social media. The COVID-19 pandemic has cast racial, gender, and class inequities into sharp relief and exacerbated them, with people of color disproportionally dying from the virus. Whether directly through climate disasters or indirectly through news reports, adult conversation, and science classes, the climate crisis will increase the pressure and anxiety many young people are experiencing—and the challenges this presents to us as educators.

Action is an antidote to worry and despair, as Cheryl and her students acknowledge. It's also critical that schools be places where students feel comfortable sharing their feelings, where they have trusting relationships with people who care about them, where they belong to a community that has their back as they try to make sense of what is going on in the world, where they develop racial and cultural awareness and skills in standing up for justice, and where they can find joy in linking arms with others in the fight for climate justice.

Schools must nurture educators as well. They must be places that strengthen our hearts and support us as we offer our gifts of active hope to our students. This chapter offers a powerful, evidence-based strategy and best practices for transforming our schools into "beloved communities" as the foundation for climate justice education. The components of the strategy, each described in a section of this chapter, are as follows:

- engage the school community in selecting and implementing a high-quality social and emotional learning (SEL) program
- develop the social and emotional skills of students and school staff

- create brave spaces for sharing feelings and strengthening relationships
- cultivate a racial equity mind-set
- institute antiracist policies and practices
- support and engage parents and caregivers
- foster student leadership
- encourage and support self-care

ENGAGE THE SCHOOL COMMUNITY IN SELECTING AN SEL PROGRAM

Social and emotional learning is the process by which we develop our capacity to understand and manage our feelings, relate well to others, deal well with conflict and other life challenges, make good decisions, and take responsibility for improving our communities—from the classroom to the world.

The principal establishes an SEL leadership team representative of the faculty and including parent and student representatives. The role of the group is to assess the social and emotional strengths and needs of the school community, review available research-based programs, choose one that addresses the school's needs, guide its implementation, monitor its effectiveness, and oversee its ongoing development. Since the program will aim to address a crucial need and will require staff training and class time, it's critical that the school community as a whole participate in the decision-making process. The Collaborative for Academic, Social, and Emotional Learning (CASEL) has been instrumental in establishing SEL as a respected field of educational practice with a strong research base. In the search for an effective program, CASEL's list of SELect programs is a good place to start.

In this chapter, I draw from Morningside Center for Teaching Social Responsibility's conception of SEL because it's high-quality, research-based, and strongly aligned with climate justice. Having shaped it, I am also intimately familiar with how it works.

DEVELOP THE SOCIAL AND EMOTIONAL SKILLS OF STUDENTS AND SCHOOL STAFF

For the culminating project of their multidisciplinary course on climate justice, seniors at the Washington Heights Expeditionary Learning School in New York City (known as WHEELS) worked in groups of four to choose a climate justice issue and create a seven-minute video. One student, introducing his group's video, said that the students had disagreed over which issue to focus on. One favored pollution; another, garbage and littering; and a third, drug addiction. "Through good listening and negotiation," he stated proudly, "we were able to solve our conflict with a win-win-win agreement." They decided to address all three—a decision that forced them to explore connections among these three major problems in the neighborhood.

Their neighborhood in the Washington Heights section of Manhattan is surrounded by highways that pollute the air and lead to high rates of asthma. A large neighborhood park is full of trees, but it's strewn with garbage, including needles from drug users. As a result, people don't use the park to enjoy its potential beauty and clean-air benefits. Because the park is underused, it's unsafe as well. The student-created video called for the school community to join volunteer efforts to clean up the park and to support neighborhood demands that the city improve park maintenance.

The students not only produced a call-to-action video for the school and wider community; by sharing the role that listening and negotiation played in their accomplishment, they demonstrated the power of SEL as an essential body of knowledge and skill for climate justice activists. Founded in 1982 by educators concerned about the danger of nuclear war, Morningside Center for Teaching Social Responsibility (originally called Educators for Social Responsibility Metro Area) started out organizing educators to advocate for a nuclear freeze and for educating a generation of young people in peacemaking. It was clear to us from the beginning that peacemaking had to be based on fairness and justice.

Our first major program and curriculum, *Resolving Conflict Creatively*, aimed to educate young people in the skills of peacemaking and conflict resolution.[2] Mahatma Gandhi was one source of our inspiration. We agreed with his belief that to achieve real peace in the world, we would have to begin with the children. And we shared with Martin Luther King Jr. and others the conviction that peace is not only the absence of war; it is the presence of active justice. Although Morningside Center now describes its work as fostering SEL and equity, our initial purpose has not changed. It is to educate for a world of peace with justice. The skills that Morningside Center teaches aim to serve that end and have remained constant over the years. They are as follows:

- create a vision of the community we hope for in our classroom and school
- understand and manage feelings
- listen actively
- be assertive (strong, but not mean)
- solve problems creatively and nonviolently
- stand up for justice
- make a difference

These skills are essential for young people to learn as they grapple with climate change—and the dislocation, anxiety, and conflict it generates. SEL builds our capacity both to weather the emotional challenges created by the crisis and to work together effectively to respond to it.

Whether we call it SEL, peacemaking, justice-seeking, or conflict resolution, this is a body of knowledge, ideas, and skills that needs to be learned, practiced, and applied in an ongoing process of growth. This is not to imply that students and adults come to SEL as blank slates. From the time we're born, we're taking in messages about how to handle feelings, relate to others, and deal with conflict. The fields of peacemaking, conflict resolution, and SEL seek to assemble and share wisdom and know-how, gleaned over many years from many sources, and share it so that people can use it to build on their strengths and, in some cases, change behaviors and ways of thinking that are not serving themselves or others well.

We foster these values, skills, and ways of thinking in our students through instruction in a research-validated curriculum. Best practice in SEL instruction for students can be summed up in the acronym RISE (regular, interactive, skills-based, and explicit): regular, because it takes practice to learn these skills; interactive, because to learn how to relate well to others, you have to interact with them; skills-based, because skills are as critical for social and emotional competence as they are for learning to read or play basketball; and explicit, because this work is so important that you need to give it focus by naming it and making it a priority.

Teachers need strong support to teach SEL curricula. Best practice is twenty-five to thirty hours of training and additional classroom coaching to support them as they teach the curriculum on a regular basis. The training is as much about developing teachers' own social and emotional competence as it is about introducing them to the curriculum. It gives teachers the opportunity to practice on an adult level the skills they will be teaching and enables them to run through practice lessons with their colleagues. To foster SEL in young people, the adults must be on a journey to improve their own social and emotional skills. All of us can benefit from lifelong learning in this area. Boosting educators' skills not only prepares them to teach the curriculum but also gives them tools to improve their relationships with students and colleagues.

Although the skill areas are consistent across the grades from preK to 12, the sophistication of the skills and the situations they address are tailored to the developmental needs and capabilities of the students. Each skill can support us as we navigate the climate crisis and work for climate justice.

Create a Vision of the Community We Hope For

In this skill area, students and teacher reflect on what they value in their relationships with other people and share their hopes for their classroom or circle group: How do I want to be treated? How will I treat others? Together, students and teacher make community agreements. Instead of taking their classroom for granted as a place where the teacher alone lays down the rules, they identify what they hope for and begin to make it a reality, with everyone taking responsibility. This is a first step in enabling students and teacher to create a supportive community and envision together the future they would like to see. It's an exercise in active hope.

Understand and Manage Feelings

Students learn that we all have feelings, and they expand their feelings vocabularies. They notice that feelings come and go and learn ways to take charge so that their feelings work for them rather than against them. For example, they learn that they can have feelings without acting on them in the heat of the moment. They can share a feeling with a friend or an adult, write about it in a journal, or shift their attention to something they're grateful for. They can take deep breaths or take a walk around the block to cool down when angry, enabling them to think more clearly about how to deal with the anger trigger. Teachers find these techniques extremely useful as well. Social activists throughout history have channeled their anger into constructive action for justice. As we cope with the climate crisis, and as we educate and fight for climate justice, we will face plenty of occasions for anger and disappointment. We must also cherish and celebrate moments of triumph and connection. Skills in managing this roller coaster of feelings are critical tools that we need as we and our students offer our gifts of active hope and sustain them for the long haul.

Listen Actively

To listen actively is to listen in a way that encourages the other person to talk. Students and teachers learn the importance of body language to send the message that they care about the speaker and are interested in what they have to say. They practice skills in paraphrasing to check their understanding of what the speaker is trying to communicate, in acknowledging and reflecting feelings the speaker is expressing, and in gentle questioning to show interest without prying. They get plenty of practice in their SEL classes as they listen to each other in pair-shares and go-rounds. Good listening is the foundation for building friendships and work relationships, for racial and cultural understanding, and for good leadership. Good listening is especially critical for climate justice because it is key in building the trusting relationships we need in challenging times. For adults, good listening is essential in building supportive relationships with students and in being fully present when students share feelings and concerns.

Be Assertive

Students and teachers learn that when they find themselves in a situation that is unfair, annoying, or not meeting their needs, they have several options: they can give in; they can be aggressive (mean); or they can be assertive, which is being strong while acting with respect for the other person. Of course, at times, it's smartest to give in, and at other times, you may have to be aggressive. The aim is to expand students' and adults' assertive options. For instance, students or adults can work in pairs to practice natural assertive messages (saying clearly and firmly what they want). They can practice creating and using "I-feel messages" in conflicts with friends or family members—rather than using "you messages" that judge and blame the other person.

This skill enhances one's comfort and effectiveness in standing up to unfair treatment of oneself and others.

Solve Problems Creatively and Nonviolently

Problem-solving skills can be used to address classroom problems and problems among friends. In Morningside Center's curricula, students explore the concept of conflict, learning that conflict is part of life. Conflict can lead to violence, but it doesn't have to, especially if people are skilled in conflict resolution. Students learn about conflict escalation—how to avoid it and how to jump off the escalator if they find themselves on it. They learn to see conflict not as a crisis or a failure but as a problem to be solved. They learn and practice skills in negotiation and mediation. Like the WHEELS students working on their climate justice video, they learn that conflicts can sometimes be solved so that everybody wins. They also learn and practice the ABCDE problem-solving method: Ask, what is the problem? Brainstorm solutions. Choose one. Do it. Evaluate how it works.

Stand Up for Justice

Students share their cultural backgrounds: What has been great about being who they are? What has been challenging? They learn to identify prejudice, stereotypes, discrimination (defined as action based on prejudice), and oppression (systemic mistreatment of people based on their group identity). They learn the terms for the forms that discrimination and oppression take, including racism, sexism, classism, anti-Semitism, Islamophobia, anti-LGBTQ oppression, and adultism. Through role-plays, skits, and activities, students and teachers learn and practice assertive strategies to stand up for fair treatment of all people—within their school and in the wide world. The relevance for climate justice is clear. When students reflect on their racial, gender, and cultural identities and listen to their classmates share theirs, those concepts are no longer abstract, but rather become concrete and personal. The imperative to identify mistreatment and stand up to it lays the groundwork for understanding how oppression has played out on the global stage in the history, economics, and politics of fossil-fuel extraction and burning. These school-based activities across the grades foster the values of understanding, respect, and fairness on a personal level and establish an age-appropriate foundation for understanding oppression on societal and global levels in the higher grades.

Supporting teachers to teach these skills lays a foundation for culturally responsive teaching and other antiracist policies and practices and is a critical step in building the "beloved community." In the training, educators share their cultural backgrounds, acknowledge and explore the realities of discrimination and oppression in our society, and learn strategies to prevent discrimination and oppression from occurring in their classrooms.

Make a Difference

Students and teachers learn stories of courageous people who are fighting for justice and the environment or who did so in the past. Students identify the strengths of these people, the challenges they faced or are facing, and what they have achieved.

We invite students and teachers to remember times when they made a difference for others in ways large or small. They identify the qualities they have that enabled them to make a difference. They reflect on other positive qualities they would like to develop and get support for developing those qualities. They envision something they hope for their family, their classroom, their school, their neighborhood, or the world, and they identify a concrete step they can take to make that hope a reality.

They also take part in a classroom exercise or project that requires them to cooperate with others to achieve a goal. Reflecting on the experience afterward, they identify skills and behavior that helped or hindered their efforts to work with others to get things done. The climate justice films that WHEELS seniors created are examples of such a project. The students readily acknowledged that to make their films, they had to exercise skills in cooperation, including all of the social and emotional skills discussed thus far.

CREATE BRAVE SPACES

It is standardized-testing time and students are stressed. Morningside Center staff developer Marieke van Woerkom opens an SEL Circle for a group of sixth graders with a mindful moment: Students listen to relaxing music while closing their eyes or viewing a fall scene on the smart board.

"As you listen to the music," she says, "breathe calmly and try to check in with yourself and how you're feeling." After the music fades and she turns on the lights, Marieke sends the Talking Piece around so that students can share their feelings about the experience. Some say they felt relaxed and peaceful; others say they felt uncomfortable.

Then one student says, "I'm tired of kids' commenting on my skin color. They call me Black," he says, "and not in a nice way!"

"What does that have to do with anything?" another student says, rolling his eyes.

Marieke explains that sometimes when we pause for a moment, important thoughts come into our minds. She sends the Talking Piece around again, inviting students to share what is on their minds. Around the Circle, students open up, sharing things that are bothering them. "I get teased for being a new kid in the school," says one. "We've got to be kinder to each other!" Several students agree and say it feels good to express their feelings. To close, Marieke sends the Talking Piece around for students to share one thing they can do to treat each other better.

One Circle won't solve this problem, of course, but students' sharing in the "brave space" provided by the Circle provides an opening to address the situation in depth in the future. A Circle such as this is relevant to climate justice education because it supports the effort to create a school that is a microcosm of what we want to see in the world: a place where all can thrive.

As teachers provide instruction for students in regular SEL classes, they are not just boosting students' social and emotional skills. Equally important, they are creating brave spaces for students to share feelings, concerns, and stories and to forge personal bonds with each other. This occurs naturally as students interact to learn and practice these skills.

At the elementary level, the format for SEL instruction is a weekly Workshop facilitated by the classroom teacher with the children usually sitting in a circle. The Workshop starts with a Gathering, a go-round in which students are asked to share something positive—that is, something new and good in their lives. Next is the Agenda Check, in which the teacher reviews a posted agenda for the lesson and invites the students' feedback. The Main Activities follow, such as an exercise to identify the behaviors of good and poor listening and an opportunity to practice good listening in pairs. Evaluation gives students a chance to share what they've learned from the lesson. The Closing ends the lesson on a positive note—for example, students might share in a go-round something they're looking forward to or, if time is short, join in a round of applause or give high fives around the circle.

The format Morningside has adopted for SEL lessons at the middle and high school levels is the Circle. Participants sit in chairs in a circle with no obstructions in the middle. On the floor in the center of the circle is the Centerpiece, an attractive piece of cloth or a circular piece of muslin that the students decorate. The Centerpiece symbolically holds the values of the Circle. The Circle begins with an Opening

Ceremony followed by the Main Activities and a Closing Ceremony. A Circle Keeper (the teacher or a trained and experienced student) facilitates the Circle. The Talking Piece is passed around the Circle in order, inviting each person to speak in response to a question or topic. The Keeper's responsibility is to build a metaphoric container in which honest sharing takes place.

The Circle directly addresses two crucial developmental needs of adolescents: belonging and voice. Circles foster strong bonding and give students a major role in shaping the process. Sitting in the Circle puts everyone on the same level. The Keeper doesn't lecture but acts as a facilitator for constructive dialogue. The students are not recipients but active participants. The best way to implement a Circles-based curriculum is through an advisory program that includes a forty-five- to sixty-minute Circle at least once a week throughout the school year.

In addition to facilitating SEL Workshops and Circles that become brave spaces for students, teachers enjoy brave spaces with colleagues by participating in SEL training sessions. The brave space develops naturally as teachers interact with each other to learn and practice the skills. Using what they learn in their training, teachers often help transform faculty meetings into brave spaces as well.

Some schools have instituted voluntary Circles to provide self-care for faculty. Often a teacher takes the initiative to organize this. The group might meet once a week before school starts. Participants choose a Keeper or have a different Keeper for each session. They might focus on sharing their thoughts and feelings about a book or article, or they might just share what's on their minds.

Whether for students or adults, the first session of a Circle or Workshop begins with participants creating community agreements to establish norms for the group. A crucial agreement is confidentiality: What is shared in the Circle stays in the Circle, while the skills learned and practiced spread out from the Circle to benefit the community.

These brave spaces provide ongoing support for students and adults and contribute to a positive school culture. They also serve the school community well in times of acute crisis. When upsetting events occur (climate disasters, mass shootings, dramatic instances of racial injustice), the school has routines and processes already in place to provide emotional support for faculty, students, and families and, when necessary, to mobilize the community for action.

CULTIVATE A RACIAL EQUITY MIND-SET

The next phase of creating the beloved community is to cultivate a racial equity mind-set throughout the school community. The purpose is to deepen understanding of racial equity among faculty, students, and parents and to instill a strong commitment to creating a truly equitable school.

The learning process to achieve this is led by the principal and the school's SEL leadership team. Having led an inclusive schoolwide process of selecting an SEL program and guiding its implementation, the principal and SEL leadership team now turn their attention to guiding the school community in exploring and coming to common understanding of key concepts, including racism, equity, and racial equity. The aim is to foster throughout the school community a racial equity mind-set: the conviction that although racism is not the only factor that diminishes the academic performance and life opportunities of Black and brown students, it is the primary factor—and the one most often dismissed and ignored.

Embracing the racial equity mind-set, educators realize that to address the needs of Black and brown students they need to understand how racism operates in their schools; to change the policies, practices, and behavior that are producing negative outcomes for Black and brown students; and to work together to create great schools where all students can thrive. The aim is racial equity, a state in which race is no longer the determining factor in students' school performance.

Because we cannot understand and eliminate racism unless we talk about it, educators need to have conversations about race. This is not easy. We live in a racialized society. We live with the history of white people having committed genocide against Indigenous people and having enslaved Black people for hundreds of years. But it is absolutely necessary to talk about racism if we're going to improve the well-being and school performance of Black and brown students. Fortunately, a school that has embraced SEL has a strong foundation to build on. Through training, coaching, and teaching an SEL curriculum to students, faculty have boosted their own social and emotional skills, strengthened their relationships with each other, and participated in brave spaces for sharing feelings.

In addition, wise guidance and educator-tested learning activities are available to support the SEL leadership team, including the work of Glenn Singleton, author of *Courageous Conversations about Race*.[3]

The principal and the SEL leadership team plan the learning process, which takes place in a series of monthly faculty meetings. Before engaging the faculty as a whole, the principal and leadership team have courageous conversations themselves, first experiencing the learning activities before introducing them to the full faculty.

Set the Stage

Once the principal and team are ready, the process of engaging the faculty might unfold as follows:

- The principal and the SEL leadership team members explain the purpose of the courageous conversations.

- It's about the students! The aim is to improve the well-being and academic performance of students by engaging faculty in an ongoing process of school improvement. The process will include analyzing data to identify school policies and practices that are producing negative outcomes, exploring root causes, introducing new approaches, and assessing their effectiveness.
- Other anticipated outcomes are to strengthen relationships among adults in the school community, strengthen relationships between adults and students, and increase the cohesiveness of the school community.

- The principal and the SEL leadership team members work with the faculty to create community agreements or add to an existing set of agreements. These agreements need to address the special challenges of talking about race, racism, and equity. For example, they might include such concepts as the following:
    - Experience discomfort. Discomfort is inevitable in conversations about race. It is through dialogue, even when uncomfortable, that change and healing can begin.
    - Expect and accept lack of closure. Don't rush for solutions. This process takes time.
    - Speak your truth. This means being open about your actual thoughts and feelings and not just saying what you think other people want to hear.
    - Stay engaged. Resist the temptation to exit even when it gets uncomfortable.
- The principal and the SEL leadership team members describe the "container" for these conversations as a brave space, not a safe space. It's a place to speak our truth, take some risks, feel discomfort, make mistakes. Growing up in a racist society, we've all taken in misinformation about other groups. This is not our fault; it's not an occasion for shame or blame. But it is incumbent upon us to take responsibility for setting things right by creating a truly

equitable school. Although we cannot guarantee a safe space, we can facilitate these conversations, and all our racial equity work, in a spirit of warmth, generosity, openness, and inclusion.

Dive in

Several learning activities have proved effective in generating great conversations. Faculty members can:

- read and discuss the poem "Invitation to Brave Space," by Beth Strano;[4]
- bring in artifacts representing their racial and cultural backgrounds and tell stories of the artifacts;
- tell the stories of their names;
- explore the definitions of key words: race, racism, equity, and whiteness;
- listen to a panel of faculty members of diverse racial and cultural backgrounds share their identities, values that were important in their families, and what has been both wonderful and challenging about being who they are (followed by pairing up to share feelings and thoughts);
- read short texts (e.g., by James Baldwin, Bettina Love, Ta-Nehisi Coates, bell hooks, Glenn Singleton, Audre Lorde) and discuss them in small groups;
- share racial autobiographies; and
- study the research on implicit bias, especially as it relates to teachers' interactions with students, and explore its implications for classroom practice.

INSTITUTE ANTIRACIST POLICIES AND PRACTICES

As we're deepening racial awareness, we also need to act by instituting antiracist policies and practices. Following are four such antiracist initiatives: restorative discipline, culturally responsive teaching, equitable classroom practices, and continuous school improvement for racial equity.

Restorative Discipline

Jason, a sixth grader, was continually disrupting Ms. Herman's class (names in this vignette have been changed). At the teacher's request, Morningside Center staff developer Daniel Coles convened a Restorative Conference in which Jason agreed to take part. Participants also included Jason's best friend, an eighth grader Jason invited to be his ally; a girl from the class whom Ms. Herman invited to join as her ally; and a teacher who joined to learn how a Restorative Conference works.

Daniel opened the conference by asking participants to share a story about a time they did something hard because it was the right thing to do, even though they really didn't want to do it. Daniel shared his story and started the Talking Piece around the Circle. It came first to the teachers, who, to Daniel's surprise, shared deeply personal stories. Then it was Jason's turn. He spoke about his parents separating and his father leaving and how painful that was.

"Now I'm the man of the house," he said, tears coming to his eyes. He pulled his sweatshirt up over his head and put his head down on the table. Jason's friend, who was sitting next to him, reached over and put his arm around Jason's shoulders to comfort him.

When it was her turn, the girl (taking part as Ms. Herman's ally), turned to Jason and said, "Jason, I connect so much with what you're saying." After describing some of the challenges she was having at home, she continued, "Jason, we all know that you've been off-task and disruptive. You've made it hard for Ms. Herman to teach and for the class to learn. But I know what you're going through, and I'd like to help." She offered to be someone he could talk to when he was upset.

The conference proceeded as participants explored the conflict between Jason and Ms. Herman. Both gained insight into the other's perspective. Both realized there were things they could do differently. "But the most important outcome," observes Daniel, "was that Ms. Herman understood what Jason was going through and saw him as a child she now felt compelled to support. Feeling heard and supported, Jason was now motivated to change his behavior as well."

Daniel recalls:

> On my subsequent visits to the school, Ms. Herman would often make a point of bringing Jason by just to say hello to me. He felt a lot of support both from the adults and from the two students in the conference. While Jason and Ms. Herman continued to have some challenges, their relationship shifted. Now Ms. Herman spoke about how much progress Jason was making both academically and socially. Also, the gym teacher, who was also the restorative practices teacher and a coach at the school, was able to connect Jason's story to his own story about his relationship with his father, and I was able to do the same. Jason saw that he was not alone in this challenge he was facing and the pain he was going through.

In this story, teacher and student pause and take the opportunity to reach across the barriers of race, gender, and age to listen, heal, and build their relationship rather than slide into a downward spiral of punishment and suspension. This exemplifies the transformation of heart, mind, and behavior that needs to occur as we work together to eliminate racism and heal our environment.

Restorative discipline is an essential pillar of an equitable school community. It is an explicitly antiracist school policy and practice. In *The New Jim Crow*, Michelle Alexander shows that punitive zero-tolerance discipline policies disproportionally target Black, brown, and LGBTQ youth, creating a school-to-prison pipeline that contributes to the plague of mass incarceration.[5]

By contrast, restorative discipline promotes belonging and responsibility, fosters SEL and equity, and provides a viable alternative to punitive approaches. A person who does harm is engaged in a process of understanding the full impact of the harm done and is held responsible for healing the harm to the extent possible. A restorative teacher, who replaces the traditional dean, meets privately with the wrongdoer(s), with those harmed, and with a staff member who represents the school community. With the consent of all parties, the restorative teacher facilitates a conference to explore the harm done and agree on steps to heal it. The conference is one among a range of restorative practices, which include negotiation and mediation for solving conflicts before harm is done, as well as restorative circles for fostering belonging and student voice. These are enormously helpful practices in both schools and in the organizations and movements we build.

Culturally Responsive Teaching

Research shows that teachers, having grown up in our racist society, tend to show bias against Black students and that bias against Black students exists among teachers of all races. Research also shows that having Black teachers can dramatically improve the academic success of Black students.[6] Teachers, however, are overwhelmingly white. In our public schools, 7 percent of teachers are Black and 82 percent are white, while 52 percent of the students are Black.[7]

Two interventions offer promise for addressing the realities revealed by this research: culturally responsive teaching and equitable classroom practices.

In *Culturally Responsive Teaching and the Brain*, Zaretta Hammond offers a powerful framework for lifting the teaching of Black and brown students to a new level of excellence.[8] Her framework,

"Ready for Rigor," is completely aligned with and builds upon SEL. The ultimate aim of Hammond's approach is to improve the skills of culturally and linguistically diverse students in the area of information processing. This is relevant to climate justice because it prepares students to grasp the complexities of climate science; to understand the politics, economics, and history that have shaped the crisis; and to connect the dots as the crisis unfolds before their eyes.

Equitable Classroom Practices

A Resource for Equitable Classroom Practices, 2010, created by the Equity Initiatives Unit of Montgomery County Public Schools, Maryland, describes twenty-seven specific practices to promote equity in the classroom.[9] Every day, a teacher has dozens of interactions with students. Chances are that our biases—in particular, biases against Black students—are subtly (or not so subtly) affecting our interactions in ways we are not aware of. Focused on student-teacher interactions, Montgomery County's equitable classroom practices are a great checklist to help teachers ensure that, at least in these twenty-seven ways, their interactions are promoting equity.

Continuous School Improvement for Racial Equity

A racially equitable school is a school that is always working hard to be racially equitable. The process will never be complete. Here are some steps to take along the way:

- Decide on areas to focus on—for example, academic performance and discipline.
- Gather data on aspects of these areas that stand out, such as graduation rates and suspensions.
- Identify racial disparities—for instance, Black students are suspended at a much higher rate than white students.

- Explore root causes of racial inequities and develop hypotheses for what the root causes are. This involves understanding the systems that are producing the negative outcomes and how they operate to do so.
- Devise strategies for addressing the root causes—that is, ways to change the systems.
- Implement these strategies.
- Gather data to see if the strategies are working.
- Based on the data, tweak and revise the strategies, or go back to the drawing board.

Of course, if you are already implementing antiracist policies and practices, such as the ones described in this chapter, this continuous improvement process should be adapted to assess how well they are working and how they might be improved.

See the appendix for resources on the science of school improvement, in particular, *Learning to Improve: How America's Schools Can Get Better at Getting Better* by Anthony S. Bryk et al.[10]

SUPPORT AND ENGAGE PARENTS AND CAREGIVERS

The Art of Parenting

Diane was in tears. She had just participated in an exercise facilitated by fifth graders as part of a workshop for parents at her child's elementary school. The students engaged the parents in "The Torn Heart," an activity they'd experienced in one of their weekly SEL lessons. They began by introducing the terms "put-up" and "put-down." Then, one of the fifth-grade facilitators told the story of Maria, a fifth grader who suffers put-downs at home and at school as she goes through her day. A construction-paper heart was taped to the storyteller's chest to represent Maria's heart. Every time Maria experienced a put-down in the story, the storyteller tore off a piece of Maria's construction-paper heart and let it fall to the floor.

Upon finishing the story, she asked the parents, "How do you think Maria is feeling?"

"Sad ... terrible ... like crying," the parents acknowledged.

"Fortunately, because this isn't real life," the storyteller explained, "we can retell the story to give Maria a better day by substituting put-ups for put-downs."

With a new heart on her chest, she told the story again, pausing just before the point where Maria had received a put-down in the first telling of the story so that a parent in the audience could provide a put-up. When the student finished the revised version of the story, the room fell silent, and then broke into applause.

"Turn and talk with a partner," the student facilitator said, "and share some feelings or thoughts that came up for you."

In the group report afterward, a tearful Diane shared that she felt terrible—that the exercise helped her see that out of frustration and anxiety she had fallen into a habit of putting her daughter down and that she was determined to stop it. She thanked the student facilitators and said she was glad they were learning about things like this in school.

Parenting can be a lonely, anxious, challenging endeavor. It's one of the most important jobs in the world, but it's undervalued, and parents receive little training or support. Schools that embrace SEL can support parents by providing workshops that bring parents together to have fun and socialize, build friendships, share the joys and challenges of parenting, and boost their social and emotional skills. The better those skills, the better equipped parents will be to support their children—and each other—as they confront the challenges of the climate crisis. Many of the practices and learning activities in this book can be easily adapted for parents.

Voice and Leadership

With full support from the principal, the parent members of the SEL leadership team join with other parent leaders to use monthly parent association meetings to keep parents informed about the progress and challenges of the SEL/racial equity work going on in the school. With help from faculty members and students, they engage parents in hands-on activities to give parents a feel for what their children are learning. When the school introduces something new—for example, a new measure regarding school safety, new pandemic protocols, changes in the school schedule to adapt to a nearby climate disaster, or a major change in discipline policy based on restorative practices—they ensure that parents get a full explanation of what's going on and why, that their questions and feedback are welcomed, and that plans are modified, if necessary, to address their concerns.

A well-informed and supportive parent body is essential to the success of serious efforts to address the true needs of students and families for racial and climate justice. As the climate crisis unfolds, a trusting relationship between the school, families, and community will be more important than ever—and social and emotional skills will help.

FOSTER STUDENT LEADERSHIP

Peer mediation programs are a natural extension of robust classroom instruction in SEL. They take SEL out of the classroom and into the lunchroom, the playground, and (at the high school level) the mediation room. They develop young people as school leaders who resolve conflicts among their peers peacefully, not through adult intervention, but with a little help from their friends.

Young students looked up to the peer mediators at Public School 24 in the Sunset Park section of New York City. "I want to be a mediator!" insisted Angel, a first grader.

"You aren't old enough yet," replied Emma Gonzalez, Morningside Center staff developer, who worked with the school for many years. "When you're in third grade, you'll have a chance to be a mediator."

"Well, can't I at least be a peace helper?"

Within a month, Public School 24 had a peace-helper program. Emma engaged seasoned peer mediators to train the younger students and worked with them and their teachers to set up peace corners in their classrooms where children could go if they were having a conflict or just wanted to cool down for a few minutes. If desired, the class's peace helpers were available to help.

Building on the peace-helper and peer-mediation programs at Public School 24, Emma introduced diversity panels as a next step for building SEL and equity into the school's culture. Drawing on students already serving as peer mediators, Emma gathered panels of four or five students, each representing a different kind of diversity, such as an English-language learner, a student with a disability, a Black student, a Muslim student, and a student who had recently immigrated to this country. In a classroom presentation, each panelist would speak about their culture or difference, stressing what they appreciate about themselves and their identity, and also sharing ways they had experienced mistreatment from other students because of these differences. After the panel presentation, a panelist would ask volunteers from the class to share something about their identity, including times they had experienced mistreatment. This would lead to a discussion about how students could make their school a place where everyone was consistently treated with respect.

Now students are increasingly creating climate clubs in their schools, as they did at Cheryl Grau's school (mentioned at the opening of this chapter). Fred (Mr.) Rogers famously shared what his mother told him to do when tragic events occur in the world. "Look for the helpers," she said. "You will always find people who are helping."[11] This is good advice! We are inspired by helpers just as Angel was inspired by his school's peer mediators. Part of creating an equitable school community is to support students' impulse to have voice and take leadership. Students can be trained to be Circle Keepers. A student advisory board can give students voice on school policy. Students can be peer mediators and peace helpers (for more on engaging students in action for climate justice and supporting their leadership, see chapter 5).

ENCOURAGE AND SUPPORT SELF-CARE

These days, self-care has come to mean "treat yourself" and often involves spending a lot of money. But Black, lesbian, feminist, activist writer Audre Lorde saw self-care differently. In her 1988 essay "A Burst of Light: Living with Cancer," she wrote, "Caring for myself is not self-indulgence. It is self-preservation, and that is an act of political warfare."[12]

Many forms of self-care support us in reconnecting with ourselves, our calling, our love for life, and our passion for justice. They help us tap the sources of energy that fuel the adventure of active hope we've undertaken. The price is right: no money changes hands. These practices can include meditation, breathing activities, stretching, dancing, deep listening to music, journal-writing, self-affirmation, or a gratitude practice.

Consider inviting students, faculty, or parents to share strategies they use to calm down and relax or find inspiration and new energy. Invite them to try out a range of strategies to find out what works best for them.

School leaders can also promote self-care in little ways—for example, by opening or closing meetings with brief activities that invite relaxation or expression of gratitude.

Implementing these best practices and teaching strategies will over time create a community—a brave and beloved space—where heart can peek out and reveal itself in countless loving interactions. The stories in this chapter capture some of those moments: Cheryl telling the students in the climate club, "I'm with you, we're in this together"; the student in Marieke's Circle having the courage to say he was tired of being called Black in a mean way—and getting support from his peers; Daniel providing the occasion for Jason and Ms. Herman to see, understand, and connect with each other; first-grade-student Angel achieving his dream of becoming a peace helper; and Diane gaining the awareness that put-downs were distancing her from her daughter.

Now, in our journey toward teaching for climate justice, we move from strengthening our positive connections with our fellow human beings to understanding and loving nature. The truth that "we are each other's harvest" applies quite literally to the relationship between humans and nature. In fact, we must welcome nature as an honored member of our beloved communities. Can we educate a generation of young people to know and understand this truth? Educators featured in the next chapter are showing the way.

CHAPTER 2

Cultivate Love and Understanding of Nature

A KEY DIMENSION of educating for climate justice is to foster love for nature, understanding of how nature sustains life, and action to restore the broken relationship between humans and the natural world.

This requires getting students outdoors to have direct experience with nature, because we can't love what we don't know. Too many of us, especially those of us growing up in cities, have little connection with nature. We take it for granted. Even people who live in the country may see nature more as a commodity than as a source of wonder to love and respect. To fight passionately for something, we need to know it, fall in love with it, and recognize its fragility. By cultivating students' love for the natural world, we increase their motivation to protect the environment from harm.

Lacking an understanding of nature, we may not realize that humans are part of nature and depend on natural systems for our very survival. We may forget that many of the resources that support human life on Earth (soil, forests, plankton, the atmosphere, to name a few) have limits that we are quickly approaching or have already exceeded. This ignorance goes hand in hand with the mind-set, deeply ingrained in our culture, that sees the Earth and its living beings as available for endless exploitation to serve the needs of relatively well-off people in industrial countries.

A major cultural shift is now gathering momentum, spurred by the climate crisis, to challenge that dominant mind-set and replace it with one based on love for the natural world, a relationship of reciprocity with all living beings, and justice for all people. This is at the heart of the Great Turning, described in the introduction, which is the aim of climate justice education.[1] As educators, we need to support this cultural shift by preparing a new generation to become stewards of the environment and fighters for climate justice.

In doing so, we build on the work described in chapter 1. The social and emotional skills, the brave spaces for sharing feelings, the active commitment to equity, and the restorative practices for building community and healing harm—these pillars of the beloved community prepare us to connect deeply with the natural world. They enable us to feel the full range of our emotions—from wonder and gratitude to sadness and grief, to love and determination to act. Chapter 1 was about striving to make the school a beloved community. Chapter 2 is about expanding the beloved community to embrace the entire natural world.

The teachers whose work is described in this chapter are cultivating love and understanding of nature in specific ways tailored to the developmental capacities of their students and the opportunities provided by their schools. What they all have in common is their ability to find various ways of immersing their students in nature. The chapter organizes teaching practices into four overlapping themes that together represent a vision of how to foster love and understanding of nature and action for environmental justice. These themes are as follows:

- Make it personal. Foster in students a positive emotional connection with nature.

- Make it local. Give students the opportunity to gain firsthand knowledge of nature in a particular place near where they live.
- Foster environmental stewardship. Engage students in acting to protect nature.
- Act for climate justice. Engage students in acting to ensure that all people have access to clean air, clean water, green spaces, and access to nature.

MAKE IT PERSONAL

In this section, you'll meet three teachers who love nature and share their enthusiasm with their students on a daily basis. They also strongly emphasize building community in their classrooms as a foundation for caring for nature. They engage students in experiencing nature with all five senses and slow things down to give students time to feel and to express those feelings in speaking, writing, art, singing, dancing, and role playing.

Liat Olenick

"Teaching science to young kids is teaching them to love—to love exploration and discovery, to love themselves as creative people, full of wonder and life, to love and care for plants and animals and by so doing come to know that our well-being is intertwined with theirs." That is how Liat Olenick sums up her philosophy of education.

A native New Yorker, Liat attributes her interest in nature and teaching to her grandmother whose home was full of flowers and who frequently took her on weekend visits to the Brooklyn Botanic Gardens and the Bronx Zoo. Early on, she came to care about plants and animals. As a youngster, she organized a stoop sale to raise money for the World Wildlife Fund.

As the science teacher for grades preK to 4 at a public elementary school in Brooklyn, Liat had her own room and classes came to her. "I try to create a magical, alive space that kids can walk into and feel special, curious, and engaged," she explains. "The room is full of plants and animals for kids to observe and take care of. There are five or six animals in the classroom at all times, including a tarantula, a bearded dragon, a turtle, hamsters, and various bugs like ladybugs and butterflies."

The room was arranged in a circle of tables, each named for an ecosystem. Kids did hands-on work at the tables with science and art materials, with Liat orchestrating their activities from the middle. The children also had access to a small fenced-in nature playground next to the schoolyard where there are trees, shrubs, and places to plant things. Liat took students on field trips to New York City treasures, such as the Bronx Zoo, the Brooklyn Botanic Gardens, Prospect Park, and the American Museum of Natural History.

Singing and team-building games reinforced the culture of the magical space, summed up in the following: "We take care of each other. We take care of living things. We take care of our classroom." Liat says, "Kids feeling joy and connection—that's my teaching priority because that's how they'll learn the best and because we need to see children as full human beings and they need to feel love and joy because that's how they're going to be their best selves. Teaching children to love themselves and love each other and love nature and living things—it's all the same thing because we're all connected."

Liat's curriculum across the grades focused on sensory experiences: touching plants and animals in the classroom, digging in the dirt and planting things in the nature playground, providing food and water to care for the animals, and taking walks around the neighborhood. And all the while, kids are noticing, observing, asking questions, and making connections. "I want them to understand that plants and animals grow and change just like they do," says Liat, "I want them to know that we have the power to take care of living things and I want to show them what that looks like."

Sophie Schwadron

When I interviewed Sophie Schwadron, she was teaching kindergarten at the Ben Murch Elementary School, a public school in Washington, D.C. (she now teaches preK). "Working with kids is absolutely draining," she acknowledges, "but spending all day with kids is basically the most fun thing there could be. Being with a group of kids in the classroom from August to June, we get to imagine the world we want to live in and then practice it—how we treat each other, how we treat nature, how we talk about our identities, how we address conflict, and how often we sing and dance and have fun. To me, that's the dream way to spend a day. It's really hard sometimes to have the energy for it, but it gives me hope every day."

The student population of her school is around six hundred students, composed of 57 percent white and 43 percent Black, Indigenous, or people of color. The school's early childhood teachers (preK and kindergarten) have adopted the Reggio Emilia approach, an educational philosophy that is student-centered and fosters experiential learning. (Reggio Emilia is the name of the town in Italy where the approach was developed in the post–World War II era.)

Sophie was turned off of science in high school and college. She thinks that this may have had to do with poor teaching, with associating science with physics and chemistry (which didn't interest her), and perhaps subconsciously with the idea that science was for men and not for women.

In any case, she loves science now. "Kids love space, kids love the earth, kids love animals," she observes. "When I began to see things through kids' eyes, it made me wonder more. I saw that science was about asking questions of real things. That's what changed it for me."

She has made understanding the natural world an integral part of her curriculum. When her school closed on March 14, 2020, she worked from home and taught virtually. Before the COVID-19 pandemic, she had plants and animals in the classroom, and her students learned by caring for them. She took her students on visits to a nearby roof garden associated with the University of the District of Columbia (UDC). They identified the flowers and vegetable plants growing there and learned about the benefits of urban roof gardens for birds, bees, and humans, including mitigating the sun's heat in the summer and providing insulation against cold in the winter. Using recycled materials, her students designed buildings with gardens on top and described the benefits. A nonprofit organization that plants trees around the city worked with fifth graders at her school to choose trees and decide where to plant them. Two of the trees were planted outside a window of Sophie's classroom. Her students named the trees Ricky and Cupcake and tracked them over the seasons. Last year, she and her students watched the live webcam that the National Arboretum in Washington, D.C., streams each year of the eagles returning to mate. Her students fell in love with the eagles, and she led them in an extended study involving books, videos, and art. Rachel Carson's book, *Silent Spring*, is credited with saving the eagles and other bird species from extinction by challenging and eventually eliminating the use of the pesticide DDT (dichlorodiphenyltrichloroethane), which was poisoning them.[2] Sophie read her students a children's book about Rachel Carson to show them that people can choose to spend their lives devoted to preserving and respecting the environment, including the eagles they had come to love.

Xochitl Bentley

"Sometimes, I think if I weren't a teacher, I'd be a full-time environmentalist," reflects Xochitl Bentley. "But then I realize that being a teacher gives me an important platform for connecting with this young generation of climate stewards."

When I interviewed her, Xochitl was teaching Advanced Placement English at a small charter school in the San Fernando Valley, Los Angeles County, north of the city of Los Angeles. More than 90 percent of the students are Latinx. "I'm a third-generation teacher," she says proudly. "It's great to grow up in a family that has always taught and has regarded teaching as the best thing you can do."

Starting out as a teacher who wanted to share her enthusiasm for reading and writing with her students, she is now equally devoted to fostering a love and understanding of nature. "I treasure my experiences with nature. I can find healing in reading a poem or taking a wonderful walk in the woods," she says. During the past year, she became a certified California naturalist. "I was really struggling with how I was feeling during the pandemic. I realized that being outside and replanting burnt areas of the Angeles National Forest was healing me in a way nothing else could," she explains.

The high school English language arts (ELA) curriculum is skills-based. Teachers have freedom to choose texts as long as they are developing the appropriate skills. In prepandemic times, Xochitl took her students into nature as part of honing their research skills. To learn about forest sustainability, they went on tours provided by TreePeople, a nonprofit organization. "The tours were actually hikes," says Xochitl. "The students loved it. Some said it was the first time they'd been on a hike. It was really exciting for them." During the pandemic, Xochitl was not able to take students on these hikes. So, when she went out to replant in burnt areas of the forest, she would interview people who work in the forest system and make videos of the interviews to show to her students.

Xochitl read *Braiding Sweetgrass* by Robin Wall Kimmerer and was deeply moved.[3] In her book, Kimmerer braids together Indigenous wisdom, science, and the teachings of plants. Inspired by the book, Xochitl decided to ask her students to write a braided essay. The essay would consist of three threads that would build on and speak to each other, the way *Braiding Sweetgrass* does. The essay would not be for an audience, but for each student personally. She introduced the students to three mentor texts, which have in common the theme of flight: "Joyas Voladoras," by Brian Doyle, a delightful essay about hummingbirds; "Victor," by Heather Swan, a poignant poem depicting bees struggling to fly while afflicted with a pesticide called "Victor," and "Musée des Beaux Arts" by W. H. Auden, which includes a reference to the tragic flight of Icarus that ends with a plunge into the sea.[4]

The students read and discussed the texts and shared the feelings that these writings evoked. Xochitl helped them identify what she calls "writing craft moves" that the authors used to enhance the effectiveness of their work. For example, repetition of "A hummingbird's heart" ("Joyas Voladoras") or ending with a question, "What war do we think/we're winning?" ("Victor"). Then students wrote braided essays with the following guidelines in mind: One of the threads should be personal and include details from memory. One should include factual information gleaned from research. Students should use at least three craft moves from the mentor texts they studied, and they should use connecting images, words, ideas, or events to get the narratives speaking to each other.

Explaining her thinking behind this exercise, Xochitl says, "I want my students to think about how a poem or essay makes them feel. I want them to use reading and writing to understand their own lives and the world around them. I want them to think about how environmental degradation (in this case, the decline in the honeybee population) makes them feel. That's why I chose the "Victor" poem. One of her students admitted, "Miss, when I think of a bee, I think of how it wants to sting me. I've never before had a positive feeling about a bee." Now her students were seeing bees in a new way, and they were also learning that these insects, which pollinate flowers and make honey, are endangered.

"It's not to create a sense of gloom and doom—I'm not into that," says Xochitl. "It's to increase awareness and promote a sense of responsibility." Poems are a wonderful way to bring nature into the classroom because many poems are so short that you can always make room for them in any curriculum. Xochitl is a fan of the poet Mary Oliver, who often wrote about nature.

In *The Sense of Wonder*, Rachel Carson wrote, "I sincerely believe that for the child ... it is not half so important to know as to feel. If facts are the seeds that later produce knowledge and wisdom, then the emotions and the impressions of the senses are the fertile soil in which the seeds must grow."[5] This makes sense. If we feel wonder, awe, excitement, and curiosity about nature, we're much more likely to pursue knowledge and understanding of nature, provided the information isn't presented in a way that deadens interest, as it was for young Sophie.

Carson explains that her experiences in nature with her young nephew caused her to conclude that the development of a child's sense of wonder required "the companionship of at least one adult who can share it, rediscovering with him the joy, excitement, and mystery of the world we live in."[6] Liat credits her grandmother with fostering her interest in nature.

Sometimes, it works the other way around. It was only seeing the world through the eyes of a child that awakened Sophie's sense of wonder, which had been dulled by schooling. Liat, Sophie, and Xochitl are providing the companionship of which Carson writes, evoking a sense of wonder in their students.

MAKE IT LOCAL

The two teachers featured in this section are in very different locations, one in New York City and the other in a small town in the Adirondack Mountains of New York State. Their schools allow them the freedom and provide the resources for them to immerse their students in rich multidisciplinary explorations of water in their local environment.

Megan Wellford

"I love exposing children to real-world issues and then coaching them toward action to solve them," says Megan Wellford. "My students and their a-ha! moments sustain me in this work. Whether the issues are local or global, it's vital to foster this sense of agency in young people. That process and the ever-increasing urgency of the climate crisis are what keep me going." Megan teaches fifth and sixth graders at Keene Central School (KCS), a public school in the Adirondack Mountains of New York State that serves some 170 students, grades preK to 12, about 40 percent of whom qualify for free lunch.

"On a basic level, I teach about climate because it is part of the sixth-grade curriculum at our school," she explains. "In actuality, I teach about climate change because it would be unfair not to. The issues surrounding climate change are intimately tied to my students' futures. They need to learn how to be critically engaged and how to advocate for the large-scale changes that are needed to solve the problems of climate change."

Megan and a third-grade teacher led their students in a year-long interdisciplinary experiential study of the Lake Champlain watershed in which they live and their school is located. Supporting the teachers' work was a year-long professional development program sponsored by the Lake Champlain Basin Program called "A Watershed for Every Classroom." Megan also took part in Shelburne Farms' Education for Sustainability programs in neighboring Vermont.

The study was entirely aligned with the mission of Keene Central School, which includes instilling a sense of place and a deep respect for the environment. The anticipated outcomes for students were to know, understand, and do. They would learn the geographical, geological, historical, ecological, and economic stories of their watershed. They would understand what the watershed is, why it's important, and what is needed to maintain its well-being. They would act as stewards of the watershed, sharing what they learned with their schoolmates and with the larger community, and acting on behalf of the watershed.

Working in multiage teams, students began by sharing stories of how they and their families interact with the watershed. Taking field trips to Beaver Pond, a fast-moving stream, and the Ausable River, all within walking distance of the school, they spent time in these three ecosystems observing and making "event maps" of the trees, plants, and animal life they saw. As the study unfolded, they hiked on Rattlesnake Mountain, a favorite tourist spot in the area. They visited Essex Farm to learn about sustainable agriculture. Studying maps, they followed the "Trip of the Drip"—the trajectory of a water droplet from a lake in Keene Valley to the Atlantic Ocean.

They took a ferry to the ECHO (Environment, Culture, History, and Opportunity) Lake Center, a self-described "seriously fun" science center that offers interactive investigations and immersive multimedia experiences. The students participated in Rock and Roll Geology, a program to explore twenty thousand years of geologic history in the Lake Champlain Basin. They visited the Chimney Point Historic Site to learn about the history of the Lake Champlain Basin, including the Indigenous people who had lived in the area for nine thousand years before Europeans arrived in 1609. They studied sources of pollution in the watershed and the impact of industries around the lake on the watershed's health. They participated in World Water Day, a United Nations observance day held on March 22 of each year since 1993. The aim of World Water Day is to promote the celebration of fresh water and raise awareness that some 2.2 billion people in the world do not have access to fresh water.

During the year, the classes made some twenty-five field trips and hosted a number of guest speakers. They shared their learnings in a Science Slam to which the community was invited. They created a quilt promoting ideas for protecting the watershed and featuring water-inspired poetry and illustrations by students. The quilt was then displayed in a prominent place in the school.

Jared Fox

Jared Fox teaches high school environmental science at Washington Heights Expeditionary Learning School (WHEELS), a preK–12 public school in upper Manhattan, New York. Expeditionary Learning Schools are based on the educational philosophy of the German educator Kurt Hahn, the founder of Outward Bound. Jared engages his students in project-based learning and in-depth case studies. Before the COVID-19 pandemic, the focus of Jared's environmental science course for seniors was New York City's water. They spent two-thirds of the year studying it.

Jared's interest in water was, in part, sparked by a course he took at the American Museum of Natural History in which he learned about the Bronx River. About twenty-four miles long, the Bronx River flows down from north of the city and through the Bronx, emptying into the East River. It is the only fresh-water river in New York City. Originally pristine and considered a possible source of water for the city, it became a dumping place for industrial waste and sewage. As Jared learned in his course at the museum, however, the Bronx River has made a dramatic turnaround. Although it still has its problems, mostly from storm runoff, it's no longer a dumping place, and its natural habitats, beauty, and water quality have been partially restored. As part of his course with the museum, Jared went canoeing in the river. "It blew me away," he says. "I couldn't believe I was paddling along in this beautiful river right in New York City."

WHEELS is in Northern Manhattan and many of its students live in the Bronx. So Jared begins his case study of New York City's water by taking his students on a visit to the Bronx River, hosted by the non-profit Bronx River Alliance. "It's captivating for students," he reflects. "Many of them are from the Bronx or their families live in the Bronx, so it has relevance and authenticity: it's happening right here, in their backyard." Students learn what an estuary is. They learn the history of the Bronx River and the ongoing efforts to restore it. They learn about species that have been restored to the river. They don waders and go into the river to collect water samples. And yes, like Jared, they get to go out in canoes. "It's a great way to immerse the kids in the topic," he says with a smile.

Students then learn about New York City's water supply: Where does the water come from? How does it get to the city? What did it take to build the aqueducts and water mains through which the water flows to the city? What brings the water into our apartments? Jared got a grant to take the students on a trip to the Catskill Mountains to one of the reservoirs so that they could see where their water comes from.

Jared explains that once students have learned where their water comes from, the next step is to learn where it goes when they're done using it. They learn all about New York City's drainage and sewage systems, water-treatment plants, and ongoing efforts to improve the system's capacity for handling storm runoff. The final phase of the water case study examines the health of New York Harbor. "We look at data available on NYC's Department of Environmental Protection website," Jared explains. "We learn that although, generally speaking, New York Harbor is cleaner than it's been in a really long time, there are still hot spots where sewage continues to flow into the harbor every time there's a heavy rain. The students learn about ways to mitigate this problem and create public service announcements to educate the public and public officials about what they can do to prevent these overflows."

"I do not know whether it is possible to love the planet," wrote professor, author, and environmental activist David Orr. "But I do know that it is possible to love the places we can see, touch, smell, and experience."[7]

Megan and Jared chose places close to home and went deep with their students. They also focused on water, a most relevant topic in this time of climate crisis. With droughts, floods, wildfires, rising sea levels, desertification, water pollution, and water scarcity affecting people in so many parts of the world, there could hardly be a more important subject for students to understand—and not take for granted.

Jared's and Megan's work demonstrates the benefits of the case study. The learning for students was holistic, involving their minds, hands, and hearts. They observed nature in habitats near their schools, and explored history, geology, biology, and ecology. They had fun and interacted with each other and with enthusiastic adults—all this as they discovered the central importance of water for all life on Earth.

Few teachers will have the freedom and resources to undertake similarly ambitious efforts. That reality is an argument for major changes in the way we educate our young. But even without a major overhaul of the educational system, there are many ways to "Make It Local" that are doable for teachers everywhere. Consider the following suggestions:

- Choose a place near your school, take your students there, and get to know it well. It might be a small garden in the schoolyard, a rooftop garden near the school, or a community garden in a lot on a city block or in a public park. Give students time to experience it at different times of the year. Slow things down. Encourage them to pay attention to what they see, hear, or touch, and invite each student to single out one thing that strikes them. Have them draw and write about what they see. Encourage them to ask questions. Have them research the names of the plants and trees.

- Develop partnerships with local agencies and organizations that can provide information and guest speakers to enhance the students' understanding, as Jared did with Bronx River Alliance, as Megan did with the ECHO Science Center, as Sophie did with the National Arboretum, and as Xochitl did with TreePeople. If a park or community garden is near your school, find out who cares for it and invite them to join your students on a visit to tell them the names of the plants, how to care for them, and why the garden is important to them and to the community.
- High school ELA teachers can take advantage of the fact that in many schools, ELA curriculum is skills-based. As we have seen, Xochitl was free to take students on forest tours with TreePeople as long as the activity was aimed at developing students' research skills.
- While focusing on getting students into direct contact with nature, link your students to national and international events that engage with environmental challenges. An example is World Water Day, in which Megan and her students participated.

FOSTER ENVIRONMENTAL STEWARDSHIP

All the teachers whose work is featured in this chapter enlighten their students about the harm human activity is causing to nature and the environment. They do so while taking the utmost care to be sensitive to their students' developmental needs and capabilities. To foster active hope, they also engage students in age-appropriate environmental stewardship activities.

Liat Olenick

Liat introduces second, third, and fourth graders to ecology and life science. In a unit on pollination, children study the parts of plants and the functions they serve, and this leads to pollination and the role of bees. They learn that the bees get food by sucking nectar from the plants and help the plants by spreading their pollen. Humans help the plants by exhaling carbon dioxide. The plants help humans by providing food and oxygen, and the bees help humans by helping the plants and making honey. So, we're all connected. The students also learn that bees are suffering and dying in massive numbers because of pesticides that poison them and destroy their habitats. Then they learn how they help the bees.

For several years, Liat involved fourth graders in a waterway restoration project in collaboration with the Newtown Creek Alliance, which is working to restore Newtown Creek, a superfund site in Brooklyn and Queens. Through the project, students learned how the creek became polluted and what strategies activists and city agencies have been using to clean it up. They focused especially on the role of oysters in filtering water and restoring the creek's ecosystem. They met with the city council representative for their school district to share what they were learning, to get more information on what the city is doing, and to advocate for stronger action to restore Newtown Creek.

As these examples show, Liat does not avoid sharing environmental problems with her second to fourth graders. She explains:

> In my experience, kids are able to understand what they're ready for. I've had first or second graders who read or hear something about climate change, but the implications are over their heads. Most kids, except maybe some fourth or fifth graders, don't really make the connections that it's going to affect them. I don't like to hide the problems. I think it's really important to be truthful as well as developmentally appropriate. I've just found that kids don't really put it together about what's going on until they get older. Their typical response is to be angry about animals getting hurt and to feel it's not fair (which is a very fourth-grade way to feel

> anyway) and they're excited about writing letters or making protest signs. It's an extension of taking care of plants and animals, which my curriculum is all about.

Liat feels that the elementary school science curricula need to be updated. She says:

> They teach what people felt was important for kids to learn thirty years ago. But now everything has changed. We can't teach about nature as a static thing. We're teaching kids about the natural world while it's actively being destroyed, and we all know this. To teach about nature, we need to teach about social justice and about humans being part of the environment and about the impact humans are having. Also, the curriculum needs to be more holistic, more connected to students' lives. Rather than having kids memorize the parts of the food chain, take them out to your own school backyard and have them look for all the living things they can find and have them consider how those living things are connected. Do place-based, hands-on learning that kids can relate to.

Sophie Schwadron

Sophie took on the issue of waste and recycling. She read her kindergarten students *Just a Dream* by Chris Van Allsburg, the story of a boy who is a litterbug but envisions a beautiful future full of wonderful robots and other inventions.[8] One night, lying in bed, he wishes he could visit the future. In his sleep, his dream comes true. He visits the future but instead of wonderful inventions, the future is full of trash. When he awakes, he is changed. Inspired by the story, Sophie and her students began collecting recyclables from home and bringing them in to use for art projects. For Earth Day, Sophie engaged the students in making floats of recycled materials and leading a parade in the neighborhood in which students from all grades and their parents participated. Sophie worked with teachers in the older grades to start a recycling club that now involves the whole school.

Xochitl Bentley

Like Liat, Xochitl introduced her students to the effects of pesticides on bees, not to create a sense of gloom and doom, but rather to increase awareness and promote a sense of responsibility for repairing the damage humans are doing to natural systems.

She also engaged her students in studying California's campaign to prevent forest fires. In the fall of 2020, Xochitl's virtual classes took place while the San Fernando Valley experienced smoky haze and unhealthy air quality. The curriculum called for developing students' skills in formulating arguments with effective calls to action. Xochitl decided that a case study of the Smokey Bear Wildfire Prevention Campaign would be a timely project. The aim was to research the major causes of wildfires and update Smokey Bear's Campaign with a specific call to action. The students studied the seventy-five-year history of the Smokey Bear Campaign by viewing an online archive of campaign posters, which showed how the campaign had evolved over time. In addition to the image of a lovable bear, the posters addressed the why of fire prevention by showing what we need to protect from fires as well as what causes wildfires and how to prevent them. They studied and assessed media coverage of the California wildfires to identify gaps in the public's understanding and the media's coverage of the situation. An important insight the students gained from their study was about the role of invasive nonnative plants in making fires spread more quickly. Consulting with TreePeople, they learned that an important fire-prevention strategy is to eliminate invasive plants from previously burned or cleared forest areas and replace them with native plants that hold hot embers for a longer period. They learned that TreePeople is doing that restoration work in the Angeles National Forest. The case study culminated with students sharing their slides and calls-to-action scripts with Xochitl and their classmates on a platform called Flipgrid. Xochitl noted that the student takeaways from the case study were many. In addition to honing their skills in argument and calls to action, students improved their media literacy and their environmental literacy, including a more nuanced understanding of the causes of wildfires and of how to prevent them. Xochitl's students also felt that Smokey's famous catchphrase, "Only you can prevent forest fires," puts the onus on the individual, whereas TreePeople's work demonstrates that concerted action by nonprofit organizations and the government is also required.

Megan Wellford

As explained earlier, Megan's year-long exploration of the Lake Champlain watershed had three dimensions: know, understand, and do. The "do" part involved serving as stewards of the watershed. The students did just that; they identified a threat to the health of the watershed and took action. The problem: dog poop.

"[Dogs] are truly man's best friend," the students acknowledged in their proposal to the Keene Town Board. "However, their solid waste, if left on the ground, gets washed into our watershed. When this happens, people (and even their dogs) can contract many harmful diseases." They proposed the installation of four dog mess pickup stations at two sites in Keene Valley. Not only did they detail the environmental impact of dog waste, they provided a web address where town officials could find out how much the recommended pickup stations would cost and order them. "[The proposal] was approved and implemented," says Megan, "thanks in large part to a few actively involved community members who got behind the students' proposal. In developing and advocating for the proposal, students honed their skills in Google maps, research, writing proposals, civic engagement, and more."

In addition to alleviating the harm done to the watershed by human and dog activity, Megan's project strengthened the school community in the town of Keene, New York, and throughout the watershed. By doing the larger watershed project in collaboration with the third grade, third graders and sixth graders got to work together, know each other, and mutually benefit by overcoming the artificial divisions of age and grade. The children reinforced one of their school's key values by creating a quilt to express the community's commitment to protecting the watershed. By engaging community members in their dog-poop cleanup campaign, the children forged relationships with the town board and many community members. By observing World Water Day, they joined a network of people around the world committed to ensuring that everyone, everywhere, has clean water to drink.

Jared Fox

Having led his students in learning all about New York City's water and how great it is, Jared posed a question to them: Does it really make sense to buy bottled water, given the cost and the environmental impact of the plastic bottles, when you have good water coming right out of your tap that is free and you can put in a reusable container? He says, "I like to get kids thinking differently about common practices that they have come to accept as normal."

Once students realize that drinking New York City's water is a better environmental choice than drinking bottled water, Jared engages them in designing an advertising campaign to promote New York City's tap water. Students work in small groups to plan multimedia campaigns (including posters and videos). Jared brings in water scientists, experts from the Department of Environmental Protection, and ad experts to sit on a panel in front of the classroom. They listen as students pitch their multimedia campaigns and critique the students' work.

By engaging their students as stewards for nature and the environment, these teachers are taking love as wonder, excitement, and curiosity to another level. David Orr reminds us of the distinction the Greeks made between *eros* and *agape*. *Eros* is romantic love that wants to possess the object of love. *Agape* is self-sacrificial love—love devoted to the well-being of the other and wanting nothing in return.[9] It is *agape* love that is needed to restore our broken relationship with nature, and it is *agape* love that the teachers featured here are trying to foster in their students.

Agape love calls on us to acknowledge the harm we humans are doing, to stop it, and to work to heal the harm we have done as best we can so that we restore our damaged relationship with nature. These are the restorative practices of the school as a beloved community expanded to embrace nature.

Agape love of nature also requires taking the time and care to pay attention to nature and understand how nature works. That is the science of ecology. The teachers featured in this chapter introduced their students to the aspects of ecology that are needed to understand how human activity is damaging natural systems.

What does it mean to live sustainably on the Earth? That should be the essential question guiding education today. Ecology should be a core subject for students from grades preK to 12. For some, sustainability is continuing on our present path of domination, only with greater efficiency. That's not the path of *agape* love for nature. It's not what the teachers featured in this chapter have in mind. Nor is it sustainable. We would do well to remember the fate of Icarus. He thought he could fly by covering himself with feathers like a bird. He seemed to be doing fine for a while, but because his understanding of nature's laws was insufficient, he ended up plunging into the sea.

ACT FOR CLIMATE JUSTICE

Water scarcity is not a problem in the Lake Champlain watershed, but it is a problem for 2.2 billion people in the world.[10] Megan has used the United Nations Sustainable Development Goals and great resources provided by the United Nations to connect her local work with students to the challenge of water scarcity across the globe.

Jared and a colleague began taking students into a vast underutilized city park near his school. He says he never could have imagined what it would lead to.

The climate and environmental crisis is not affecting all people equally, and Jared and Megan have inspired their students to do something about it.

Megan Wellford

Megan and her students read *A Long Walk to Water*, by Linda Sue Park, which tells the story of a young boy, Salva, and girl, Nya, in South Sudan who are about the same age as Megan's students.[11] Nya cannot attend school because she spends her days on long treks to get water to bring back to her family. During the study, students located South Sudan on a map and learned about the history of the conflict there and the scarcity of water. Observing World Water Day, they learned about the growing problem of water scarcity around the world. The students heard a guest speaker from an organization that digs wells for villages in South Sudan, and a club at the school helped students raise funds to support the organization's work.

Erick Espin, Genesis Abreu, Jared Fox, and the Clean Air Green Corridor Project

One block from Jared's school is Highbridge Park, a 119-acre urban park that runs north from 155th Street some two miles along the banks of the Harlem River in the Washington Heights section of

Manhattan. Certain parts of the park, dotting the street access, are popular and frequently visited; however, much of the interior with forest and trails is notably underutilized because of minimal access, a lack of maintenance, and decades of neglect.

From 2017 to 2020, WHEELS required teachers to pair up and create week-long intensive courses on topics of their own choosing—this in addition to their regular classes. Jared teamed up with history teacher Erick Espin to develop "Restoring Highbridge Park."

Recalls Erick, "Jared brought in the environmental science, and I provided the historical context to explain how the Park became what it is today. The course only lasted a week, but we and the kids liked it so much that we taught it five more times during the next three years."

Through the course, students learned about the importance of green space in cities. They learned why the neighborhood around their school has so little green space. They learned how the construction of the Harlem River Drive in the forties reduced the community's access to the park and contributed to its deterioration.

But the worst blow came in the seventies, when New York City suffered a fiscal crisis and severely cut the budget of the Parks Department. All parks suffered, but the damage was not equally distributed. As Erick explains:

> Broadway divides Washington Heights into two parts. You have a more affluent, whiter population west of Broadway. East of Broadway you have more immigrants and people of color, predominately Latinx. That's the part of Broadway I grew up in. The more affluent neighborhoods were able to rebound because they could draw on private money. With little public or private money available, Highbridge Park, east of Broadway, fell into disrepair.
>
> The first part of the week-long intensive class on Restoring Highbridge Park introduced students to the big issues. Toward the end of the week, we would zoom in on the block of the school

> to involve the kids in some hands-on activities like fixing up the school's two gardens and cleaning up the block in front of the school.
>
> The second or third time we taught the class, we thought, "Why stop at the block in front of the school?"

In collaboration with the New York Restoration Project, a non-profit organization that took over management of the north half of the park, Jared and Erick made several trips into Highbridge Park with their students to pull invasive plants, plant native species, pick up litter, and restore walking trails.

"Once we started doing that, we were thrilled to see the kids' reaction," Jared recalls. "They were so excited just to be there. Many said they had never been to the park. They loved being down in the forest where nature really takes over. They really got into it and wanted more."

The visits to the park led to dreaming and what-if questions: What if students, their families, and people from the community could have safe access to the park on a regular basis? What if we could pedestrianize the street outside our school and create a plaza where students could relax and socialize? What would that look like?

The dreaming and the work in the gardens, the block, and the park had a powerful impact on the students. Recalls Jared, "Students were saying 'I never really thought about the environment I go through walking to school and how that impacts me and my family. I never thought about how I have the right to live in a place that is just as clean as someone who has more money than we have or has a different skin color.' They really latched onto the possibility for change. Once you give kids that understanding, you can never take it away."

Gradually, a powerful vision took shape of a green corridor five blocks long on 182nd Street from Broadway to Amsterdam and then to Highbridge Park. Along the corridor trees and plants would beautify the streets, purify the air, and provide shade from the summer heat. Needles and trash would no longer litter the streets. Thousands of residents, including students attending five other schools along the corridor, would have clean, safe, and green streets and access to a restored park and waterfront. And young people would lead the way.

Futures Ignite, originally called Friends of WHEELS, is a nonprofit organization "dedicated to amplifying youth and community power by inspiring, guiding, and advocating for youth to identify and persist in reaching their college, career, and leadership futures." Erick recalls that the director of Futures Ignite, Molly Delano, saw the kids working on the street one day and was intrigued. She secured a grant to support the students' work and the Clean Air Green Corridor Project (CAGC) was born.

Thanks to fundraising by Molly Delano (in collaboration with the students), CAGC Project now has a full-time organizer. Genesis Abreu is a person of color with Indigenous roots and Salvadoran and Dominican ancestry whose pronouns are they and them. Says Genesis, "I was born and raised in Washington Heights and Inwood. From a young age I saw how toxic hazardous waste has negatively affected this community. I grew up in a place near a sanitation parking lot, an MTA bus depot, and an MTA subway yard—and I knew that none of that was by accident. Growing up in this environment radicalized my understanding of environment and sustainability."

Genesis sees the CAGC Project as rooted in a long history of resistance, transformation, and youth leadership:

> In the sixties, the Young Lords in East Harlem set fire to all the garbage cans, because the Department of Sanitation wouldn't pick up all of the refuse in the streets. The water protectors put their bodies on the frontline at Standing Rock, and spoke out about environmental racism. I emphasize the legacy of environmental justice and how young people of color have been the backbone of

> it. The students are realizing that we *are* like the Young Lords. We *are* like the water protectors. We are doing this work and we have always done this work.

Greening and beautifying a block may seem like a simple matter. Not in New York City! Since coming on staff in November 2021, Genesis has supported the students as they meet with local political leaders, officials of city agencies, and the project's many partners.

On Tuesdays after school, CAGC youth leaders do stewardship work along the corridor, tending the tree beds and picking up trash on the sidewalks and street. "We think community members have noticed the students' picking up after them and are now taking more responsibility themselves," says Genesis with a smile, "because there's now a lot less trash for us to pick on Tuesdays than there used to be!" The stewardship youth leaders have also prepared a community survey to gather information from tenants, store owners, street vendors, service providers, and other stakeholders about the issues they face and to get their ideas for the CAGC.

With support from an organization called NYCH2O, students have created ArcGIS story maps, in which they use photography and video, text, music, and art to describe current reality on the corridor and their vision for the future. The story maps are a vehicle for inspiring the schools, the community, and public officials with the CAGC vision and for developing students' communication skills in a variety of media.

Working with Columbia University's Center for Resilient Cities and Landscapes (CRCL), Genesis won approval from the city to make the school's block of 182nd Street an "open street," free from cars and available for student and community activities. To date, this has allowed the CAGC Project to close the street to traffic and parking about once a month for a block party. The August block party brings current and former WHEELS and Green Corridor students together to have fun, celebrate their accomplishments, and share what they are learning with each other, the community, and public officials.

A recent collaboration with CRCL has engaged students with the issue of extreme heat. "We've talked a lot about air pollution and access to green spaces, but this was a new topic for us," says Genesis.

> It's especially important because Washington Heights lacks adequate green space to provide shade. The project involved learning about the dangers of extreme heat, identifying "heat islands" in Washington Heights, evaluating the city's plans for addressing our community's needs, and working with local officials and the mayor's office to improve city policies.
>
> We have also developed an urban ecology citizen research project. This is a collaboration with the New York Restoration Project and Columbia University's E3B Program (Ecology, Evolution, and Environmental Biology). With graduate students from Columbia, our students go into Highbridge Park and Sherman Creek (another park in upper Manhattan) to collect data to inform park improvement. Students are learning to do research using best practices, including how to measure soil moisture and temperature, tree canopy and vegetation, water quality and turbidity. Last summer and again this summer the students held a digital community forum for students, community members, our nonprofit partners, and elected officials. They described their research project, shared their findings, discussed the health of these two local parks, and made recommendations to the city.

This urban ecology research project was a high point for Genesis. They recall:

> I love seeing how students' perceptions of the environment change. At the beginning they're curious but nervous. "I don't want to go

into the woods. I don't want to get dirty. You want me to be sweating outside all day!?" I remember how they felt on the first day and how their attitude has changed as they come to the end of the program. I see myself in them. That's how I got started. I had teachers and facilitators who were passionate about science and the outdoors and encouraged us to step out of our comfort zone. If it weren't for that, I wouldn't understand why it's so important for Black and brown folks to be connected to nature and the environment.

After immersing her students in a rich local study of water, Megan reads her students a powerful young adult novel to introduce them to the issue of clean-water scarcity around the world, the United Nations Sustainable Development Goals, and a way they can make a difference.

The CAGC Project engages youth from a low-income underserved community to envision environmental justice for their community and to roll up their sleeves to make it happen. In so doing, they are living the idea that "green" is "justice" and "justice" is "green."

What opportunities can you seize to build bridges between green and justice for your students?

CHAPTER 3

Educate for Deep Understanding of the Climate Crisis

BAYARD FAITHFULL IS part of a network of educators that held a conference on climate change in 2018. Of the teachers who shared their work to educate students about the climate crisis, fifteen were science teachers and only one, Bayard, was a social studies teacher. "The climate crisis must make its way into the social studies curriculum," says Bayard, "because it's not just about science. It's about history, economics, politics, and social justice. I hope I've had some influence in that direction."

For twenty-three years, Bayard taught at The Beacon School, a public high school in Manhattan, New York City. He mentored the student environmental club that recruited one thousand Beacon students to take part in the September 20, 2019, youth climate march in New York City. Several of his students were leaders in organizing the citywide march and in coordinating New York City Fridays for Future, the student strikes that drew many young people to protest at the United Nations every Friday. For the day of the march, Bayard organized a teach-in at the school with thirty-three workshops presented by faculty and parents on topics ranging from "Global Warming: The Chemistry of Greenhouse Gases" to "The Green New Deal and the Politics of Climate Change."

For nine years, he taught a semester class for seniors on Global Environmental Politics that complemented and supported the work of the environmental club. Bayard and his students explored global warming, biodiversity, food and food justice, population policy, scarcity and waste, water shortages, sustainability, environmental philosophies, and environmental activism.

"The centerpiece of the class was 'good talk,'" explains Bayard.

> I expected students to use evidence to support their arguments, assess the validity of different arguments, and try to understand different perspectives on the world. I expected them to participate actively in classroom discussions, be respectful of their classmates and their views, and be prepared to be challenged when they spoke. The class involved discussion, debate, simulations, and mock trials. I'd put tangible issues on the table, give kids some factual background, introduce them to different perspectives, and then invite dialogue.

Summing up his philosophy of education, Bayard says, "Deep learning takes place when we move from purely studying something to trying to come up with ways to create social change. For all of us who care about climate justice, it's good to read about it, it's good to study it. But if you've truly grasped what's at stake with your heart and soul, you have to act."

To play a constructive role as active participants in a democratic society, we all need to have a deep understanding of the climate crisis. Young people should develop this gradually from grades preK to 12 in age-appropriate ways. To educate our students effectively, we educators need to keep improving our own understanding as well.

"Deep understanding," as I use the term here, is the knowledge and insight required to inspire wise decision-making and action aimed at sustaining all life and promoting human well-being based on social justice.

To seek deep understanding of the climate crisis, we must explore four key questions:

- What is the predicament?
- How did we get here?
- What do we need to do?
- How are we doing?

To answer these questions, we must explore the climate crisis from multiple perspectives and across multiple disciplines—not only science but also history, economics, politics, current events, literature, art, music, and social justice.

We also need to identify root causes. Deeply entrenched systems, institutions, and ways of thinking are driving the monumental changes taking place on our planet. Only if we understand them do we have a chance of changing them to create a just and sustainable future.

This chapter provides my answers to each of these four questions as well as descriptions of outstanding work by classroom teachers aimed at bringing their students to deep understanding of what's happening to the world they're growing into.

All the educators featured in this chapter teach middle school or high school because deep understanding of the climate crisis is not an appropriate goal for elementary school students, cognitively or emotionally. The priorities for younger children are building the beloved community, developing love and understanding of nature, being "helpers" in their school community and beyond, and learning the stories of people working now and throughout history to build a better world.

QUESTION 1: WHAT IS THE PREDICAMENT?

Global Warming

The Secretary General of the United Nations has called global warning a "code red for humanity." On August 7, 2021, the United Nations Intergovernmental Panel on Climate Change (IPCC) published the Summary for Policymakers of its Sixth Assessment Report on the physical science basis of climate change.[1] The IPCC's six reports are the gold standard in climate-change assessments. This particular report is a consensus document of some two hundred scientists from around the world who examined fourteen thousand scientific papers on the topic. The report was approved by 195 countries.

The 2021 report is remarkable in three respects. First, it is based on much more data than the IPCC's previous reports and reflects more accurate computer modeling. Second, it came out during a summer of extreme climate events around the world: wildfires, floods, droughts, and heat waves, which demonstrated just how serious and immediate the threat is. And third, the report is far more conclusive than its predecessors. In it, scientists express complete confidence in these major takeaways:

- The climate is changing, and these changes are due to human activity that is increasing the amount of carbon dioxide (CO_2) and other greenhouse gases in the atmosphere. These gases act as a blanket absorbing heat from the sun and warming the planet. The report flatly rejects the lie, promulgated by the fossil-fuel industry for decades, that there is debate among scientists about this.
- Each decade for the past forty years has been hotter than the one before it, and all four have been hotter than any previous multiple-decade period for at least 125,000 years. Scientists predict that even if we immediately take strong action to reduce

emissions, the world will continue to get warmer for at least the next thirty years. That's because it takes a long time for CO_2 in the atmosphere to break down and become harmless.

- Through new attributive computer modeling, scientists have established *beyond a doubt* that the extreme weather experienced worldwide in 2021 resulted from global warming. As the climate continues to warm in the next thirty years, the floods, droughts, hurricanes, and wildfires are likely to increase in frequency and intensity. Climate change is not a dark cloud on the horizon. It's here and now.
- The report offers a glimmer of hope. We have a window of opportunity to prevent things from getting even worse if we act aggressively now to reduce greenhouse emissions and eliminate them entirely by 2050. Increased warming of the planet is baked in, so to speak, for the next thirty years. But if we act immediately, we can avoid the worst.

Deterioration of Nature Worldwide

Nature is deteriorating rapidly and dramatically around the world. This is a threat to human well-being equal to that of global warming. That is the message of the 2019 Global Assessment Report of the United Nations Intergovernmental Science-Policy Platform on Biodiversity and Ecosystem Services (IPBES).[2] This report is the work of 150 experts and 350 contributing authors who analyzed fifteen thousand scientific papers as well as a substantial body of Indigenous and local knowledge. This was the first such report in fifteen years.

Those of us who get our food from a supermarket, our medicines from a pharmacy, and our water from a tap may underestimate the gifts nature gives us. The report lists eighteen specific contributions, including food, energy, and medicines, regulation of climate, regulation of air and freshwater quality, and the formation and protection of soil.

Did you know that two billion of the world's people depend on wood as their primary source of energy and that four billion depend on nature as their primary source of medicines? I was also surprised to learn from the report that 75 percent of global food crops depend on animal pollination. We had better keep those pollinators thriving and happy! And I had no idea that marine and terrestrial ecosystems mitigate the warming of the planet by sequestering (storing away) some 60 percent of the carbon that we humans recklessly emit into the atmosphere. Mother Nature is doing everything she can to help us—if we would just let her.

The world's population has more than doubled in the past fifty years. In 1971, it was 3.7 billion. As of 2022, it had reached 7.8 billion. More food, energy, and materials are being supplied to people in most places than ever before, but this is increasingly diminishing the capacity of nature to sustain humans in the future and frequently undermines nature's other contributions in the present.

In cutting down a forest to provide land for agriculture, we are losing the forest's essential service of sequestering our carbon emissions. Relying on fertilizers made from fossil fuels, we are exhausting the soil and polluting water. Using pesticides to protect crops, we are killing off pollinators. Through overfishing, we are threatening the future of the marine food system on which billions of people depend for their food and livelihoods. As our activities send CO_2 into the atmosphere and produce global warming, the oceans absorb CO_2 and become more acidic, threatening coral habitats and plankton, which provide the foundation for the marine food chain and life in the seas. A million species are facing extinction, and for every species lost, more are endangered because every species depends on other species for food and other services.[3]

The benefits and burdens of our current systems to meet human needs are not equally distributed or experienced. Although we produce enough food to provide a healthy diet for everyone on the planet,

11 percent of the world's population is undernourished, and some two billion people lack regular access to safe drinking water.

These assaults on the natural world are not sustainable.

The Future That Lies Ahead

A group of leading Earth system scientists have delved deeply into the workings of Mother Nature. They have studied the resilience of ecosystems around the globe. They have identified the factors that have enabled them to function reliably for so long and have also determined the points at which these systems would start to fail. They have created what they call the Planetary Boundaries Model, which identifies nine thresholds we dare not cross.[4]

Following are the nine lights on our planetary-boundaries dashboard:

- climate change
- ozone layer depletion
- air pollution
- biodiversity loss
- land conversion
- freshwater withdrawals
- fertilizer use
- chemical pollution
- ocean acidification

If we can stay within boundaries the scientists have identified in these areas, we are safe. But if we cross even one of them, we endanger our entire life-support system. According to the scientists, we are close to exceeding the thresholds of safety in four of these areas. The four lights on our dashboard now flashing red are global warming, biodiversity loss, conversion of natural habitats to land for agriculture, and fertilizer use.

Scientists have reached broad consensus that if we act immediately and boldly (not to mention effectively!), we can avoid the worst. But what if we don't act immediately and effectively? What's "the worst" they are referring to? The hurricanes, wildfires, floods, and droughts we are already experiencing give us some sense of what could be in store. But what's coming in the next hundred years, if we don't change course, will be utterly devastating.

Looking at trends already well underway, naturalist and natural history filmmaker David Attenborough sees the following as a likely scenario for the next eighty to one hundred years if we continue with business as usual:

- Damaged by continued clear-cutting to make land available for agriculture and resource extraction, by 2030, the Amazon Rainforest reaches a tipping point that triggers a phenomenon called "forest dieback," which rapidly transforms what's left of the rainforest first into a dry seasonable forest and then into a savannah.
- The Amazon Rainforest is home to one in ten of the world's species. The local extinction of these species has domino effects throughout the biosphere as sources of food for other species disappear.
- A healthy Amazon Rainforest respires huge amounts of water vapor into its canopy, which is swept up by clouds and comes back down to Earth as rain, not only on the rainforest but on a wide region beyond it. With the rainforest gone, rainfall is reduced in large parts of South America, causing water shortages in major cities and droughts in farmlands created from the deforestation. Thirty million people must leave the watershed, including three million Indigenous people.
- During the whole of the current geologic era, the Holocene (some eleven thousand years), the Amazon has been locking away CO_2—a total of some one hundred billion tons. With

the rainforest now gone, fires in the dry season release that long-sequestered carbon into the atmosphere, further warming the planet.

- Arctic ice is already melting. As global warming continues, the arctic ice melts completely, raising sea levels and further increasing global warming because the white ice is no longer there to reflect the sun's rays.
- This jump in warming accelerates the thawing of the permafrost, the frozen soil beneath the tundra and forests in northern Alaska, Canada, and Russia. As the soil thaws over time, it releases huge amounts of greenhouse gases that have been locked away in the frozen ground for thousands of years, and the planet warms ever further.
- As more and more carbon enters the atmosphere, the ocean absorbs increasing amounts, forming carbonic acid and making sea water more acidic. This threatens coral and plankton, the foundation of the marine food chain. The livelihoods of half a billion people are directly affected, and a major source of protein for humans begins to disappear.
- A land-based food crisis occurs as well, as overuse of fertilizer reduces the productivity of land, and pesticides and habitat destruction decimate insect species that provide pollination.
- Destruction of natural animal habitats also makes another pandemic likely. Scientists are beginning to understand the connection between the health of nature and the health of humans. An estimated 1.7 million viruses of potential danger to humans hide in mammals and birds. By bringing animals and humans closer together, the destruction of animal habitats increases the likelihood that viruses will be transmitted to humans. Think of a virus as contagious as COVID-19, but with a higher death rate.
- If the developments described above unfold as predicted, by 2100, global warming will have reached four degrees Celsius

> beyond pre-industrial levels, sea-level rise will inundate coastal cities around the world, and more than a quarter of the human population will be living in areas too hot for human habitation. The result will be a mass migration to drier and milder regions of the world, overwhelming our fragile political and economic systems and triggering cataclysmic conflict and suffering.

As Attenborough points out, this is a series of one-way doors. Once these developments occur, they are not reversible. If we don't change our ways, our marvelous life-support system, responsible for sustaining human life on the planet for millions of years, is headed for collapse.[5]

Pause and Breathe

A friend once told me, "Don't forget to breathe!" I laughed. But she had a point. I came to realize that it's good, every so often, to pause, take a deep breath (or two), and connect with yourself. If you've just read "What is the predicament?" this may well be a good time to do just that. Chances are that what you just read is not new to you, but take a minute or two to let it sink in. And don't forget to breathe—deeply! What feelings, thoughts, and images come up? You may want to write in your journal, take a walk in the park, or take turns sharing feelings with a trusted partner. You might want to cry or rage. That would be all right, too!

Stories from the Classroom

Once you've done whatever you need to do to take good care of yourself, let's turn to the classroom. How do we bring the predicament into the classroom? The bland language of the UN reports is one thing. But what on earth do we do with David Attenborough's series of one-way doors?

There is no one right answer. You'll have to figure out what makes sense for you and your students. What I offer in this book are stories from the classrooms of real teachers who are wrestling with that very question. I hope that their work will provide inspiration and insight that will help you, as you wrestle with the unprecedented challenges of educating young people in this time of climate crisis.

Here, we'll discuss the work of three teachers. You have already met Bayard Faithfull. Next you will meet two science teachers: Beth Mowry and Cynthia (Cindy) Vitale.

Beth Mowry Beth Mowry taught high school science at Brooklyn Collaborative Studies (BCS) in New York City. Most of her students live in the Red Hook section of Brooklyn, a low-income community that suffered extensive damage when Hurricane Sandy devastated parts of the city in 2012.

For seven years, through the end of the 2020–21 school year, Beth taught a year-long course in climate change, which nearly all the students took during their four years at the school. The course integrated science, history, current events, and public policy.

To connect the class to her students' lives, Beth engaged them in a case study of Hurricane Sandy. The course began with the documentary *Inside the Mega Storm* and was framed by the question: Was Hurricane Sandy a weather event or the result of climate change? It was both, as students discover in their explorations. First, they learned how the sun drives the Earth's energy furnace. Then they looked closely at Hurricane Sandy and the science and data behind the storm. Finally, students created infographics summarizing their findings and made presentations in the Red Hook community.

The students went on to study the Earth's climate system, including the carbon cycle and how humans are altering that cycle. The key question for the second semester was, Will climate change be the end of New York City? To provide insight into this question, students looked to the past to see what might happen in the future. "We watched a video, a History Channel documentary called *Little Ice Age, Big Chill*," explains

Beth. "I've used that for a very long time, and it happens to be one of the kids' favorite parts of the curriculum. I'm not sure why! The video shows how the climate changed during the period between 1350 and 1850 and how that affected agriculture, food security, human health, politics, and warfare. It's a really good way to do interdisciplinary work in a climate-change class because it's social studies, history, and science; it's learning from the past to prepare for the future."

Next, students homed in on Sandy's impact on New York City. They conducted fieldwork, which involved mapping out the flooding caused by Sandy in their neighborhood. They learned about measures that could mitigate the impact of future storms and presented their recommendations to city officials. "Real work on real problems," says Beth. "That's our school's motto."

Cynthia Vitale Cynthia (Cindy) Vitale taught life and environmental science for twenty-five years at Summit High School, a comprehensive public high school in Summit, New Jersey, a predominately white, upper-middle-class suburban town of some twenty-one thousand people.

Cindy brings up climate science regularly in all her classes and shares the "small things" she does to reduce her carbon footprint. Cindy explains:

> I've always been a nature and animal lover. I've always enjoyed being outside, exploring and observing, watching, touching, smelling, and listening to all the wildlife around me. It was always my happy place. Teaching has been a great way for me to share my passion. Although I try to do many things in my everyday life that are good for the environment, I have found much satisfaction in educating and inspiring students to be responsible citizens of this planet. Students see me as a "mom" figure. I make a point of connecting with them and I'm there when they need me.

Cindy says that her goals in teaching about the environment boil down to these three: "I want students to view themselves and their fellow humans as organisms in an ecosystem rather than rulers of the environment. I give them the message that their generation is pivotal in turning climate change around. I emphasize that even small things they do can make a difference."

Cindy teaches two elective environmental science classes. Together, they include units on population, food and agriculture, pollution, climate change, energy, environmental policy, and careers in environmental science. In one unit, students work in small groups on a semester-long project of green planning for their town. Their plans have to address energy, waste, water, food, housing, education, public safety, and transportation (because many residents of Summit commute to New York City). Students do environmental cost analyses with resources Cindy provides from the US Environmental Protection Agency and other sources.

In this and other classes, she keeps students up to date on current events relevant to environmental policies. The school subscribes to Newsela, a student news service. She assigns students to find articles on Newsela related to climate and to write blogs responding to the articles based on prompts she gives them.

"Kids love interesting documentaries," Cindy observes. "Call it a movie and they're on board." In the population dynamics class, students watched *Inconvenient Sequel* and *Before the Flood*. In another class she showed *Food, Inc.* Two students told her that they have stopped eating meat as a result. Her favorite is *A Life on the Planet*, by David Attenborough, which she shows to all her classes. "It's one of the best two hours of TV I've ever seen," she says. "The best thing is that during the last part of the documentary, he talks about what we can do and the solutions that are possible now. It's very uplifting."

Cindy does a lot of environmentally green things. She recycles, composts, and shops at farmers markets. Until recently she had a summer home in Chincoteague, an island off the coast of Virginia. There she has a small greenhouse, rain barrels, and rain gardens, and she made videos to show her students how they work. She shares all her practices with the students.

Cindy mentored a student environmental club at the high school a couple of years ago before turning it over to another teacher. She says, "A lot was attempted, some of it successful: recyclable lunch trays, reusable water bottles, reusable plastic bags. The group researched and put together a proposal to convert the school to solar panels. Their proposal was denied, but they learned a lot." She has stayed in touch with the young man who was leader of the club. He is planning a career as an environmental activist. "He told me that my sharing the little things I do for the environment has been an inspiration for the path he is taking in life."

New Jersey has adopted the Next Generation Science Standards (NGSS), versions of which have been approved by nineteen states (see the appendix). These new standards call on science educators to go beyond rote teaching of scientific facts to foster students' understanding and application of basic scientific principles, including those having to do with the environment and climate change. Cindy is happy with the NGSS. "They are much more heavily ecology based than the old standards were and give me the opportunity to teach what I want to teach."

Following are some notable takeaways from the work of Bayard, Beth, and Cindy:

- Whether through mentoring student climate clubs or engaging students in project-based learning, all three teachers supported students in taking action.
- All three made good use of films.

- All three are experienced teachers highly respected in their schools. If you're relatively new to teaching or to your school, make alliances with teachers like these.
- Beth focused her curriculum on a local environmental issue. This strategy has potential for schools around the country because most communities have environmental challenges. Even in areas where climate change is still considered "controversial," there may be support for students tackling a local climate issue.
- Bayard and Beth were fortunate to work in schools based on a philosophy of "real work on real problems." Their schools belong to a network of schools called the Consortium, which fought hard to get their schools waivers from the New York State Regents Exams. Instead, they assess students' learning with Project-Based Assessment Tasks (PBATs). Because of their schools' participation in the Consortium, Bayard and Beth didn't have to teach to the tests and were able to create the innovative project-based curricula described in this chapter.
- Cindy's school is more traditional—and more typical. Her school needs to navigate a trickier political terrain than those in Manhattan and Brooklyn. Still, Cindy has found creative ways to infuse climate and environmental awareness into all her classes. She is no doubt able to do this partly because of her status as an experienced, well-liked, and highly respected science teacher. She is grateful that New Jersey has approved the NGSS, which has opened up space for climate and environmental education.

What did you take away from the stories of Bayard, Beth, and Cindy?

QUESTION 2: HOW DID WE GET HERE?

The History, Economics, and Politics of Global Warming

Fossil-fuel extraction and consumption took off with the invention of the steam engine in 1750, which marked the beginning of the

Industrial Revolution. This story became interwoven with colonialism and slavery, as the steam engine powered ships to go all over the world in search of fuel to extract, forests to cut down, minerals to mine, and people to exploit.

The mind-set that justified unlimited extraction of fossil fuels was the idea that humans had been granted dominion over nature. The mind-set that justified the exploitation of people through slavery and colonization was racism: the idea that differences in skin color made some people more human than others—and that those who deemed themselves to be "more human" had license to exploit other people and their lands.

Fossil fuels have brought benefits, of course. They have created great wealth for the rich nations that did the extracting and the exploiting, while all along the way, low-income people of color and Indigenous people in the Global South have paid the price. This population bears the least responsibility for the climate crisis and now is first in line to suffer its impact. In the United States as well, low-income people and people of color suffer the most from a warming climate and environmental degradation.

For forty years, it has been clear that our way of life based on fossil fuels is not sustainable. We urgently need to stop using fossil fuels and stop destroying the natural systems that take our CO_2 emissions out of the atmosphere. We urgently need to make a transition to sources of clean, renewable, and sustainable energy.

Furthermore, we have a moral imperative to join our efforts to sustain all life with equally powerful efforts to promote equity, eliminate racism, and ensure that people of marginalized communities in the United States and around the world participate meaningfully in creating the sustainable economic, social, and political arrangements that are just and fair for all people.

Climate justice means that rich nations compensate nations of the Global South for the wealth they have stolen. It means that they strive to heal the harm they have done by providing ample resources to help marginalized nations and communities mitigate and adapt to the climate emergencies they are facing. It means putting an end to the ongoing exploitation of their people and the degrading of their lands. It means helping them establish vibrant climate-friendly economies that provide nutritious food, clean water, and clean air for all. It means that the voices of Indigenous people and people of color help shape the movement to sustain all life and the new economic and political systems that grow out of it. It means instituting humane immigration policies.

Climate justice means cleaning the lead-contaminated water in Flint, Michigan, and ensuring that what happened in Flint never happens again, anywhere. It means stopping the air pollution that produces high rates of asthma in the South Bronx and other neighborhoods of color.

The Drivers of Nature's Deterioration

The 2019 Assessment Report of the Intergovernmental Science-Policy Platform on Biodiversity and Ecosystem Services identifies five direct drivers of damage to biodiversity and ecosystems:

- Changes in land and sea use—for example, agribusiness corporations acquiring arable land and converting it from small farms to large plantations for monocrops (corn) to make biofuels.
- Direct exploitation of species—for example, overfishing.
- Climate change and the extreme events it brings—for example, droughts, floods, hurricanes, and wildfires, and as the climate warms up, less productive crops, leading to food insecurity.
- Pollution—for example, marine plastic, which has increased tenfold since 1980, affecting 267 species, including 86 percent of marine turtles, 44 percent of seabirds, and 43 percent of marine mammals.

- Invasion by alien species—for example, by attacking native species that haven't developed defenses to protect themselves, endangering crops and leading to food insecurity.

The Assessment Report also identifies the following five *indirect* drivers:

- Production and consumption patterns. The United States has 5 percent of the world's population and consumes 25 percent of the world's energy.
- Population dynamics. The world's population has doubled since 1970. Providing food, energy, and materials to all these people is degrading the capacity of nature to meet these needs in the future.
- Trade. Transporting food and materials in ships, planes, and trucks around the world requires huge amounts of fossil-fuel energy and is a significant contributor to CO_2 emissions. Global trade also spreads invasive species around the world.
- Technology. Rather than serving human needs, many existing technologies produce profits for the few at the expense of the climate, nature, and Indigenous and low-income people around the world.
- Governance at the local and global level. To date, governments have generally incentivized economic growth with little regard for the environmental damage it causes.[6]

Root Causes: The Systems and Underlying Assumptions Propelling Humanity to Catastrophe

The good news is that global warming and the deterioration of nature are not caused by an unpreventable act of nature. They are caused by humans—humans like us, living and working day in and day out, wittingly or unwittingly, to unleash the forces that are leading us to disaster.

As scientists have reported, we have already done much irreparable damage to natural systems. We and future generations will have to live with the impact of that damage. But, as discussed earlier, scientists emphasize that we can avoid the worst if we act immediately.

To direct our efforts intelligently, we need to look deeply into root causes. Behind the extreme events we're experiencing, the trends the scientists are seeing, and the drivers they have identified are powerful systems and institutions channeling human energy in ways that spell misery for billions and a future Earth that may well be uninhabitable for humans.

For a full answer to the question of how we got here, we need to identify those systems and institutions and the mind-sets they are based on. My efforts for deep understanding lead me to the following conclusions: The system driving us to disaster is capitalism, or, more accurately, what Bill McKibben calls the "particularly rapacious variant" of capitalism that has developed during the past fifty years in the United States.[7] Within this system, the institutions most responsible for our predicament are the fossil-fuel industry and industrial agriculture.

Fossil-Fuel Industry The fossil-fuel story is well-documented. Forty years ago, scientists at Exxon-Mobil, the world's largest publicly traded fossil-fuel company, accurately predicted how much CO_2 would be in the atmosphere in the 2020s if we continued with business as usual. They termed the consequences as "potentially catastrophic."[8]

But instead of disclosing what their scientists had learned, Exxon-Mobil eliminated that division of the company and spent millions of dollars in a massive disinformation campaign to discredit independent scientists who had come to the same conclusion. Thus began what Bill McKibben calls the "most consequential lie in human history."[9] They used their wealth and political clout to block meaningful governmental action to address global warming and protect the environment. At the same time, they moved ahead more aggressively than ever to promote the extraction and burning of fossil fuels—with the result that half of all carbon emitted into the atmosphere since the beginning of the Industrial Revolution was sent up during the past thirty years.

In this same period, neoliberal economic policy (deregulation and tax legislation favorable to corporations and the wealthy) enabled a relatively small number of people and corporations, including fossil-fuel interests, to become fabulously wealthy and wield undue political influence. (In 1978, the top 1 percent in the United States owned 23 percent of the nation's wealth. Since then, their share has doubled. Three people now own more wealth than that owned by the bottom 150 million people taken together.[10]) Driven in many cases by a radically individualistic political ideology, these wealthy corporations and individuals have been wielding political influence far beyond their numbers.

They have set about undermining our democratic institutions; opposing improvements in the economy, health care, and the social safety net; and preventing action to address the climate crisis. In 2012, more than 60 percent of all campaign contributions came from less than 0.05 percent of the population. In 2016, networks funded by Koch Industries, the huge conglomerate with substantial interests in fossil fuels, spent nearly three-quarters of a billion dollars to support Republican candidates in congressional and state races.

Agribusiness and Industrial Agriculture The industrial food industry is controlled by a small number of large corporations. Since the Nixon era in the seventies, they have received substantial subsidies from the federal government. During the past fifty years, they have transformed much of the world's agriculture from small farms and traditional peasant agriculture to huge one-crop farms that pollute the local water supply and erode the soil. Lacking crop diversity, these farms are less resilient to climate disasters.

Industrial agriculture uses 70 percent of agricultural resources to provide 30 percent of the world's food, while Indigenous and peasant communities sustainably provide 70 percent of the world's food with only 30 percent of the resources.[11]

Increasing numbers of industrial farms don't even produce food but grow corn to make ethanol for the gas tank. Industrial agriculture is responsible for 50 percent of global greenhouse gas emissions, a third of which comes from livestock, and accounts for 85 percent to 90 percent of all agricultural emissions. It also depends on intensive use of pesticides and fossil-fuel-based fertilizers that ruin the soil, adding chemicals to the land, water, and crops.

During the past fifty years, agribusiness has grown into a transnational power, gobbling up land and resources, pushing peasants and Indigenous people off the land, depriving them of their livelihoods, undermining their cultures, and diminishing their well-being. Not only has agribusiness received substantial subsidies from the US government for years, but the World Bank and the World Trade Organization have instituted loan and trade policies favorable to agribusiness at the expense of peasant and Indigenous farmers in countries of the Global South.

Pause and Breathe

Here's another place for pausing, taking a breath, and letting what you've just read sink in—or putting your attention on something that brings you joy or makes you laugh. How we got here is not pretty. What feelings, thoughts, and images arise? Again, do what you need to do to take good care of yourself—a listening exchange, journaling, walking, working out, whatever works for you.

Stories from the Classroom

The teachers featured here, Xochitl, whom you met in chapter 2, and Cindy, whom you met earlier in this chapter, use novels to give students important insights into our second question: How did we get here? See what you can take away from their experience.

Xochitl Bentley Xochitl Bentley had her Advanced Placement (AP) students read *Parable of the Sower*, the dystopian novel by Octavia Butler. The book gave her the opportunity to introduce her students to a model for systems thinking.[12]

Originally published in 1993 and set in the 2020s, *Parable of the Sower* made it to the *New York Times* Bestseller list in 2020 because of its relevance to the climate and political challenges we face today. The novel's narrator and central character is Lauren, a young Black woman who lives with her parents and three siblings in a walled-off section of Robeldo, near Los Angeles. Lauren can see beneath the surface of the wildfires, rising sea levels, water scarcity, extreme poverty, and social collapse that threaten her family and herself. She realizes that the hoped-for return to normal will not happen because the systems driving the collapse are still in place.

Lauren keeps a journal in which she gradually develops "Earthseed," a collection of verses expressing her view of God and how to live. The central tenet of Earthseed is that God is Change. We need to adapt to Change, but we aren't powerless. "With forethought and work," she writes, "we shape God."[13] Lauren envisions Earthseed as a diverse, equitable community based on Earthseed truths and fostering personal, community, and environmental well-being. Surviving the destruction of her family and community, she sets out on a dangerous journey committed to gathering reliable partners to join her in "shaping God" into her new Earthseed community.

Xochitl's students immediately recognized Lauren's leadership qualities and repeatedly described her as able to "think outside the box." "I pushed my students to unpack this cliché and dig deeper," says Xochitl in a blog she wrote for Moving Writers. "We noticed that a key feature of Lauren's emerging leadership was an ability to see the flaws in systems and the need for improvement."

To deepen students' understanding of Lauren's way of thinking, Xochitl introduced them to the iceberg model, a tool for systems thinking.[14] "The part of the iceberg visible above the waterline represents events to which we often need to *react*," she explains.

> Just below the waterline are patterns and trends. If we identify these, we can sometimes *anticipate* what is likely to happen next. Beneath patterns and trends are the underlying structures that influence the patterns. If we identify these structures and their flaws, we may be able to *design* structures that create better patterns and events. Finally, at the bottom of the iceberg are the mental models, the beliefs, assumptions, and values that shape the structures and keep them in place. If we can change these mind-sets, we may be able to go beyond tweaking or reforming the structures to *transform* them.

Xochitl says that her students' journals showed that they recognized the power of Lauren's ability to see patterns and anticipate events. This was in contrast to the adults around her, who were in denial about the forces driving the changes taking place, and who were just reacting to events and grasping for false solutions. A key takeaway from *Parable of the Sower* is that good leadership in this time of environmental and social crisis requires the imagination to envision and enact new ways of living based on a clear view of unfolding reality.

Xochitl's use of *Parable of the Sower* to introduce systems thinking pairs nicely with a novel that Cindy Vitale assigns to her AP science students.

Cynthia Vitale After the AP science exams are over in the spring, Cindy assigns her AP students the novel *Ishmael* (1992) by Daniel Quinn. Like *Parable of the Sower*, it was published nearly three decades ago and continues to have great relevance for today.[15]

Ishmael is the story of an unlikely Socratic dialogue between Ishmael, a wise and highly educated gorilla who communicates by telepathy, and an unnamed educated, middle-class white man. They meet when the man answers an ad posted in the local paper by Ishmael: "Teacher seeks pupil. Must be interested in saving the world." Through an extended process of questioning and reflection, Ishmael leads the man to recognize the underlying cultural mind-set that is driving modern civilization to destruction. "You're captives of a civilizational system that more or less compels you to go on destroying the world in order to live," argues Ishmael.[16] His aim is to educate his pupil so that the pupil can spread the message to a hundred people, each of whom can spread it to a hundred more, and so on—in this way saving the world. The assumption shaping modern civilization, asserts Ishmael, is that humans are set apart from nature and that our destiny is to conquer and rule nature. Ishmael gets his pupil to understand that this is not true—that humans are part of nature and subject to nature's laws.

"I feel this is such a timeless book," reflects Cindy. "It's been around for decades, and it's more appropriate now than ever. It has such a simple message—and it's one of key ideas I want students to take away from my classes: We are organisms in a complex biosystem. We need to take and give in ways that are sustainable."

"Some students thought the book was silly," Cindy acknowledges. "But many liked the book and felt that they were walking away with a new perspective and some powerful information."

In her blog, Xochitl reflects that reading Octavia Butler's *Parable of the Sower* was a slightly eerie experience because so much of what occurs in the novel is happening now. Although the situation Lauren lives through and triumphs over is horrendous, her heroine's journey is compelling and inspiring, offering students a person their age to emulate. Like Lauren, Xochitl was "thinking outside the box" to assign the book to her students and help them understand the qualities that make Lauren such a good leader.

Cindy's assignment of *Ishmael* is an equally bold move, inviting her AP biology students to ponder how deeply engrained cultural assumptions shape events, patterns, and systems. These assumptions need to be critically examined, especially when the systems they have inspired are leading us to disaster.

Both are provocative books for young people to read at this time.

What are your take-aways from Xochitl's and Cindy's use of novels with their students? Is there a relevant poem, essay, short story or novel that you would like to share with your students?

QUESTION 3: WHAT DO WE NEED TO DO?

The climate crisis gives humanity the opportunity to transform destructive and oppressive systems into new social, political, and economic relationships that enable humans to live in balance and harmony with each other and all living beings. Chapter 4 will describe the contours of that new world by presenting visions for the future—not pie in the sky, but living examples of what is possible thanks to the work of imaginative, persistent, and courageous warriors for climate justice around the world.

Next, I present just three steps we need to take *right now* to set us in the right direction. They aren't perfect. They don't include all of the changes we need to make. But they will buy us some time—and time is crucial, because it's running out.

1. Reduce Greenhouse Gas Emissions

The United Nations has called on the world to reduce greenhouse gas emissions by 45 percent by 2030. This will get the world off to a good start in bringing emissions to zero by 2050, which is necessary to prevent global warming from going beyond the critical tipping point of 1.5 degrees Celsius beyond pre-industrial levels.

But think about what that means. Reduce our fossil fuel use by 45 percent in one decade? They must be kidding! But they're not. Let's take a moment to imagine what would be involved.

To cut emissions by 45 percent by the end of this decade will require bold steps to support the transition from fossil fuels to renewable energy, including the following:

- ending the huge government subsidies to the fossil-fuel industry, and subsidizing, instead, the scaling of renewable sources of energy;
- constructing a whole new energy infrastructure, including wind turbines and solar panels and mass transit and electric cars;
- developing the human infrastructure as well as supporting people who will lose their jobs in the fossil-fuel industry and training them and others for jobs in the renewables industry;
- phasing out coal, halting construction of new fossil-fuel infrastructure, and keeping in the ground all fossil fuels that haven't yet been extracted; and
- undertaking serious efforts to cut consumption and waste of energy.

There is a precedent for the economic, political, and societal mobilization that this monumental transition requires: When the United States entered World War II after the attack on Pearl Harbor, the country came together under the leadership of President Franklin D. Roosevelt to support the war effort—everything from blackouts and Victory Gardens to retooling the entire manufacturing sector to create the weapons of war.

2. Save the Rainforests

Rainforests are among nature's most precious gifts to humanity. They generously give us oxygen and rain and mitigate global warming by locking away huge amounts of carbon. Unfortunately, rainforests are in serious trouble, and we must act immediately to save what is left.

The three largest rainforests in the world are located in the Amazon, the Congo River Basin, and Southeast Asia (primarily Malaysia and Indonesia). As recently as 1960, 80 percent of Indonesia was forested. The demand for pulp, paper, plywood, and palm oil has spurred a massive land grab and resource rush by corporate interests seeking profits by cutting down and burning forests to clear land for plantations to grow these commodities. The deforestation has proceeded so rapidly that just under half of Indonesia's original forest cover now remains. Instead of sequestering carbon, Indonesia is now the third largest emitter of greenhouse gases after the United States and China, with 85 percent of its emissions coming from forest and peatland degradation.[17]

The Amazon is on the verge of following suit if rapid deforestation is not rapidly reversed. Only the rainforest in the Congo currently has enough standing forest to remain a strong net carbon sink.[18]

Effective action will require governments working in concert to drive systemic change, which must include blocking industrial agriculture corporations from grabbing land and cutting down forests, incentivizing sustainable ways of doing business, and supporting small landholders, Indigenous people, and local communities as stewards of the land. If US corporations are involved in destroying rainforests for profit, they need to be called out. The international community needs to use its leverage to encourage Brazil, Indonesia, and Democratic Republic of the Congo to advance their long-term national interests by protecting these precious treasures.

3. Help Small Countries of the Global South Address Climate Change

At the UN Climate Change Conference (COP26) in November 2021, small countries of the Global South asked that the rich nations commit to provide $200 billion per year to help them deal with climate change. They want help in transitioning to renewable sources of energy, and in mitigating and adapting to changes in climate that affect their vulnerable countries. They are also asking for compensation for damage already done. They raised the issue of climate migration and called for the international community to include them in negotiating humane policies to address migration, which will only increase as the climate crisis continues to unfold. They also want the rich nations to make a binding and enforceable commitment to reduce their carbon emissions by 45 percent by 2030. These are reasonable demands from countries that did little or nothing to create the climate crisis and now stand in the frontlines to bear its impact.[19]

QUESTION 4: HOW ARE WE DOING?

The Good News

The Climate Movement Is Alive and Well Millions of people continue to work, day in and day out, to educate the public about the climate emergency, protest government inaction, and promote viable alternatives to dominant systems for producing energy and growing food. Despite the disruption caused by the pandemic, the climate movement is growing. On November 5, 2021, twenty-five thousand young people marched in Glasgow to urge world leaders attending the COP26 climate change summit to take decisive action. The next day, one hundred thousand adults and young people marched in Glasgow for climate justice. Joining them were protestors participating in some three hundred local actions around the world.[20]

The Public Wants Action Recent polls in the United States and around the world have found that strong majorities of the public are deeply concerned about the environment and climate change. According to recent polls by the Pew Research Center, 60 percent of adult Americans believe climate change is a major threat to the country, up from 44 percent in 2009. Two-thirds believe that protecting the environment should be the top priority for the president and Congress (up from 41 percent in 2011), and 52 percent say that addressing global climate change should be top priority (up from 28 percent in 2011). Seventy-nine percent say the priority for the country's energy supply should be developing alternative sources, such as wind and solar. Only 20 percent say the priority should be expanding production of oil, coal, and natural gas.

The polls reflect the partisan political divide. Nine in ten Democrats believe the government is doing too little to reduce the effects of climate change compared with only 35 percent of Republicans. However, 52 percent of Republicans born after 1980 see protecting the environment and dealing with global climate change as a priority.[21]

The UN Development Programme commissioned a poll of a million people across fifty countries and found that two-thirds of respondents say climate change is a global emergency. In all fifty countries, a majority agreed.[22]

Alternatives to Fossil Fuels Are Affordable and Ready to Scale All that is needed is a boost from governments to build the infrastructure for the new energy system. The International Monetary Fund estimates that the fossil-fuel industry received more than $5.3 trillion in direct and indirect subsidies from governments during 2015 alone. That's $10 million a minute. In comparison, the US wind-energy industry has received only a total of $12.3 billion in direct subsidies since the year 2000.[23] It's high time for our government to end subsidies for the fossil-fuel industry and to invest in the scaling of clean sources of energy, which eight in ten Americans favor over continued production of fossil fuels.

In 2020 Americans Voted for the Environment A solid majority elected Joe Biden, who promised to make protecting the environment and reducing global warming a top priority.

President Biden Has Been Delivering on His Promise On September 8, 2022, President Joe Biden signed into law the Inflation Reduction Act (IRA), the most significant piece of climate legislation ever passed in the United States. It provides $369 billion in new federal subsidies for electric vehicles, wind farms, solar power, and other clean energy technologies. The federal dollars will spur trillions of dollars in private sector investments in clean energy as well. This is a major step toward Biden's goal of cutting fossil-fuel emissions in half by 2030.[24]

The climate movement can take credit for this major achievement. Every protest, every campaign to block construction of a fossil-fuel pipeline, every scientific report on the impact and causes of global warming, every youth climate march—all important in their own right—helped create the shift in public conscious that made passage of the IRA possible. The Sunrise Movement, 350.org, Environmental Defense Fund, Extinction Rebellion, and many more organizations did their part, as did the scientists and engineers who developed the new clean energies technologies the IRA can now fund to scale.

COP27: The Good, the Bad, and the Ugly

COP27 was the twenty-seventh annual meeting of the "Conference of the Parties." It brought together negotiators and representatives from the 196 countries (and the European Union) that have signed on to the United Nations climate framework aimed at stabilizing and reducing greenhouse gas emissions. Also attending were UN officials and observer groups, such as nongovernmental organizations, universities, private companies, and lobbyists. It took place in Egypt from November 6–18, 2022. A brief overview of decisions made at COP27 provides a snapshot of where the international community currently stands on climate change.

The Conference produced one significant breakthrough: It established a fund to provide aid to the world's smallest and most vulnerable countries when they suffer climate harm. However, COP27 made little progress in getting agreement on specific ways to cut greenhouse gas emissions. Few countries had followed through on boosting their emission-cutting pledges, as required by COP26. Nor had rich countries delivered on their commitment to provide $100 billion to help small countries make the transition to clean energy. While affirming the target of keeping global warming at no more than 1.5 degrees Celsius above preindustrial levels, the Conference couldn't agree on specific targets to achieve that. "Too many parties are not ready to make more progress today in the fight against the climate crisis," European Union climate chief Frans Timmermans told weary negotiators. "What we have in front of us is not enough of a step forward for people and the planet."[25]

That said, the agreement to create a fund to compensate small and vulnerable countries for what the UN calls "loss and damage," shows that the COP process can empower these countries to demand justice. The United States and other rich countries had resisted making such a commitment in the past. But with a third of Pakistan under water from catastrophic floods, Pakistan's negotiators organized a block of 130 nations to demand creation of a loss and damage fund. Digging in their heels, they said they would not leave the Conference without an agreement. "If there is any sense of morality and equity in international affairs," argued Pakistani negotiator Munir Akram, "then there should be solidarity with the people of Pakistan and the people affected by the climate crisis. This is a matter of climate justice."[26]

They got what they demanded, though much work remains to be done. A transition committee will work out the specifics—how large will the fund be, where will the money come from, how will it be distributed, and for what purposes. Reflecting on the achievement, Harjeet Singh, head of global political strategy for Climate Action Network International, said, "COP27 has sent a warning shot to polluters that they can no longer go scot-free with their climate destruction."[27]

Other bright spots included the announcement by Lula da Silva, the newly elected President of Brazil, that, unlike his predecessor, he is strongly committed to saving the Amazon Rainforest. Two attractive pavilions eloquently expressed the perspectives of children and youth and of advocates for climate justice. And President Biden was able to cite the IRA as an example of the kind of bold actions governments need to take to reduce greenhouse gas emissions.

But, on the whole, COP27 leaves a sour taste in the mouth. The Egyptian government arrested and detained civil society activists, who have always been an accepted presence—and a moral compass—at previous COPs. As COP27 delegates and observers met in posh hotels, environmental activists were on hunger strike in prison. A number of world leaders, including the Conference's Egyptian hosts, used the gathering to promote their fossil-fuel supplies. Six hundred and thirty-six official fossil-fuel lobbyists attended the Conference,[28] and Coca Cola, the world's leading plastic polluter, was allowed to be a major sponsor of COP27 despite a challenge from an online petition that garnered 238,000 signatures. The British government, which had hosted the climate talks in Glasgow in 2021, had barred fossil-fuel companies from sponsorships. Wrote Georgia Elliot-Smith, a delegate to COP26 who launched the petition, "Plastic is suffocating our planet, and, year after year, one company leads the pack of polluters—Coca Cola."[29] In closed door sessions, Saudi Arabia and

China pushed back against language calling for phaseout of all fossil fuels, and blocked a proposal that nations set more ambitious targets for cutting greenhouse gas emissions.[30] Saudi Arabia is transitioning its economy to clean energy so that it will have more oil to sell to the rest of the world.[31]

This account of how we are doing shows the power of the fossil-fuel industry, with major oil-producing nations and industry lobbyists working hard to hijack the UN's annual global warming conference. Tragic as it is, this is not surprising. No one said it would be easy to transform the energy foundation for everything we do and the companies and nations that profit from it.

Fortunately, we also see the power of the global climate movement. It has come a long way in waking up the world to the perils of global warming and the need to make the transition to clean energy as soon as possible. With red lights blinking on the planetary-boundaries dashboard, we need a vibrant, vigorous climate movement more than ever.

The past year's developments offer two accomplishments the movement can build on. The movement can advance climate justice by supporting the block of 130 small and vulnerable countries in establishing an effective, well-funded loss-and-damage fund. Although COP27 agreed to create the fund, the details need to be worked out—and the details will make all the difference. This hard work, led by representatives of the 130-nation group, will need strong support and generous allocations of resources from wealthy countries. The United States should lead in providing and organizing this support.

The IRA offers unique opportunities and challenges for the climate movement in the United States. While the movement must maintain its efforts to block the construction of new fossil-fuel extraction and infrastructure, the IRA provides the resources to begin building an economy based on clean energy. This gives the movement the opportunity, and the responsibility, to support the transition to green energy we have been fighting for. This will involve supporting effective implementation of green energy solutions for everything from transportation to home heating and cooking. It will mean selling green-energy solutions to the public and resisting fossil-fuel-funded efforts to stir up opposition at national and local levels. And, since we live in a capitalist economic system, it will mean holding profit-making companies, including big utilities, accountable for implementing the IRA in ways that truly serve the needs of the people and the planet and do not just fill corporate pockets with federal cash. A tall order for the climate movement! But it's what we get for creating this opportunity.

Now we turn to two more stories from the classroom, showing how master teachers educate for deep understanding of the climate crisis.

Stories from the Classroom

Next you will learn more about Bayard's extraordinary work and meet middle school teacher Lesley Younge, who engages her students in a simulation of an Indigenous Peoples' Climate Summit. See what you can take away from their work.

Bayard Faithfull Bayard pulled no punches in educating the students in his Global Environmental Politics class about the severity of the climate crisis and how we got here. Because there is no high school textbook that deals with the global politics of the climate crisis, Bayard assigned books such as *Soil, Not Oil* by Vandana Shiva, *The Omnivore's Dilemma* by Michael Pollan, and Bill McKibben's *Eaarth*—"Eaarth" being McKibben's name for the uninhabitable planet we are rapidly turning our beloved Earth into. Bayard's students viewed films such as *Food, Inc.* and *The World According to Monsanto*.

His students took part in the C Roads Project (see the appendix), a simulation exercise in which students work in groups representing a variety of countries and do climate negotiations. "They experience the sticking points," explains Bayard. "When wealthy countries ask countries of the Global South to cut their carbon emissions, those countries say, 'Listen, you have a big head start on us. You've been burning fossil fuels for 250 years. It's up to you to take the lead in cutting emissions and help us catch up with sustainable technology!' "

For the food unit, the class visited East New York Farms, a social justice project run by people of color. It's a learning center that trains kids in how to farm and run a farmers market. The farm is empowering for kids to learn not only about growing but also about selling and maintaining a small business.

Bayard brought in guest speakers, including activists with the Sunrise Movement and 350.org and officials from New York City's Department of City Planning, who focus on strengthening the city's resilience against hurricanes like Sandy.

For an environmental philosophies unit, he divided students into groups and gave each group a reading that expresses a particular perspective—for example, Indigenous, feminist, racial justice, socialist. Students examined the strengths and weaknesses of these different arguments and realized that they believed some parts of all of them. Bayard says the readings helped students make connections among the various movements and see them as paths toward achieving the same goal.

Although his priority was to support student activism for major governmental and corporate policy changes, Bayard also encouraged students to make individual changes in their lives. "Achieving a vision like the Green New Deal would involve broad policy changes but also millions of individual changes," he explains. "Our society is based on consumption and waste. All of us can lower our carbon footprint."

He gave them a challenge. During a designated month-long period, they were to choose ways to live more sustainably. He gave them a long list of actions they could take to lower their carbon footprint. The list was divided into four categories: power, reduce/recycle/reuse, food, and organizing for change. Points were assigned to each action. For example, the top item for food was eating vegetarian (four points per week). Students kept journals of what they did and brought them in each Monday for four weeks. The goal was to earn twenty-five points per week. "Usually by the end of the month," says Bayard, "somewhere between a third to a half of the kids had moved from being carnivores to being vegetarians!"

For two years in a row, Bayard took students to Ecuador during spring break as part of this class. "Basically, we were looking at the decimation of the Amazon," he recalls. "We met with various environmental groups. Ecuador is a relatively poor country. They wrestle with questions about land. Should they sell it off for mining and oil companies to exploit or keep it as national park, which makes them a lot less money but it's more sustainable? It was a really powerful experience for kids to understand some of the reasons why the Amazon is being destroyed so quickly and what impact that has on our world."

Bayard arranged the trip through Global Exchange, a nonprofit organization that does social justice tourism around the world. They use proceeds from the tourism to help fund social change organizations within the countries. Part of the money Bayard and his students paid for the trip went to the organizations they visited.

Lesley Younge Lesley Younge loves teaching middle school students. "They're finally old enough for people to stop coddling them," she explains. "Their eyes are open to some of the greatest concerns of the world and they're looking for answers. Giving them the opportunity to explore big issues in ways that are both intellectual and personal brings power into the classroom. I love helping them harness that energy of wanting to know and wanting to do and helping them find a direction."

During the 2019–20 school year, she taught at the Whittle School and Studio, an independent school in Washington, D.C. A teacher with seventeen years of experience, Lesley was part of a small middle school team that also included an art teacher, a performing-arts teacher, and a STEM teacher. "We decided that the first six weeks of our seventh-grade curriculum would be a project for the kids to engage in," she recalls. After considering various options, they agreed on "The Indigenous Peoples' Climate Summit Role Play," developed by Rethinking Schools (see the appendix).

The role-play exercise was inspired by the actual Indigenous Peoples' Global Summit on Climate Change that took place in Anchorage, Alaska, in April 2009. Representatives of Indigenous groups from around the world came together to share experiences and agree on a strategy for leading a global campaign. Explains Lesley, "We started with the materials provided by Rethinking Schools and built on it, adding a substantial research component, a multimedia arts component, and a performance component."

The teachers organized their nineteen seventh graders into six small groups, each representing an Indigenous group from one of the six areas of the globe represented at the Anchorage Summit. Students read and discussed a one-page handout with information about the Indigenous group they would be role-playing, including the specific climate-related challenge the group is facing and how they are trying to address it.

The Indigenous groups chosen for the role-play were the Diné (Navajo), who are dealing with a long drought in the southwestern United States; the Yup'ik (Alaska Native), who are experiencing Arctic warming and the melting of permafrost; the Bambara of Africa, where the Sahara Desert is expanding rapidly, taking over grasslands and trees; the Kiribati (central Pacific Islands), whose existence is threatened by sea-level rise; the Taino, Caribs, and Arawaks (Indigenous people of the Caribbean), who are plagued by hurricanes, droughts, and threats to the coral reefs; and Indigenous peoples of the Amazon, where the precious rainforest is being damaged by droughts and incursions by loggers, miners, oil companies, and ranchers.

Discussing the handouts was just the first step. Next, the students conducted research on the Indigenous peoples they would be representing. The research involved multiple disciplines, including geography, history, politics, economics, and science.

"We wanted the students to learn enough about the Indigenous group they would be role-playing so that they could try to think from the perspective of that group," reflects Lesley. "We had a lot of conversations about taking the role-play seriously. It was a good cultural competency exercise for the students to try to represent a group of people very different from themselves, while realizing they're not that group of people. It takes sensitivity." Lesley's one regret was that she wasn't able to connect with an Indigenous group to consult directly with the students. However, they did visit the National Museum of the American Indian and talk with Indigenous people there.

Supported by the art teacher and performance-art teacher, each group developed a multimedia presentation to introduce themselves to the other groups participating in the summit and to share their perspective on the climate crisis. The presentations addressed what they most wanted the world to know about how climate change was affecting them; what steps they were taking to deal with it; what actions they would like rich nations to take; what concerns they had about the future; and, should they need to leave their homeland, how they would want the world to respond to them as climate migrants. Finally, the six groups negotiated to agree on a common set of demands and a strategy for a campaign.

"In the course of this six-week project," says Lesley, "the students developed their skills in listening, empathy, speaking up, and negotiation. They developed their skills in research and presentation. They came away with a global perspective on climate change, which was really wonderful. The students really got into their work on the summit and owned it."

Simulations and role-plays, used to great benefit by Bayard and Lesley, are excellent ways to foster deep understanding. I'm sure that Lesley's students will never forget the Indigenous peoples they studied for six weeks and role-played in their simulation of the Indigenous Peoples' Climate Summit. What an engaging way to learn about Indigenous people from six areas around the world—and to explore so much geography, history, and environmental science in the process. Lesley affirms that the teachers enjoyed it, too. They liked working as a team on a multidisciplinary core project—and they also learned a lot. Our middle and high schools need to restructure themselves to enable teachers and students to work together on projects like this.

What are your take-aways from Bayard's and Lesley's work?

So here we are at the conclusion of chapter 3. This is a tough chapter. It's not pleasant to dive into the wreck and come to terms with what is happening to our beautiful planet and life-support system. It's necessary, of course. We won't be able to move forward if we don't understand our predicament, how we got here, what we urgently need to do now, and how we're doing. But it's a heavy lift emotionally and intellectually, especially for educators, who work on a daily basis with young people, who are growing into a seriously damaged world and facing a precarious future.

This underlines the importance of the foundational dimension of our vision: building the beloved community. To move forward, joyfully working to save what we can save, we need our trustworthy relationships and equitable communities of support, our social and emotional skills, and our brave spaces for sharing feelings and concerns.

The teachers featured in the chapter did not shield their students from the knowledge required for deep understanding. Bayard had his students read Bill McKibben's *Eaarth*. Beth framed the second semester of her climate change course with the question, Will climate be the end of New York City? Ishmael makes no bones about where he thinks our civilization is headed if we don't change our relationship with nature. Nor does David Attenborough in *A Life on Our Planet*, which Cindy shows to all her students. Lesley engages her students in deep understanding of the challenges Indigenous peoples are facing around the world. Xochitl has her students read a decades-old dystopian novel set in 2020, which describes horrible events that are eerie extensions of events actually happening now.

These teachers certainly didn't coddle their students. But their teaching methods did foster community and agency. Bayard's Global Environmental Politics course complemented and supported his mentoring of powerful young climate activists. Beth's students shared their learnings with their local community and their mitigation and adaptation strategies with city officials. A self-described "mom figure" for the students, Cindy enthusiastically shares all the green things she does and encourages her students to do the same. Lesley's simulation connected students with each other and strengthened their social and emotional skills. In leading her students' exploration of *Parable of the Sower*, Xochitl focused on Lauren as a model of shrewd and courageous leadership for her students to emulate.

Although they revealed to students the truth about our situation, the teachers engaged them actively, introduced them to new ideas and experiences, increased their knowledge, strengthened their sense of agency, helped them develop new skills, and opened their eyes to new opportunities—in ways that were often fun. Although none of the teachers sugarcoated the crisis, my bet is that students came away with greater awareness of what is needed and what is possible.

Chapter 4 builds on this sense of possibility by introducing a tough-minded, resilient conception of hope, not as something we have, but as something we do. While chapter 3 has focused on what we're fighting *against*, chapter 4 provides real-life visions of what we're fighting *for*: the building blocks of a new world in which humans live in balance and harmony with each other and with nature.

CHAPTER 4

Practice Active Hope: Envision a Just and Sustainable Future

JESSICA SUDY TRACES her passion for teaching Earth science and climate to her childhood. "Growing up in a small town in western Michigan, I was always outside," she recalls. "My mom has a love for nature and the rule was when it's nice out we were outside playing, if I'd try to stay inside, intent on watching TV on a sunny day, she'd say, 'You can be inside all day. We can mop, sweep, wash the clothes, all of it.' "

So, growing up, Jessica was rarely inside. Instead, she was outside, studying the bugs that lived by the creek that flowed through the woods around her house. Climbing trees, she learned that pine sap doesn't come off hands easily. She built forts, collected specimens, and let her imagination take the lead. "Now as an adult," she says, "I am comfortable in nature because it became a second home for me as a child."

After teaching middle school in Beaverton, Oregon, for several years, Jessica moved to Grand Rapids, Michigan, and got a position at East Kentwood High School. What drew her to the school was its diversity. Many of the school's 1,800 students come from other countries.

Although new at the school, she managed to trade classes with another teacher so that she could teach Earth science—and climate change. Then she struck up a relationship with a space science teacher. They hatched the idea of an Earth and space science class based on "what-if" scenarios: What if the sun explodes? What if an asteroid crashes into the Earth? What if aliens invade? They agreed that this would be a sure way to engage the students. It was a bold idea, but Jessica wasn't afraid to try it. "I'm not a shy person," she acknowledges. "People learn pretty quickly where I stand, and I attract people who are similar."

In the class, students moved from learning about the universe, galaxies, stars, and our solar system, to the possibility of life on other planets and the idea of an alien invasion. They explored questions such as: Why would aliens want to invade our planet in the first place? What about our planet is unique? Why is it habitable? "And that," says Jessica, "brought us to Earth science. Kids realized that for us 'There is no Planet B.' So don't get comfortable with the idea that you have a backup because you really don't. We will survive a lot better by fixing the problems that we have created on this planet. Here, we have an awesome functional spaceship that's giving us everything we need. So let's stop sabotaging it!"

With every question the class explored, they took on an engineering design challenge as a "fun, creative thinking exercise." For example, in a brainstorming session on the question, "What if the sun explodes?" a student proposed that "we could build giant reflecting panels to reflect the sun's light so the explosion wouldn't warm the planet so much."

The class then turned to thinking about more immediate challenges, like melting ice caps and sea-level rise. They researched how many people live in coastal areas and would be displaced. Where would they go?

Jessica and her coteacher learned that what-if scenarios are fun and not only can spark students' imaginations but can also heighten their interest in both space and Earth science. Their experience echoes that of Jared Fox and Erick Espin (chapter 2), whose students were so excited by their visits deep into Highbridge Park that they asked a slew of what-if questions that are now being realized as the Clean Air Green Corridor Project.

Dreaming like this—looking at reality, asking what-if questions, tapping our imaginations for creative answers, and envisioning boldly—is an essential skill and practice for addressing the climate crisis. It's a starting place for active hope, the focus of this chapter. The chapter addresses three questions: First, how can we find hope in the face of the formidable challenges ahead? Second, what are we fighting for? We know what we're up against. But what visions do we have for the future? And third, how can we and our students discern the best ways for each of us, personally, to help create that future?

PRACTICE ACTIVE HOPE

What if a global movement involving hundreds of millions of people rose up to create a world order based on climate justice? This could happen! In fact, millions of people around the world are working hard to bring this about, probably including you. In their book, *Active Hope: How to Face the Mess We're in Without Going Crazy*, Chris Johnstone and Joanna Macy call this the Great Turning.[1]

Johnstone and Macy see the Great Turning as one of three stories that are being enacted in our time—scenarios that inform the way we understand our world and live our lives. One of these stories, Business as Usual, currently holds sway. It depicts modern life as a wonderful (if perhaps somewhat flawed) success story and insists that the future must provide more of the same. Unlimited economic growth, more goods for more people, nature as an unlimited source of commodities to serve human needs—these are our birthrights as humans. Despite growing awareness that this is not sustainable, the story is maintained by powerful systems, wealthy individuals who have outsize influence in politics, and deep-seated, widely held assumptions that this is how things are and must continue to be.

A second story, the Great Unraveling, is where Business as Usual is taking us. As we face climate disasters, the pandemic, and dire scientific predictions for the future, we may feel like throwing up our hands in despair. Many of us are actually living out both of these stories at the same time: We plan our lives based on the assumption that life will continue to be what it is today. But as upsetting events occur around us, we get the feeling that society is collapsing and that there's nothing we can do about it.

Then there is the Great Turning: People around the world rise up to establish a just and life-sustaining global society.[2]

Three stories—and a choice! Each of us needs to decide which of these stories will inform the way we live our lives. Chances are you have made your choice. You have chosen to embrace the Great Turning—and are reading this book to bolster your resolve.

I think of the story of the Great Turning as having four themes. They are active hope, adventure, discovery, and abundance.

"Active hope is not wishful thinking," write Johnstone and Macy. "Active hope is not waiting to be rescued by the Lone Ranger or by some savior. Active hope is waking up to the beauty of life on whose behalf we can act."[3]

One kind of hope is optimism. Another kind is what we hope *for*. Active hope is the latter kind of hope. We envision what we hope for and consider how we can best contribute to bringing it about. Once we've discerned the place where, in the words of Frederick Buechner, our "deep gladness meets the world's deep hunger," we get to work.[4] Active hope is not something we have; it's something we do.

Active hope launches us on an adventure. The stakes couldn't be higher. The challenges couldn't be greater. The ultimate outcome is not determined. Of course, there are risks, as there are in any adventure. But we accept those risks as we work to create a habitable world for our children and grandchildren, for all those we love, for people around the world, and for all living beings. We feel privileged to be alive at this critical time in the history of life on Earth and to join millions of others in playing our part. The Great Turning is the adventure of our time.

The adventure will inevitably stretch us, and this leads to discovery. As we offer our gifts of active hope, we discover new strengths in ourselves and others, new sources of personal and collective power, a richer experience of community, and deeper connections with our fellow humans and with nature.

The work will test our limits. Sometimes we will have to stretch ourselves until we ache and pain all over. But the reward will be abundance. We have chosen a life of great meaning and purpose. We have accepted the opportunity to develop our strengths and our power to make a difference. We are enjoying the companionship of close friends and comrades. All this, rather than the accumulation of material goods, becomes our conception of the abundant life.

For the Classroom

In a go-round, invite your students to share a gift they would like to give to the world, and why. Begin by sharing a gift you would like to give and explain your reasons.

Follow up by inviting your students to write and/or prepare to tell a story in which a protagonist (themselves or a person, animal, or superhero they imagine) decides to offer a gift to the world and, upon doing so, has adventures, makes discoveries, and ultimately triumphs. Encourage students to let their imaginations flourish.

Do this yourself. Write and/or tell a story you have imagined.

ENVISION A JUST AND SUSTAINABLE FUTURE

What new world does the climate crisis give us the opportunity—and the necessity—to create? Active hope begins with envisioning what we hope for and discerning how we might best contribute to making our vision a reality.

We don't have to start from scratch. Many courageous, creative, persistent people around the world have envisioned a just and sustainable future and are working to make it a reality.

The following is but a sampling of living visions of what a just and sustainable future might look like. The examples are categorized into seven areas: economy; energy; agriculture, land, and food; women and girls; nature; Indigenous wisdom; and education.

Economy: Put People and the Planet First

The economic system that has been ascendant for the past 275 years has hit a ceiling. This system, based on fossil fuels, unlimited growth, and private profit-making, produced a staggering amount of food and material goods for an exploding human population. It created unprecedented wealth, although most of it went to the richest people in the Global North.

Now it's clear that humanity has paid a terrible price for these achievements. The climate is warming; natural systems are deteriorating; and inequality is rampant. A recent study estimated that the richest 16 percent of the human population is responsible for 50 percent of humanity's impact on the living world.[5]

Many people believe that tinkering with this system won't be sufficient. We need a whole new economic paradigm. This new model of economic relationships, based on climate justice, aims to:

- bring human activity into harmony with nature, respecting the boundaries specified in the Planetary Boundaries Model and aligned with Ishmael's peace-keeping law as well (chapter 3); and
- ensure human well-being, which means decent housing, clean air and water, nutritious food, energy, education, income, and a voice in shaping the institutions that affect our lives—not just for the richest among us, but for everyone.

This new economic system will be based on a different conception of growth—not growth in production and consumption of material goods but on growth in protecting nature and in fostering human happiness. Profit will be not for the enrichment of a few but will be distributed equitably to support nature and humanity. In the new climate justice economy, power will shift from unelected corporate executives who make life and death decisions based on profitability to democratic institutions accountable to the people.

Is this a pipe dream? Many would call it that. But it seemed like a pipe dream when William Wilberforce and his colleagues began their work to end the slave trade in England, and when Mahatma Gandhi began his struggle for Indian independence, and when Nelson Mandela began his fight to end apartheid in South Africa.

The work of social transformation is always grounded in a vision—an impossible dream.

How might we as educators engage our students in exploring such expansive visions? Consider inviting students to dig into two practical proposals that begin to flesh out a new economic paradigm based on climate justice: the Happy Planet Index and the Green New Deal.

The Happy Planet Index During the past seventy years, nations around the world have adopted one overarching goal: economic growth, as measured by gross domestic product (GDP). GDP measures the quantity of material goods produced and services provided. In this economic model, the success of companies and national economies is measured by the amount of goods and services produced and consumed and, crucially, by the percentage of *growth* in production each year.

Unfortunately, even as GDP has risen, inequality has soared, and even in the world's richest economy, most Americans are financially insecure. Meanwhile, continuous growth, even so-called green growth, is no longer sustainable on our finite planet.

In 2016, the New Economics Foundation created a new way to measure economic success that takes the well-being of people and the environment into account. It's called the Happy Planet Index (HPI). It assesses a nation's economic success by measuring the three Ps: profit, people, planet, with profit distributed equitably to support nature and humanity. Judged by the HPI, the most successful economies are New Zealand and Costa Rica, not the United States and China, which currently lead in GDP.[6]

> **For the Classroom**
>
> Invite students to:
>
> - research how well the United States measures up on the HPI;
> - identify areas for improvement; and
> - envision ways to address them.
>
> Engage students in dialogue on such questions as:
>
> - What should really constitute success for a company or national economy?
> - What is the good life—and how might an economic system support it?

The Green New Deal The Green New Deal (GND) is an aspirational resolution proposed in February 2019 by Representative Alexandria Ocasio-Cortez (D-NY) and Senator Ed Markey (D-MA) and supported by a wide range of climate justice advocates. It's a vision for the future based on a story about where we are, how we got here, and what values we need to guide our way forward. Rhiana Gunn-Wright, one of the authors of the GND, explains the concept. The goals are to:

- achieve a zero-carbon economy by 2030 through a fair and justice transition for all communities and workers;
- create millions of high-wage jobs;
- invest in the infrastructure and industry we need to meet the challenges of the twenty-first century;
- secure clean water and air, climate and community resiliency, healthy food, access to nature, and a sustainable environment; and

- promote justice and equity by stopping current, preventing future, and repairing historic oppression of frontline and vulnerable communities.

The GND proposes two broad strategies for achieving these ambitious goals: major projects to eliminate carbon emissions (such as building and installing hundreds of thousands of wind turbines) and government policies to reduce inequity and protect vulnerable Americans from the disruption and instability that moving away from fossil fuels will create.[7]

Story from the Classroom

Soon after the GND (H.R. 109) was introduced in February 2019, Bayard Faithfull of The Beacon School in New York City engaged students in his Global Environmental Politics class in a project. They were to work in groups of three. Each group was asked to prepare an eight- to ten-page single-spaced policy memo for the resolution's sponsors explaining the best policies to achieve the GND. "Good policy weighs multiple factors: costs, constituencies, political feasibility, and likely outcomes," read the instructions for the project. "Good policy is supported by research from credible sources. Refer to relevant legislation and research."

To support the students, Bayard provided twenty-six links to information on federal policy, including the text of the resolution, state policies, policy proposals from think tanks, climate research, and scientific and technical analysis.

In addition to the policy memo, each group was asked to prepare a four- to five-minute slide presentation explaining the key features of their proposal and why it would be most effective.

Reflects Bayard, "We ended the unit with kids saying, 'Hey, this is not so hard.' And that's my take on it, too. If we can mobilize the political will and get Exxon out of the way, we can actually do this transformation relatively easily. We ended on a hopeful note with kids saying, 'Wow, this is really possible. This is not just tree-hugger pie-in-the-sky stuff. If you look at the science and you look at the math, and you look at the technology, everything is in place for us to make this transformation.' "

Energy: Shift to Renewables, Democratically Controlled

The energy vision is to achieve a sustainable energy system that is in sync with the economic model described above. In this system:

- clean and renewable sources of energy completely replace fossil fuels; and
- energy production and distribution is controlled and managed democratically, not by private profit-making corporations.

Renewable Energy Renewable energy is energy collected from sources that are naturally replaced on a human timescale, not like fossil fuels, which took millions of years to form. Wind, sun, rain, waves, tides, water, and geothermal heat are examples of renewable energy sources. They are also clean, emitting no carbon or other greenhouse gases into the atmosphere. Renewables are key to our efforts to reverse global warming and create a sustainable future.

Wind turbines are a good example of the benefits of renewable energy. The highly regarded Project Drawdown ranks onshore wind energy second among the eighty most promising solutions it has identified for reversing global warming. According to Drawdown, some 314,000 wind turbines are now in operation around the world to turn wind energy into electricity. Some are in the ocean; most are on land.

Currently, wind turbines supply only about 4 percent of the world's electricity. If Drawdown has its way, they will soon provide much more. Wind turbines can be built quickly at relatively low cost; their operation produces no carbon or pollution. Because they take up only 1 percent of the land on which they stand, grazing, farming, and recreation can occur simultaneously with energy production. It's estimated that the wind in three states, Kansas, North Dakota, and Texas, could serve the electricity needs of the entire United States.

This technology does have some downsides, although they pale in comparison with those of fossil fuels: Because wind is variable, there are times when the turbines are not turning. But interconnected grids over a wide area can shuttle power to where it's needed. Wind turbines can also be enormous. Some are higher than the Statue of Liberty, with blades that turn in a circle with a diameter the length of a football field. They transform the landscapes where they are sited, which sometimes leads to local opposition. Some renewable energy advocates argue for smaller scale, decentralized wind and solar systems that serve the homes and communities around them. These smaller systems also have the potential to make the country's power grid more resilient and reduce the amount of electricity lost in transmission.

If our government shifted its resources toward building wind and solar energy (in whatever form) and away from subsidizing the fossil-fuel industry, these renewable sources could meet most of our energy needs within the next decade or two, according to Drawdown.[8]

Energy Democracy Unfortunately, wind and solar still supply only a small fraction of the world's energy needs, and the production of fossil fuels is expanding as well, as the world's economy continues to grow. Currently, renewables are not growing fast enough to replace fossil fuels, but they simply make more growth possible. As one advocate put it, "Renewable energy is galloping forward at a snail's pace."[9]

We need to reorient the energy sector to protect the environment and equitably fulfill human needs. Many believe that we will not be able to accomplish this within the parameters of our current energy system based on profit-making and unlimited growth. We need a whole new model: democratization of the energy sector based on energy justice.

In this vision, energy (clean and renewable, of course) would be seen as a public good. Public utilities would build the infrastructure for renewables and manage their production and distribution, overseen by federal, state, and local governments.

Energy systems would be shaped by the public to serve the people and the planet, not controlled by private profit-making corporations, accountable only to boards of directors and shareholders with their eyes fixed primarily on the bottom line. Advocates for a publicly run energy system argue that the CEOs of fossil-fuel companies have brought humanity to the brink of catastrophe. They and the private profit-making system they created have forfeited any legitimate claim to call the shots now or in the future.

Of course, challenges aplenty lie ahead in making this transition, not the least of which is the huge wealth and political clout of the fossil-fuel industry. It will take a broad-based democratic movement to set us on the right path. The need for this movement is urgent and imperative. This may very well be the only chance we have to get things right.

A precedent exists for these democratically controlled and managed renewable energy systems: the two thousand public utilities that currently operate state and local energy systems in the public's interest around the United States. The customers of these public utilities pay 15 percent less for their energy and experience fewer blackouts than customers of private energy companies. Under energy democracy, public utilities not only would manage the system but also would be the *producers* of energy (e.g., those manufacturing the wind turbines and solar panels), accountable to the public and established with public money to serve the common good, not private actors driven primarily by the profit motive. To be successful, the movement for renewable energy must go forward in tandem with the movement for energy democracy.[10]

Renewables open another avenue for democracy as well: they give local communities more freedom to adapt the energy system to their needs. This was impossible under the fossil-fuel monopoly, which has required extraction of oil and gas around the world; pipelines and tankers to move crude oil to plants for processing; huge, centralized power plants; and a centralized electrical grid.

Renewables allow cities or local communities to create their own energy system or adapt their existing one. For example, according to their website, UPROSE, a nonprofit climate justice organization in the Sunset Park section of Brooklyn, is in the process of creating a solar farm to provide low-cost clean energy for its low-income community.

Story from the Classroom

In chapter 3, we met science teacher Beth Mowry and learned about her course in climate science at Brooklyn Collaborative Studies. Beth also taught a class in green engineering with coteacher Phil Schoolman.

In the fall semester of the 2019–20 school year, the green engineering class focused on this question: How does our school building get and use its energy? Students traced the journey of New York City's electricity from its origin to their classroom. They conducted an energy audit of carbon emissions and learned ways to make their school more sustainable. The culminating activity was a poster presentation about the true cost of the energy used in the building.

In the spring semester, students became wind turbine engineers. They learned how wind turbines generate electricity and conducted scientific experiments using model wind turbines they constructed. "The green engineering class was a big highlight of the school year," reflects Beth. "When we had to shut down in-person school in March 2020 because of the COVID-19 pandemic, the kids had already begun work on their performance-based assessment tasks (PBATs), which involved conducting experiments about factors affecting the efficiency of wind turbines, such as the number, length, and curvature of the blades for the rotor. Phil and I had to figure out how the heck kids were going to get data for their graduation requirement paper." The solution: Phil took the lab supplies home and set up a model wind turbine in his basement with a fan. Working with small groups of students on Zoom, Phil implemented their experiments on the model in his basement while students watched on Zoom and collected the data.

"A wind turbine engineer from Denmark Skyped with the class through a program called 'Skype a scientist,'" Beth recalls. "She joined one of our Zoom sessions with the students and explained what's it like to be a wind turbine engineer. She also sat on a couple of PBAT panels in which students shared their knowledge, described their experiments, and presented their data. It was awesome!"

Food, Land, and Agriculture: Shift to Agroecology and a Plant-Based Diet

The major cause of biodiversity loss is the conversion of wild habitat to farmland. In the year 1700, humans were farming about one billion hectares of land. Now we are farming five billion hectares (a hectare is 2.47 acres). This process has accelerated in the past three decades as agribusiness has used its money and political clout to seize land around the world and clear it to make way for its large single-crop plantations.

In addition to reducing biodiversity, the destruction of these wild habitats contributes significantly to global warming by releasing carbon from plants that are cut and burned and from soil that is plowed. The expansion of industrial agriculture has also forced many peasants off their land, depriving them of their livelihoods and ways of life.

Industrial agriculture is also not sustainable because it depends on fossil fuels, which have no part in a viable future for humankind. Nor are they good for the soil. Under natural conditions and sustainable farming practices, soil regenerates and sustains itself. But industrial farmland is artificially sustained by pesticides and fertilizers made from fossil fuels, which destroy the soil's natural processes and eventually deplete it.[11]

According to the website of Cooperative Climate Futures, industrial agriculture is inequitable as well: It uses up 70 percent of agricultural resources to feed 30 percent of the world's population. Peasant and Indigenous agriculture uses 30 percent of the agricultural resources to feed 70 percent of the world's population, and it does so sustainably.[12]

We need to stop converting wild habitats to industrial farmland. But how can we produce more food on less land and do it sustainably? Following are two living examples that point toward a better future for the poorest and most marginalized people of the world as well as for all of humanity and the natural world: agroecology and a plant-based diet.

Agroecology Agroecology is the holistic approach to designing sustainable agriculture and food systems. According to Cooperative Climate Futures, it seeks to foster mutually beneficial relationships among plants, animals, humans, and the environment—while giving people a choice over what they eat and how that food is produced. It draws on knowledge of Indigenous and peasant farmers gleaned over thousands of years. It sees food production and distribution as an opportunity to strengthen social bonds in local communities.

Food sovereignty is the heart of agroecology. La Via Campesina, a global food justice and peasant rights organization, envisions food sovereignty as a social movement based on the principles that food is a human right; that it should be produced, consumed, and controlled locally; that food production should develop the skills of people in the local community; and that it should grow out of a reverent and reciprocal partnership with nature.

East New York Farms, where Bayard took his students on a field trip, is a living example of food sovereignty. Founded in 1988, the organization works with young people and adults to address food justice by promoting local sustainable agriculture and community-led economic development. According to their website, they operate two farmers markets, three urban farms, and one community garden. Two of the farms are located in low-income New York City Housing Authority projects. They provide an intensive nine-month internship program in which thirty-five young people learn and practice sustainable farming, environmental stewardship, and farm marketing.[13]

For the Classroom

Research whether any of the organizations, farms, community gardens, or farmers markets in your area could provide students with a view of an alternative agricultural system. Schedule a visit and then engage students in a discussion about how this local effort connects to the broader movement for climate justice. Invite students to consider ways their school might connect to the organization, farm, or market.

Forest gardens and regenerative agriculture are two key practices of agroecology. Forest gardens (multistrata agroforests) mimic natural forests, which support a variety of life-forms from the microorganisms in their soil to plants on the ground to mammals and birds up to their highest branches. Indigenous people have cultivated forest gardens for thousands of years by planting trees whose products sustain humans, such as macadamia, coconut, pineapple, banana, coffee, cacao, rubber, and trees for timber. The benefits to the environment are many, including preventing erosion and flooding, restoring degraded soil, supporting biodiversity, and sequestering carbon.[14]

There are some 250 million acres of food forests around the world, primarily in the tropics. These are generally small plots of dense, diverse layers of trees and crops planted close to where people live. Their central purpose is feeding families, but they can also provide medicinal plants and other items that can be sold. By providing food security, some income, and climate benefits, forest gardens are the ultimate in sustainability. Most common crops are coffee, cacao, fruit, vegetables, herbs, and fuel. Forest gardens are ideal for small landholders who live in densely populated areas.[15]

Regenerative agriculture restores degraded land and prevents land from becoming degraded in the first place. No tilling is involved, because tilling exposes the soil and sends its carbon into the air. Farmers use only organic fertilizers, plant a variety of crops, plant cover crops to restore the soil, and use crop rotation. The purpose is to promote healthy soil by restoring (or maintaining) its carbon, which plants capture from the atmosphere through photosynthesis. Carbon is what makes soil naturally fertile by drawing in the millions of microorganisms that protect the roots and the plant, by attracting the worms that deposit nitrogen to enrich the soil, and by improving the soil's ability to retain water. Drawdown ranks regenerative agriculture as number eleven of its eighty solutions to reverse global warming.[16]

Industrial agriculture has produced food cheaply by not paying for the damage it causes to soil, water, birds, beneficial insects, human health, and the climate. Regenerative agriculture and food forests and gardens provide an alternative and hopeful vision for the future.

Plant-Based Diet Humanity has many reasons to shift to a plant-based diet, especially in the Global North. Our meat-rich Western diet requires too much agricultural land, emits too much greenhouse gas, and is bad for our health. In addition, the concentrated animal feeding operations (CAFOs) where cows, hogs, chickens, and other animals are grown for food, cram these creatures (and their waste) together in concentrations that are not healthy for the animals or the land.

Nearly 80 percent of farmland worldwide is used for meat and dairy production. Much of this space is not for livestock, but for crops and corn, often grown in a different country, as feed for cattle, chicken, and pigs. Beef makes up a quarter of the meat we eat. It provides only 2 percent of our calories, but we devote 60 percent of our farmland for raising it.[17]

The most conservative estimates hold that raising livestock creates 15 percent of global greenhouse gas emissions. The most comprehensive estimates, which take into account direct and indirect emissions, put the figure at 50 percent. If cattle were their own nation, they would be the third largest emitter of greenhouse gas. Project Drawdown ranks a plant-rich diet as number four of its eighty solutions to reverse global warming.[18]

A study from the University of Oxford found that the transition to a plant-based diet between now and 2050 could reduce emissions by as much as 70 percent for a vegan diet and 63 percent for a vegetarian diet (which includes cheese, milk, and eggs). A 2016 report from the World Resources Institute found that "ambitious animal protein reduction"—focused on reducing overconsumption of animal-based foods in regions where people devour more than sixty grams of protein and 2,500 calories per day—holds the greatest promise for ensuring a sustainable future for global food supply and the planet.

On average, adults require about fifty grams of protein each day. In 2009, the average per capita consumption globally was sixty-eight grams, 36 percent more than necessary. In the United States and Canada, consumption of protein averaged ninety grams. Where plant-based protein is abundant, human beings do not need animal protein, and too much of it can lead to heart disease, strokes, and certain cancers.

This will be a challenging transition, because meat-eating has become embedded in culture and tradition. It's encouraging that plant-based meat alternatives are gaining traction. It will be necessary to reframe meat as a rare delicacy rather than a staple. It would help for the US government to end price-distorting subsidies to the US livestock industry so that prices would reflect the true costs of meat.[19]

For the Classroom

Engage students in an exploration of their own food choices and the impact they have on the environment and their own health. Invite them to consider changes to make their diet more sustainable, healthier, and kinder to animals. Show the film *Food, Inc.* as Cindy Vitale did (chapter 3). Try Bayard Faithfull's sustainability challenge (chapter 3).

Women and Girls: Educate and Empower, and Achieve "Peak Human"

The climate crisis is not gender neutral. Plagued by existing injustices, women and girls are disproportionally vulnerable to climate change impacts. Most affected are girls and women of color, those in the Global South, and those who are rural and Indigenous. Members of the LGBTQ community are extremely vulnerable as well.

Girls' education advocate Malala Yousafzai has said, "One child, one teacher, one book, one pen can change the world."[20] Lots of evidence says she's right. Educated girls and women earn higher wages. Their rates of maternal mortality are lower, as are mortality rates for their babies. Their agricultural plots are more productive. Education is the most powerful lever for breaking the cycle of intergenerational poverty. Education also strengthens resilience from climate change impacts. A 2013 study of the experiences of 125 countries since 1980 concluded that educating girls is the single most important social and economic factor associated with reducing their vulnerability to climate disasters. This finding extends to their children and families as well.[21]

Drawdown also ranks girls' education as number six of its eighty best solutions for reversing global warming.[22]

How could this be?

We know that humanity must stay within the boundaries of the natural systems that make our planet habitable for humans. To achieve this, the human population cannot continue to grow at its current rate. The United Nations has projected that if current trends continue, the human population will peak (i.e., level off) early in the twenty-second century at about 11 billion people, which is 3.2 billion more than today.

This is not sustainable. Even now, with a global population of 7.8 billion, we are approaching or exceeding the carrying capacity of our planet. Can we make "peak human" come sooner?

The answer is yes. Evidence shows that distributing resources more equitably and improving the lives of all will reduce the human population. As human well-being increases, societies experience a leveling off of the population. The path for achieving this is to end poverty, build health-care services and networks, provide education, ensure energy security (from renewables, of course), and empower women to decide how many children they want to have. According to the Brookings Institution, a woman with no education has an average of four to five more children than one with twelve years of education.[23] When investments in girls' education are joined with investments in family planning, the impacts are complementary and mutually reinforcing. In 2014, the United Nations Intergovernmental Panel on Climate Change (IPCC) began including access to reproductive health services in its reports and identified population growth as a factor in greenhouse gas emissions.[24]

Family planning is not a hard sell for many women. According to Drawdown, 214 million women in low-income countries say they want the freedom to choose whether and when to become pregnant, but they lack access to contraception. The result: seventy-four million unintended pregnancies each year.[25]

Efforts to reduce population growth are controversial. Barriers include social and religious norms, opposition to birth control by sexual partners, lack of contraceptive resources, and lack of sex education. Call it what you will, it comes down to sexism—a scourge we must end to ensure the well-being of women, girls, and the planet.

In *All We Can Save: Truth, Courage, and Solutions for the Climate Crisis*, editors Ayana Elizabeth Johnson and Katharine K. Wilkinson argue that leadership by women and girls is shaping the climate justice movement and is critical to its success. Their book proves their point. It consists of dozens of short essays and poems, all by women who are serving the movement in a variety of ways: doing research, organizing protests, running organizations, creating art, planning strategy, creating policy, carrying out climate-friendly government programs, advising presidents, and more.[26]

For the Classroom

Read *A Long Walk to Water* to your students, as Megan Wellford did (chapter 2).[27] Introduce your students to the barriers girls face in attending school in other parts of the world. Engage your students in learning more about this inequity and in taking some action to address it, as Megan's students did.

Nature: Rewild the Earth

I love David Attenborough's injunction that we "rewild" the Earth. It's an exciting way to name what many of our visions for the future are all about: making more room for nature, our dear partner here on Earth, to flourish. Nature is amazingly resilient. If we can change our ways—and do so quickly—we can "rewild" the Earth. Reimagining economics and growth; keeping fossil fuels in the ground; shifting to renewable energy; halting the land grab by agribusiness; using agroecological farming practices; moving to a largely plant-based diet; fostering the education and empowerment of women and girls; and reaching peak human as soon as possible—all of these transformations will give nature space to grow back and room to breathe.

The following examples briefly describe three other critical ways to rewild the Earth.

Rewild the Seas Our oceans are in trouble. Chapter 3 discussed the threat to the marine food chain as coral dies and coral reefs are destroyed by the warming and acidification of the ocean. Ending our use of fossil fuels is the way to address this.

The other threat is overfishing. The ocean has far fewer fish than it had even fifty years ago. By rewilding the seas, we can accomplish three critical goals at once: we can capture carbon, restore biodiversity, and supply more food. The healthier and more biodiverse the oceans are, the more fish there will be. This is a life-and-death matter for the billion people, mostly in poor areas, who depend on fish as their primary source of protein.

At present, we're doing the opposite of what we need to do to restore our oceans to health. We are fishing some places and some species too much; we use fishing techniques that are wasteful and indiscriminate; and we fish everywhere. As Attenborough puts it, "There is nowhere in the ocean to hide."[28]

Attenborough calls for five solutions:

- Significantly increase the number of marine-protected areas (MPAs) and expand the area they cover. MPAs are fishing-free areas that enable fish to propagate undisturbed and grow to full size, thus maintaining and ultimately increasing fish populations. The aim is to be able to fish forever, not just for a few more decades.
- Use smarter fishing techniques—for example, nets with escape hatches for nontarget fish.
- Eliminate subsidies to the fishing industry by some governments, including the United States, which encourage fleets to overfish waters that otherwise would not be profitable.

- Replace unsustainable practices, now rife in the aquaculture (fish-farming) industry, with sustainable ones.
- Encourage ocean forestry.

By cooperating to agree on a set of rules and practices that are fair and farsighted, the nations of the world can protect the amazing gifts the oceans give us, instead of destroying them for short-term profit.[29]

Support a Circular Economy People who have grown up in the past few decades probably don't realize that the disposable society in which we now live is relatively new. This must not be the way of the future. In nature, nothing is wasted. Everywhere, life eats life: one living being's life, remains, or waste is another's food. Our current way of life, based on *take* (from nature and the Earth), *make* (some product or commodity), *use* (often only once), and *discard*, is not sustainable. Our vision for the future, the "circular economy," would be modeled on nature. Everything would be reused. For example, products would be built to last. They would have interchangeable parts that could be replaced when they wear out. Manufacturing would need to be standardized so that parts would be more easily available. Materials that went into building products would be recycled to create new products as needed. "The cleverness," says Attenborough, "is in designing ways to do so." Such cleverness would be possible in an economy based on what's good for people and the planet, rather than on growth in GDP and short-term profits.[30]

Create Cities Friendly to People and Nature The number of people living in cities is increasing. Some predictions see 68 percent of the world's population living in cities by 2050. Often seen as a scourge on the environment, cities can be friendly to nature if planned creatively with nature in mind. Their high population density can be an asset, with mass transit and bicycles carrying people to and from work at much less cost to the environment than cars.[31] The Green Corridor Project being developed by students at the Washington Heights Expeditionary Learning School (WHEELS) in New York City (described in chapter 2) exemplifies a creative way to bring city dwellers and nature into a mutually beneficial relationship.

Indigenous Wisdom: Heal Our Broken Relationship with the Earth

Educator, writer, and activist Sherri Mitchell, Weh'na Ha'mu Kwasset, Penawahpskek Nation, points out that the racist ideologies used to justify the exploitation of Indigenous people and their lands also relegated Indigenous knowledge to obscurity. Because Indigenous people didn't share European ideas about land, commerce, and humans' relationship with nature, the colonizers saw Indigenous people as primitive and ignorant.

With growing awareness that the views and practices of the colonizers are driving the world to disaster, people are increasingly turning to Indigenous ways of knowing and working with nature. Indigenous people have another critical asset as well. Although Indigenous people account for only 5 percent of the global population, they occupy lands with approximately 80 percent of the world's biodiversity and an estimated 40 percent to 50 percent of the remaining protected places in the world. These areas also have the largest carbon stores on the planet. Writes Mitchell, "This makes the protection of Indigenous rights, along with our lands and ways of life, critical to the well-being of the planet, and it makes us natural partners in the race to address climate change."[32]

Gratitude Despite the barriers, Indigenous people are doing their best to keep their knowledge and traditions alive. Children attending the Onondaga Nation's school in upstate New York begin each week, not with the Pledge of Allegiance, but with the Thanksgiving Address, a tradition of the Haudenosaunee people.

The address is also known as "The Words That Come Before All Else," because it is delivered in Native Haudenosaunee languages at the beginning and end of social gatherings and meetings.

"Today we have gathered," the address begins. "We have been given the duty to live in balance and harmony with each other and all living things." Reading and reciting the address, the children and their teachers offer greetings and thanks to specific aspects of the natural world, including the Earth, water, plants, animals, trees, sun, moon, and stars, for the gifts they bestow upon us. Each expression of thanks ends with, "Now our minds are one."[33]

Our modern society, based on a market economy, views nature primarily as a commodity, an unlimited source of things to buy and sell to fulfill human needs and desires, including making money and accumulating wealth. This is the mind-set driving the political and economic systems that are destroying the environment.

In *Braiding Sweetgrass*, Robin Wall Kimmerer eloquently invites us to embrace a perspective that sees nature in a radically different way. Braiding sweetgrass is a metaphor for the stories she braids together from her Indigenous heritage, from science (she is a professor of botany), and from her life—they are stories "meant to heal our relationship with the Earth."[34]

The foundation is gratitude, as exemplified by the Thanksgiving Address. When we regard nature, we need to see her for what she really is: our partner on this Earth and a most generous bestower of gifts. We owe everything to nature. Without nature, humans wouldn't even exist. Gratitude should indeed be "the words that come before all else."

Reciprocity As I read aloud the version of the address in *Braiding Sweetgrass*, I slow down and pause for a moment to take in the special gifts we receive from each part of the natural world and picture the children reciting the address. I am deeply moved. We do, indeed, owe nature a huge debt of gratitude for all these gifts—and repayment of this debt needs to go beyond gratitude as well, Kimmerer asserts. We need to honor the gifts nature gives us by giving to nature in return.

This chapter opened with an invitation to discern and share our gifts of active hope. Kimmerer's discussion of gifts—and specifically the gifts nature gives us—deepens my understanding of active hope and what it means. She helps me see my gifts of active hope in the context of humans' broken relationship with nature. I offer my gifts of active hope in return for nature's bountiful gifts to me and to restore, as best I can, the harm I and my fellow humans have done and are continuing to do to nature.

The Honorable Harvest To live, we take from the lives of other living beings. This is a given: life eats life. Our food is a gift and often a sacrifice of another living being. Although we must live with this reality, love for nature calls us to do so respectfully. What sensibilities and practices should guide our harvesting? Kimmerer introduces us to the Indigenous canon of principles and practices that govern the exchange of life for life. It's called the Honorable Harvest.

"The guidelines for the Honorable Harvest are not written down or even consistently spoken of as a whole," Kimmerer writes. "They are reinforced in small acts of daily life."[35] She lists what some of the guidelines might look like, if written down. Reading her list, I gather precepts such as these: Ask permission. Take only what you need and don't waste it. Use what you take in a way that is worthy of the sacrifice the giver made. Give in return for the gifts you are getting.

You get the idea. It's a completely different way of relating to nature. I'm struck by how far our society is from practicing the Honorable Harvest. Guided by this sensibility, sustainability is not about how we can keep on taking from nature. It's about what we can give to nature. The visions described in this chapter, if implemented, would go a long way toward restoring our broken relationship with nature. I also wonder what small acts I might integrate into my daily life to reinforce my living in tune with the Honorable Harvest.

Education: Teach for Climate Justice

This is the shortest section of this chapter, not because it's less important than the others, but because this entire book presents a vision for transforming education to contribute to the Great Turning. I offer a meditative practice that may help you stay centered as you offer your gifts of active hope through your work with your students.

Pause for Centering and Renewal

Pause for Centering and Renewal is a regular practice, adapted from one developed by Joanna Macy and Chris Johnstone, which aims to keep us focused, centered, and strong as we live our adventure of active hope.

We can do the practice alone, with a partner, or in a group. It has four parts:

- Come from gratitude. We take some time to identify what we're thankful for and express thanks to those human or nonhuman beings responsible for making them happen.
- Honor our pain for the world. We allow ourselves to focus on sad or difficult things going on in our lives or the world and feel our feelings.
- Discover. We identify ways we are growing, things we are learning, new experiences we are having, and new sources of inspiration we are finding.
- Go forth. We bring to mind something we hope *for* the world—a contribution we can make to the Great Turning. We commit to taking a step, large or small, to offer this gift of active hope.

This practice can be tailored for adults and students of all ages. It can be a private meditation to start off the day, a meditation with a partner, or sharing in a series of go-rounds with a small group.

In this chapter, we have explored gifts and visions, active hope, and impossible dreams. Of course, these dreams for the future are not at all impossible. They are alive in the work of people around the world who are dreaming and acting boldly. But can these visions, and the wisdom and values they embody, shape the future? Human history knows times of transformation when, to quote the poet Seamus

Heaney, "The longed-for tidal wave/Of justice can rise up/And hope and history rhyme."[36]

These tidal waves don't just happen. Chapter 5 explores the next dimension of my vision for education in this time of climate crisis: the art of civil resistance.

CHAPTER 5

Teach for Civil Resistance: The Power of Grassroots Movements to Effect Transformational Change

A MOVEMENT FOR CLIMATE JUSTICE is underway around the world. Many people are contributing, including scientists, engineers, United Nations (UN) officials, government officials, Indigenous people, journalists, teachers, activists, political leaders, and people from all walks of life. All the visions described in chapter 4 come from the work of those who care deeply about the climate and about justice. Their visions are essential for this movement. They show us what the future can be and give us the tools to create it.

It is not enough, however, to know where to go and take incremental steps to get there. The urgency and magnitude of the crisis call for more—much, much more. How can we muster the political will to bring about the Great Turning? That is the central question of our time. We need a major transformation in public consciousness and motivation to enact the monumental changes necessary. At this time, the mainstream political institutions in the United States show no signs that they can deliver this without a big boost from the people. Dark money, entrenched power, and a toxic political climate are blocking progress.

Enter civil resistance. In embracing civil resistance as our best hope for the future, we join a long tradition of freedom fighters who envisioned a better world and worked courageously and creatively to bring it about. This tradition includes the slavery abolition movement, the labor movement, the women's suffrage movement, the civil rights movement, the women's rights movement, Black Lives Matter, and the gay rights movement. Inspiring stories from other countries include the abolitionist movement in nineteenth-century England, Mahatma Gandhi's movement to free India from British colonial rule, and the anti-apartheid movement in South Africa.

Our students need to study these transformative movements for the inspiration and lessons they provide. They also need to know that the practice of civil resistance is alive and well in the world today. Witness the campaigns of the Indigenous water protectors and Extinction Rebellion.

Civil-resistance movements can produce moments of transformational change in public consciousness that appear to come out of nowhere. For instance, when millions of people around the country viewed images on their television screens of police in Birmingham, Alabama, attacking children with fire hoses and police dogs, active support for the civil rights movement increased dramatically.

Such events may seem spontaneous, but they aren't. In fact, scholars and activists have assembled an impressive body of knowledge and skill about how to develop effective civil-resistance movements, create transformational moments, and build on the public's newfound awareness to make substantive change. In so doing, they have elevated unarmed uprising to the status of an art.

STORY FROM THE CLASSROOM

For students, these points in history provide teachable moments about the ways nonviolent mass movements can bring about change. The following story illustrates how one teacher made civil resistance come alive for her students.

Sarah Outterson-Murphy

Sarah Outterson-Murphy, who teaches English language arts at a public high school in Cedar Rapids, Iowa, noticed that her ninth graders perked up when, as required, she had them examine Dr. Martin Luther King Jr.'s "I Have a Dream" speech as an example of persuasive speaking. Her students told her they wanted to know more about the civil rights movement.

"Tell me what you'd like to know," she said.

"We don't know anything about it," they replied, "except what you've told us about Martin Luther King."

The students brainstormed questions, and Sarah condensed and combined them into two: "Why did white people treat Black people so hatefully?" and "How did the civil rights movement force racist laws in America to change?"

To address these questions, Sarah decided to show students clips from *Freedom Riders*, a PBS documentary featuring dramatic footage of Ku Klux Klan and white vigilante violence against activists protesting segregation on buses and in bus-station waiting rooms and restaurants. It was 1961, and the Supreme Court had already twice ruled that segregation in interstate travel was unconstitutional. But states and cities across the South had ignored the ruling, and the federal government had done nothing to enforce it. The Freedom Riders were Black and white activists who would ride interstate buses to challenge segregation.

The violence began with the firebombing of the first Freedom Rider bus in May 1961, followed by the brutal beating of passengers fleeing the burning bus. Mob brutality and threats of violence persisted as protestors continued the rides. The violence received national and international news coverage and generated sympathy for the Freedom Riders' cause. Volunteers from around the country joined the Freedom Rides to keep up the pressure on local authorities and the John F. Kennedy administration. When Attorney General Robert F. Kennedy called for a cooling-off period, James Farmer, head of the Congress on Racial Equality (CORE) replied, "We have been cooling off for 350 years, and if we cooled off anymore, we'd be in a deep freeze."[1]

During the summer of 1961, the protest escalated, with some sixty Freedom Rides crisscrossing the South, most ending in Jackson, Mississippi, where some three hundred protesters were arrested. The Freedom Rides ended in September with a victory when the Kennedy administration finally forced the Interstate Commerce Commission to begin enforcing the law.[2]

Before beginning this study, Sarah wrote an email to her students' parents.

"I would like to let you know about our next set of lessons in our language-arts class," she wrote. "We are studying how people use words to persuade others to take action or change their perspective on issues. To do this we focus on the civil rights movement as part of the larger history of antiracist movements in America."

She then shared the two questions that had grown out of the students' brainstorming. To address them, she wanted to show clips from the PBS *Freedom Riders* documentary. She explained:

> You should know that the documentary shows multiple real-life examples of hateful language about Black people as well as images of real-life violence toward Black and white student activists.... I recognize that seeing hateful language, ideas, and actions can be painful. Racism is not acceptable in our school community or in

> my classroom. I will personally not use hate language or allow students to use it in my classroom. At the same time, your students have told me that they want to understand what actually happened, and I believe these readings and videos will help us all learn.

She concluded by asking parents to let her know by email or phone of any concerns or questions they had about the unit. "I am always happy to hear from you. Thanks."

Sarah received thank-you notes from one white and one Black family, and no responses from the others. (About half the students in her school are white, a quarter are Black, and a quarter are African immigrants from Congo, Rwanda, and Zimbabwe.)

Sarah showed the students the film, pausing at intervals to give them a chance to jot down their thoughts, including what they noticed and what they wondered about. In a typical response, one girl wrote: "It would be horrible going somewhere, knowing you would be discriminated against and [it] would be dangerous. I was surprised at how young these Freedom Riders were. It took so much courage for them to know they are likely to get killed and still go." She wondered: "How do these white people benefit from discriminating against people of color? How did that girl build up the courage to go help them after she just saw what the other people could do to her?"

Using the Freedom Rider activity in "Teaching SNCC" from Zinn Education Project (see the appendix), Sarah asked the students to write a persuasive letter to their family, pretending that everything about their life was the same, but they were college students in 1961 who had decided to head South as Freedom Riders. She gave students detailed instructions about their letters: They had to decide to whom they were writing (e.g., mom, dad, grandparents, caregivers). They had to provide background on the Freedom Rides and explain their reasons for going. They should address the concerns their family member might have, and conclude by saying what, if anything, they'd like their family member to do. As an example, she gave them a brief statement from well-known Freedom Rider John Lewis in which he explains his reasons for becoming a Freedom Rider just a few weeks before he was scheduled to graduate from American Baptist Theological Seminary.

Subsequent assignments included reading a speech by George Wallace, the segregationist governor of Alabama, and listening to former president Barack Obama's eulogy for John Lewis. The school's curriculum for that quarter called for students to write a research paper asserting and defending a claim. Sarah changed that assignment into a poster project to conclude the unit on the civil rights movement. Students could choose something they wanted to change in the world, research it, and create a poster making the case for the change. One student, inspired by Obama's eulogy for John Lewis, designed an online poster arguing for reforms that would enfranchise incarcerated people and eliminate measures that make voting more difficult in low-income communities of color.

"I was pleased with the way the unit turned out," reflects Sarah.

> The kids really got into it. I was really surprised by how little they knew and how interested they were. Some of the students focused on why white people behaved this way. I think they were able to get to a place where they understood that it was about protecting their sense of superiority and feeling defensive and not seeing Black people as human. The documentary has a really good section that shows Attorney General Robert F. Kennedy following the movement rather than leading it. In our discussions, I leaned into that, and some of the students, especially the more advanced ones, began to think a lot about how movements make change.

Good teaching practices contributed to the success of Sarah's curriculum. She built the study on students' expressed interest and their questions. She let parents know what she was planning and invited their feelings and concerns. She found a powerful documentary and, in showing it to the students, paused at intervals to allow them to note the points that struck them and comment on what they still wondered about. Having them assume the role of college students in 1961 and write letters explaining why they became Freedom Riders helped them walk in the shoes of the young activists they were studying.

We'll now delve into the art of civil resistance to understand why it has the power to make transformational change and why Sarah's decision to introduce her ninth graders to the Freedom Riders' story made sense.

THE ART OF CIVIL RESISTANCE

Civil resistance, also called nonviolent direct action, is a strategy for advancing social justice by provoking conflict. Conflict is a disagreement or an argument: people with different interests, desires, needs, or opinions oppose each other. Violence, by contrast, is physical or mental force exerted to violate, damage, or abuse. Conflict can lead to violence, but it doesn't have to, especially if people respect each other and have skills in conflict resolution.

In situations of injustice, conflict and violence exist, but they may be latent or repressed. Civil Resistance forces the conflict and violence out into the open. It breaks an unjust peace by making conflict visible and aims to create a new peace based on active justice. Instead of obeying an unjust law, people join with others in mass disobedience to challenge the status quo.

Gene Sharp: The Social Theory of Power

There are many examples of successful civil resistance campaigns (or "experiments in nonviolence," as Gandhi called them). Gene Sharp, the first scholar of nonviolent direct action, studied hundreds of civil-resistance campaigns and identified 198 tactics, which he grouped into three categories: power and persuasion, noncooperation, and actively interrupting normal daily activities. Sharp did not embrace nonviolence as a moral code, although it takes on that dimension for many people. He embraced nonviolence because he saw it as the best path to leverage change.

To explain what enables civil resistance to shift power to people who are being marginalized and treated unjustly, he developed what he called the social theory of power. The common understanding of power is that it resides in political and corporate leaders. But, as Sharp pointed out, the power of these authorities depends on the great majority of people obeying, serving, and cooperating with them. If the people withdraw their goodwill, obedience, and cooperation, the power of these rulers dissolves.[3]

Further development of the social theory of power led to the insight that people don't generally relate to society as individuals but rather as members of groups or networks of people. This led Sharp to identify "pillars" that hold up the edifices of power. Examples of these pillars are religious institutions, financial institutions, the education establishment, industries, unions, the police, the military, the health-care industry, the legal system, the business community, and the entertainment industry. If support from one or more of these pillars erodes, a leader's power may crumble. A clever, shrewd, and persistent civil-resistance campaign brought down Slobodan Miloševi , president of Serbia, when activists succeeded in eroding pillars of his support, including independent media, entertainment, university professors and intellectuals, the police, and the military.

Erica Chenoweth and Maria J. Stephan: The 3.5 Percent Rule

Building on Sharp's work, two scholars of social movements, Erica Chenoweth and Maria J. Stephan, with support from the International Center on Nonviolent Conflict (ICNC), have compiled the largest collection of empirical data on civil resistance ever assembled. Before

Chenoweth and Stephan began their research, the ICNC agreed that it would publish the findings no matter what they revealed—even if they found, for example, that civic resistance was not nearly as effective as advocates wanted to believe. They focused on campaigns, violent and nonviolent, to remove leaders (such as Miloševi) from power or to force a foreign military out of a country. They identified and studied 323 such campaigns around the world. They coded a campaign as "successful" if it achieved the full removal of an incumbent leader or the expulsion of a foreign military. They coded a campaign as "effective" if it did so within a year of its peak. They found that nonviolent campaigns were more than twice as likely to succeed as violent ones. They also found that during the past fifty years, nonviolent campaigns had grown more numerous and successful, whereas violent ones had become increasingly rare and less successful. These findings confirm the wisdom of nonviolent strategies for advancing justice, as exemplified by the successful transformative campaigns of the civil rights movement in the United States.[4]

Why are nonviolent campaigns generally more successful than violent ones? The main reason is that they can recruit many more people from a wider demographic. Overall, Chenoweth and Stephan found, nonviolent campaigns attracted four times as many participants as violent ones. The more supporters a campaign had, the greater the potential for widespread disruptions such as general strikes, for example. Also, nonviolent actions are generally easier to discuss openly, with the result that news can reach a wider audience.

Chenoweth and Stephan's research also produced another insight, which they call the 3.5 percent rule. Says Chenoweth, "No campaign failed once they'd achieved the active and sustained participation of just 3.5 percent of the population." (In the United States, that would be about eleven million people.) Although the ultimate goal is to achieve a strong majority support for a cause, a campaign must first engage a core group of supporters who actively participate in such ways as showing up for demonstrations, staffing phone banks, contributing money, voting with the movement, persuading others, and advancing the cause through their personal and professional networks.[5]

To galvanize a base of supporters, leaders of successful social movements do not try to appeal to the center by splitting the difference between opposing points of view. They stake out highly principled positions, even if they seem "unrealistic," and seek to rally support for them. They think boldly, aiming to inspire first their base, then eventually the public, with a vision of transformation, as Martin Luther King Jr. did in his "I Have a Dream" speech.

Bill Moyer: Stages of Successful Campaigns

Analysis of successful civil-resistance campaigns shows that they generally go through stages. Activist Bill Moyer mapped out those stages in his book *Doing Democracy*.[6] The first stage is *planning*: a small group of activists carefully plans the campaign. For example, Farmer and his colleagues at CORE had to decide the routes the Freedom Rides would take, the training the riders would receive, the messaging and outreach to the media, the means of maintaining communication with the Riders, legal support, and much more.

In the second stage, the campaign launches with a *trigger event*. This can be a spontaneous event that the organizers decide to highlight or an event they manufacture themselves. In the case of the Freedom Rides, of course, they created it themselves by publicizing the campaign and sending Riders on that first bus.

The campaign takes off in the third stage through the interplay of four factors: *disruption*, *sacrifice*, and *escalation*, with activists practicing disciplined *nonviolence* all the while. The Freedom Riders are a great example of this. By challenging segregation with their bodies, they disrupted business as usual. When they were met with violence, their courage and steadfastness generated sympathy for their cause. When they escalated their campaign in the face of persecution by sending bus after bus into the South with new volunteers from all over the country, they demonstrated the depth of their support and sent the message that "we shall not be moved." At the same time, they maintained nonviolent discipline. To transform public consciousness in support of their cause, they could only resist nonviolently. Any violence had to come from racist mobs or the police.

The fluidity of the situation required ongoing decision-making and improvisation on the part of the campaign's leaders. When the governor of Mississippi ordered that the Riders be arrested upon their arrival in Jackson and sent to a hated prison for hard labor, instead of being held in a local jail, the campaign responded with a successful call for hundreds more Riders to arrive in Jackson to overwhelm the prisons.

By September 1961, the Freedom Riders had succeeded in creating a *whirlwind*, the fourth stage and the peak of a successful campaign, in which a social problem is transformed into a public social crisis. A whirlwind can't last forever. Movement organizers need to know when to declare victory and end the campaign for now. Moyer acknowledged that after all the excitement there is likely to be *letdown* (the fifth stage). People may even begin to wonder what they accomplished. At this stage, it's important for activists to share their feelings honestly and try to come to a balanced perspective that enables them to celebrate their achievements and acknowledge that there will always be more to do.

In the wake of the whirlwind, the challenge is to make agreements that *institutionalize* (the sixth stage) the progress made possible by the campaign. This may require negotiation and communication skills different from those needed to orchestrate a successful mass mobilization. Fortunately, the negotiation now occurs in a new context. In the case of the Freedom Rides, by September, the Kennedy administration, which had called for a "cooling-off period" in June, finally required the Interstate Commerce Commission to begin enforcing the Supreme Court's decision to end segregation in interstate travel. Other transformational events followed, and the shift in public consciousness set the stage for successful campaigns in Birmingham and Selma that led to the March on Washington and passage of the Voting Rights Act of 1965.[7]

Division and Polarization

As the Freedom Rides demonstrate, although civil resistance is nonviolent, there is nothing passive about it. Without question, the Freedom Riders were divisive. They got in the faces of their opponents, standing up to them, interrupting deeply held habits of behavior and mind, and preventing them from living their "normal" lives based on racism. This made people uncomfortable, even those who considered themselves sympathetic to the cause. King's famous "Letter from a Birmingham Jail" was directed not at racist opponents but at "the white moderate ... who constantly advised the Negro to wait until a more convenient season."[8]

The protests galvanized racist opponents, and backlash and violence followed in their immediate aftermath. But the long-term effects of polarization were positive, pumping life into the movement, activating the African American community, and engaging student activists nationwide—including me. Polls showed that in the wake of Birmingham Commissioner of Public Safety Theophilus Eugene "Bull" Connor's attacks on protesters, the percent of the public that saw civil rights as "the most urgent issue facing the nation" sharply increased. As support for civil rights grew in the sixties, major social institutions began to abandon the racist order.[9] Division and polarization are part of civil resistance. As Frederick Douglass wrote: "If there is no struggle there is no progress. Those who profess to favor freedom and yet deprecate agitation, are men who want crops without plowing up the ground, they want rain without thunder and lightning. They want the ocean without the awful roar of its many waters. This struggle may be a moral one, or it may be a physical one, and it may be both moral and physical, but it must be a struggle. Power concedes nothing without a demand. It never did and it never will."[10]

Importance of Electoral Work

The Freedom Rides demonstrate another key point about the art of civil resistance: the strategic importance of having allies in governmental seats of power. Despite its initial foot-dragging, the Kennedy administration ultimately forced the Interstate Commerce Commission to enforce desegregation of interstate travel. After successful campaigns in Birmingham and Selma and the March on Washington, the Kennedy administration introduced civil rights legislation, and in 1965 President Lyndon B. Johnson signed the Voting Rights Act. These victories followed effective civil-resistance campaigns and would not have occurred without them. But the legislative victories validated the hard work and sacrifices of activists and were crucial for institutionalizing progress when the transformative moment was strong.

Climate justice activists need presidents, governors, mayors, senators, representatives, and state legislators sympathetic to our cause and susceptible to the pressure our movements can apply. To achieve this, we must work to ensure that elections are fair and that, when administered effectively as they were in 2020, they have the trust of the people. A systematic and well-funded campaign is now underway to undermine democracy in the United States. Developments such as the January 6, 2021, attack on the Capitol, the ongoing attempt to discredit the 2020 election, and new state laws that have made it more difficult to vote, especially in communities of color, all have led the International Institute for Democracy and Electoral Assistance to add the United States to its list of "backsliding democracies."[11]

Although civil-resistance campaigns are crucial for achieving transformational change, advocates for climate justice in the United States must also work to safeguard voting rights, resist efforts to weaken the integrity of our elections, and reduce the role of "dark money" in politics. Civil resistance for climate justice and electoral work must go hand in hand.

Teaching Idea

In 2011, Erica Chenoweth and Maria J. Stephan published the findings of their research in *Why Civil Resistance Works: The Strategic Logic of Nonviolent Conflict.*[12] This book is not only of interest to other researchers. In 2017, a group of fifteen people in England began meeting to consider why campaigns to mobilize people to address the climate crisis had failed and how to make them successful. Inspired by *Why Civil Resistance Works*, they concluded that "the only way to overcome entrenched political power is through extensive campaigns of large-scale nonviolent direct action." Within a year, the organization they created, Extinction Rebellion (XR), organized a civil-disobedience campaign that led to the arrest of a thousand people and finally put the climate crisis on Britain's political agenda. There are now chapters of XR in major cities around the world.[13]

Invite your students to research XR and the creative tactics its members use to engage the public in addressing the climate crisis.

STORY FROM THE CLASSROOM

Elementary school children are not too young to learn about civil resistance. When my daughter Emma Rose was a third grader, she experienced a curriculum about the Montgomery bus boycott that culminated in a play created by the children and their teacher. The play and the boycott occurred a long time ago, but there's nothing outdated about them. A video of the performance took me back to March 10, 1994.

Donnie Rotkin

"We'll walk hand in hand. We'll walk hand in hand. We'll walk hand in hand someday. Oh, deep in our hearts, we do believe, we'll walk hand in hand someday." The twenty-five children in Donnie Rotkin's class of third and fourth graders are standing in a line holding hands and facing the audience on the stage of the packed auditorium of Central Park East I School (CPE I) in East Harlem, New York City, at the conclusion of their play.

Most of the kids are Black and Latinx. Five are white, including Emma Rose. My wife and I have tears in our eyes, remembering the many times we ourselves sang that song at demonstrations. When the song ends, the students, school faculty, parents, grandparents, and neighbors in the audience rise for a standing ovation.

Before the performance, Barry Solowey, the school's music teacher with a special talent for getting children to sing on key and with heart, had warmed up the auditorium by inviting everyone to sing "This Little Light." Then Donnie welcomed the audience:

> I am very pleased to present *The Montgomery Bus Boycott*, a play with music by my class. This play comes at the end of two-and-a-half months of hard work on the part of my class. The theme of this play is fair and unfair. The children acted out scenes from their own lives when they had been treated unfairly. They read books. They watched videos of events in Montgomery. They made the sets, collected props, and did all the things necessary to produce a play. It's important to remember that the civil rights movement was real. It really happened. The true events in this play took place in 1955. But the children in the play are acting, performing. They're being someone they're not. When they're a bus driver saying, "Get out of here! Go the back!" it's not the child saying that. It's a bus driver back in 1955. When you see the children acting, remember they are actors and actresses. Enjoy the show!

The play has eight scenes, each depicting a major event in the story of the boycott: people riding on a segregated bus, Rosa Park's arrest, Dr. Martin Luther King Jr. speaking in a church, people walking to work, a demonstration with people carrying picket signs, a sit-in at a lunch counter, protesters being arrested and put in jail, and elation over the Supreme Court's decision that bus segregation in Montgomery, Alabama, was unconstitutional. In each scene, the children sang a freedom song: "Oh, Freedom!" "We Shall Not Be Moved," "If You Miss Me in the Back of the Bus," "Keep Your Eyes on the Prize," "We Shall Overcome," and a song Donnie wrote for the play.

Donnie taught at CPE I for twenty-five years beginning in 1981 and served five more years coaching teachers at the school. Over the years, he has taught all the grades from kindergarten to grade 6. His teaching was theme-based with all subjects integrated into the theme. Science-and-environment-related themes included birds, mini-beasts, and the sky. Social studies themes included fair and unfair (grades K–2), the civil rights movement and the Montgomery bus boycott (grades 3–6), and slavery and the Underground Railroad. Another theme was garbage, related to both social studies and science.

The unit on the Montgomery bus boycott integrated reading, writing, social studies, art, music, and social and emotional learning. It began with class discussions about what's fair and what's not fair. Donnie prepared questionnaires for students to use when interviewing parents and other family members about the topic. In response to their children's questions, parents shared their thoughts about societal issues and told stories about their personal experiences as well. In class, students shared stories and feelings about times they felt mistreated or had witnessed others being mistreated. In small groups, they created skits to explore these situations and to practice ways to stand up for themselves and others. Donnie says that this work was based on the ideas of Vivian Gussin Paley, who wrote *You Can't Say, You Can't Play*. Donnie also invited parents to come in and tell their stories. This exploration of what's fair, what isn't, and what to do about it provided the framework for exploring the Montgomery bus boycott and other forms of discrimination.

Reading for the two-and-a-half months of the project focused on the struggle for freedom and justice, including the civil rights movement, the boycott, Martin Luther King Jr., and Rosa Parks, as well as Althea Gibson, Mahalia Jackson, Jesse Owens, Harriet Tubman, Sojourner Truth, Cesar Chavez, Malcolm X, Jackie Robinson, Muhammad Ali, and Dolores Huerta. Donnie had multiple copies of books in his classroom library. All the students would read the same book, but they would read it to each other in small groups, often sharing feelings and acting out scenes from the book, just as they had previously acted out scenes from their own lives. Donnie also read a book to the whole class called *Selma, Lord, Selma* about two girls, ages nine and eleven, who become organizers.

Once the students had learned about the boycott through books and videos, Donnie presented each of the eight scenes to them, one after the other. In small groups, they acted out the scenes. Through students writing down dialogue that developed in their improvisations, the scripts for the narrator and each of the scenes emerged. Meanwhile, Barry, the music teacher, worked with all the kids, and the chorus/choir in particular, on Donnie's song and the five other freedom songs they would be singing in the play. Song lyrics also served as homework assignments. The students' art assignment for the project was to design and paint the two large murals of the bus and the stained-glass windows in the church as well as the protest signs.

A rich curriculum like this leads to some great classroom discussions. Kids asked, "Why and how do people become racist? Why do people want to mistreat others based on the color of their skin?" Donnie used the Rodgers and Hammerstein song "You've Got to be Carefully Taught," from *South Pacific*, to address these questions. "We had many discussions about that song," says Donnie. Songs can give movements and curricula soul, as the civil rights movement and Donnie's theatrical project demonstrate.

Another question arose from the Latinx students in his class. "Where do we sit?" they asked. "The whites are sitting in front and the Blacks are sitting in back. Where do we go?" Latinx parents and students shared their experiences of discrimination.

On rare occasions, a parent expressed concerns that "my child is too young for this." Donnie would listen and then share his thinking: "This is completely age-appropriate. This is about feelings. This is about the world and how to be powerful in the world and how to stand up against unfair treatment of yourself and others."

My daughter Emma Rose has vivid and fond memories of the Montgomery bus boycott play. She recalls, "I had seen it when I was in first or second grade, and when I got to third grade, I was thrilled to take part in it. It was really fun working with all the other kids and learning the songs and singing in the chorus. Learning about the ways whites treated Blacks in Montgomery in 1955, I was so glad to be working with friends and classmates of different races, all on an equal basis, to put together something so cool!"

Like the Freedom Rides, the Montgomery bus boycott is an excellent example of the art of civil resistance and its power to bring about transformational change. The planning by E. D. Nixon, Rosa Parks, and their colleagues at the local National Association for the Advancement of Colored People (NAACP) chapter; building solidarity in the Black community; seizing on Rosa Parks's arrest as a powerful trigger event; orchestrating a campaign of disruption, sacrifice, and escalation; maintaining morale through regular mass meetings in the churches; and following strict nonviolent discipline despite violence from racist opponents are all best practices in the art of civil resistance. Together, they produced a campaign successful on many levels, not the least of which was to educate a new generation of civil rights leaders in strategic nonviolence, including Dr. Martin Luther King Jr., and to provide a model of nonviolent direct action that activists in the sixties would build upon.

The play that Donnie, Barry, and the children created is a great example of how to teach and learn for climate justice. It engaged students' hearts, minds, hands, and bodies in fighting for justice, building solidarity, and living the beloved community—a community that encompassed not only their classmates but also the ancestors whose roles they were playing and on whose shoulders they stand. It does all this in a way that is appropriate to the age of the students, as it focuses on issues they are wrestling with in their young lives: What is fair? What is unfair? How can we work together to create a world that is fair and friendly for all?

STORY FROM THE CLASSROOM

Ursula Wolfe-Rocca

"Ask a high school student to list examples of civil disobedience," observes Ursula Wolfe-Rocca, "and they are likely to include Rosa Parks. A few might throw in Thoreau's refusal to pay taxes to support war. Throughout all my years of teaching social studies, students almost always came into my classes seeing civil disobedience as a relic of the past, not as something alive in their own time."

When Ursula viewed a powerful hour-long film documentary about the ongoing civil resistance campaign to block construction and operation of Enbridge Energy's new Line 3 oil pipeline in northern Minnesota, she saw a great opportunity to correct that falsehood and to educate students about the climate crisis.

Ursula taught social studies for twenty years with high school students in Lake Oswego, a wealthy, primarily white suburb of Portland, Oregon. In addition to her teaching, she serves on the editorial board of Rethinking Schools and is a writer, organizer, and teacher-educator with the Zinn Education Project.

Ursula says that her philosophy of teaching is encapsulated in a story Toni Morrison told in the lecture she gave upon receiving the Nobel Prize in Literature in 1993. There's an old woman who is blind and wise, the story goes. Some young people visit her, perhaps bent on showing her up for the fraud they think she is.

Standing before her, one of them says, "Is the bird I am holding alive or dead?"

After a long silence, the old woman says, "I do not know if the bird you are holding is dead or alive, but what I do know is that it is in your hands."

The young people feel reprimanded, shamed by her response, and they react with outrage. "We have heard all our short lives that we have to be responsible. What could that possibly mean in the catastrophe this world has become.... Our inheritance is an affront.... How dare you talk to us of duty when we stand waist deep in the toxin of your past?"

"I get that it's not *all* a catastrophe," Ursula acknowledges.

> But I feel young people have every reason to be totally cynical, demoralized, and really, really pissed off, especially when it comes to the climate. That's the premise from which I operate. My responsibility is not to tell them what their responsibility is, which I feel is what lots of civics education tries to do. No, my job is to use everything I've learned to help them understand how things are and how we got here, and then, of course, what folks have done in the past to organize toward a different future and how that might happen now.

In 2015, Enbridge Energy announced its intention to expand its pipeline network by constructing a new Line 3 along a different corridor. Leaders of Indigenous Anishinaabe bands objected, saying that the new pipeline (and the current one as well) would threaten their treaty-protected land and water rights for fishing, hunting, gathering, and farming, including cultivating wild-rice habitats central to Anishinaabe culture. It would threaten the pristine ecosystem, rich in biodiversity. It would also represent a huge new investment in fossil-fuel infrastructure at a time when keeping fossil fuels in the ground is an urgent priority.

Based in Canada, Enbridge is the world's largest oil-pipeline company. Its sole purpose is to profit from continued expansion of the fossil-fuel industry by transporting crude oil to refineries and refined oil to consumers. Its new Line 3 pipeline would transport 760,000 barrels of crude oil per day from the tar sands oil fields in Alberta, Canada, through a pristine area of Minnesota with some two hundred interconnected bodies of water, including the headlands of the Mississippi River.

In the documentary *Necessity: Oil, Water, and Climate Resistance*, we meet the Indigenous people who are leading the campaign to stop the pipeline. We meet the retired white people who broke into Enbridge company property to turn the valves and shut down the flow of oil. We meet the activists who chained themselves to block the entrance of a Wells Fargo Bank in Duluth, Minnesota, to protest the bank's investments in the Line 3 project. More than a thousand of these "water protectors," as they call themselves, committed civil disobedience and after being arrested planned to use what is known as the "necessity defense" at their trials.

The necessity defense is typically used when someone breaks the law to save another person's life. The water protectors argue that this defense applies to their acts of civil disobedience: they break the law to prevent a greater harm—that is, the damage fossil fuels are doing to the environment. The documentary also introduces the lawyers who represent the water protectors in court and the medical doctors and climate scientists who are called in as expert witnesses.

When she first watched *Necessity*, Ursula immediately saw a way for teachers to engage students with the film. She created a lesson for the Zinn Education Project called a "mixer," a role-play to prepare students to get the most from the film. She wrote role sheets for each of the nineteen people profiled in the film. Teachers would distribute the role sheets to their students, each of whom would study their role and review a list of suggested activities, such as "Find someone who broke the law as a form of climate resistance. Who is this person? What did they do and why?" Then the students would get up, mix and mingle, and, playing their roles, have conversations with each other. The role-play would build a sense of anticipation for viewing the film and deepen students' understanding of where the people profiled in the film are coming from.[14]

Ursula says:

> When I introduce this lesson to teachers, the feedback I get often runs along these lines: "I really, really liked this: so much fun, so much great information, so many great people to introduce the kids to. But I notice that you didn't include Enbridge, you didn't include any of the pro-fossil-fuel folks in your mixer." These teachers seem to feel it's self-evident that this is a flawed lesson because everyone is on the same side.
>
> My response is that this lesson is not seeking to set up a debate about whether we should continue building fossil-fuel infrastructure or get rid of it. It's seeking to help students understand how differently positioned people build solidarity together to achieve a common end. To me, what's so powerful about the film is that people are acknowledging their differences in class, race, age, geographic locations, and expertise, and they are using those differences to figure out how to build a potentially successful and sustainable movement. The frame is solidarity, not the pros and cons of fossil fuels.
>
> I feel a lot of our curricula fall into what I call the "T-chartification" of curriculum. Everything has to be on a T-chart

> with pros on one side and cons on the other, and you have to have a debate. You're not telling the kids the truth if you're not debating. I understand where the multiple-perspectives idea comes from. Of course, I shouldn't be indoctrinating students, and I should be giving them a sense of the broad spectrum of perspectives on things. But if we don't start with the right questions, we miss what's most important.

For Ursula, the right question for this lesson is not whether fossil fuels in general, and Line 3 in particular, are good or bad. That question has already been answered most definitively. The appropriate question is, how can we build a movement to avoid the catastrophe the continued use of fossil fuels is creating. "To me," says Ursula, "teaching social justice is showing students that social movements don't just happen. They happen because people join together, share their talents and resources, and work hard to make them happen."

Throughout her teaching career, Ursula has taught American history. The entire fourth quarter of the class has been the Black freedom movement. Explains Ursula:

> It's true, what the kids tell the wise, old, blind woman in Toni Morrison's story: They "stand waist-deep in the toxin of the past." True—and we're also standing waist-deep in a wonderful history that's too little talked about. We don't know the ancestors we could look to and model ourselves after. And that's what I want for students. I want them to meet people through the curriculum I'm teaching and feel, "This person is with me and I'm with them and perhaps I can learn something and get some inspiration," as people all over the world have drawn inspiration from the civil rights movement, and still do today.

"Kids need to know," for example, "that a decade before the end of the Civil War, the vision of full emancipation, full abolition, and uncompensated emancipation was unthinkable. The pro-slavery folks were winning victories left and right. You have *Dred Scott* and the Fugitive Slave Act. The role of cotton in the economy is enormous. The abolitionists are fringe radicals. How amazing that such a huge transformation could take place in one decade!"

Ursula's aim in teaching about Rosa Parks is to turn kids away from the individualist narrative that we all are accustomed to and build kids' understanding of collective action. "Rosa Parks," she emphasizes, "doesn't come out of nowhere, and she doesn't do it alone."

She wants students to know that the Rosa Parks story is about taking a leap and not knowing how things are going to turn out. Citing Jeanne Theoharis's biography, *The Rebellious Life of Mrs. Rosa Parks*, she says Rosa Parks had no reason to believe that her arrest was going to be any different from all the refusals and protests in the past. Although Parks worked for the NAACP and was helping to plan its campaign against bus segregation in Montgomery, her refusal to give up her seat on that particular day was her own spontaneous decision. She was nervous about the mass meeting two nights later, fearing people would be angry with her for acting on the spur of the moment. Parks was a real live person, not an icon. She had fears, doubts, and feelings like the rest of us.

Ursula wants students to walk away with a better understanding of the role of radicals. She explains:

> The standard version of history that kids get from seeing *Forrest Gump*—I can't tell you how often kids reference that movie in history class—is that there is the mainstream good civil-rights movement, and then there is the bad civil-rights movement, the militants, the guys who wore leather jackets and berets and carried guns. I want students to understand how absolutely false that dichotomy is. There's this incredible picture of Rosa Parks at a

conference in the seventies. She's gray-haired and wearing this incredible print dress, and she's holding this poster of Malcolm X and gazing at it with such admiration. She said that he was one of her personal heroes.

I teach the Black freedom struggle as a long civil-rights movement. Reconstruction is not over; reconstruction continues. We did not win voting rights with the Fifteenth Amendment. We won a battle but not a war. We didn't win voting rights with the Voting Rights Act of 1965. I have no easy answer for a student who says, "Are you telling me that what people were struggling for in 1877 are the very same things people are struggling for today?" Yes, without diminishing the real victories, we must acknowledge the incompleteness of those victories.

We have to help kids see that you keep going, you keep trying, and there are no stars in the skies saying this time it's going to be successful. But we do have these examples, like Rosa Parks and Reconstruction, where, for whatever reason, there's a particular set of ingredients that leads to the possibility of real transformation.

We show the kids the long story and hope they feel empowered by it, not demoralized. We endeavor to leave them clear-eyed and with a sense of possibility, which is the best any of us can hope for.

INDIGENOUS YOUNG PEOPLE LEAD FOR CLIMATE JUSTICE

In April 2016, a group of Native American teenagers set up a "prayer camp" near the Standing Rock Indian Reservation in North Dakota to protest the proposed completion of the 1,200-mile Dakota Access Pipeline. This final section of the pipeline would carry oil under the Missouri River half a mile upstream from the reservation. The 8,200 people residing in the reservation, 41 percent of whom live below the poverty line, depend on the river for drinking water, irrigation, and fish. The pipeline would also threaten a nearby lake they consider sacred and an ancient burial ground as well.

The young people were members of a tight-knit group from the Cheyenne River Reservation in South Dakota. They had come together to address the epidemic of suicide among Native American youth. Calling themselves the One Mind Youth Movement, they had set up a safe house for teenagers and were providing counseling, urging the young people to look after each other and get involved in their movement. They had also joined the ongoing protests against the proposed Keystone XL pipeline, which, if approved, would transport oil from Canada to Nebraska, cutting under the Cheyenne River just upstream from their reservation. The Indigenous Environmental Network (IEN) (see the appendix) had enabled the young people to get training in organizing and civil resistance.[15]

A group of these young people decided to set up a prayer camp on the neighboring Standing Rock Reservation, modeled on one IEN had established on their reservation as part of the campaign against the Keystone XL pipeline. They built a teepee where they slept, lit a sacred fire, and began a spiritual retreat, with drugs and alcohol strictly prohibited. As word spread on social media and across their friendship networks, other young people joined them. For some, it was the first real home they had ever known. They also found purpose in the campaign to protect the tribe's drinking water and to protest fossil fuels. During the next six months, as word continued to spread, people and donations flooded into Standing Rock and the prayer camp became a movement, uniting environmentalists, conservative farmers, radicals of the American Indian Movement, traditional chiefs from hundreds of tribes, and young people seeking family and a sense of purpose. The camp provided emotional support, spiritual sustenance, and training in nonviolent direct action as well as shelter, food prepared on-site in makeshift kitchens, a legal clinic, and twenty-four-hour medical care.

Using a strategy from Native American cultural tradition, the youth leadership organized a run of 1,800 miles from Standing Rock to Washington, D.C., there to present petitions signed by 140,000 people to the US Army Corps of Engineers demanding that the company's request for an easement to begin construction be denied. Along the way, the runners gained new supporters, additional runners, and publicity for their cause. By the time the runners made their run and presented their petitions, the whole world knew about Standing Rock and the fight over the Dakota Access Pipeline. Nevertheless, on July 29, 2016, the US Army Corps of Engineers approved the easement, and construction on the pipeline began in mid-August.[16]

Late August saw a huge influx of supporters pour into the protest camps in what organizers called "the big boom." Hundreds of water protectors now became thousands. Tribal elders and the tribal council now got completely on board, erecting a traditional Council Lodge and formally deputizing the youth leadership as leaders of the campaign.

Support continued to grow in September as the media showed images of militarized police and private security agents using batons, tear gas, mace, attack dogs, and fire hoses against the water protectors. By then, some ten thousand people were living at the camp. In November, as temperatures dropped below freezing, police continued to turn their fire hoses on the protesters. Then, late in November, the US Army Corps of Engineers withdrew the permit for the camp.

At this bleak time, the youth leadership was finding it increasingly challenging to maintain nonviolent discipline. They needed to do something to remind people why they were there. On December 2, they saw an opportunity. On Facebook, the Morton County Police Department was soliciting donations as a gesture of support for their officers, who were under lockdown at the police station so that they would be immediately available, if needed. The young people gathered granola bars, warm clothing, and water, and organized a march to present the donations to the officers. At the police station, the leader of the march, Thomas Tomatiuh Lopez Jr., gave a speech. "You have brutalized us," he said, "But we won't brutalize you. Do you know why we brought you water instead of soda? We want you to be healthy. *Mni wiconi!* Water is life!" The officers accepted the donations.[17]

The Obama administration gave the water protectors an unexpected victory on December 16 when the US Army Corps of Engineers denied the easement for construction of the pipeline. Believing it was too tentative a victory, the young people were reluctant to close the camp. But with temperatures now below zero, they decided to disperse for the winter. In January 2017, after a month apart, they reconvened in Washington, D.C., to join protests against Trump's Inauguration. They were there when they learned that President Trump had issued an executive order allowing the Dakota Access and Keystone XL pipelines to go forward.[18] The Dakota Access Pipeline was completed in April 2017 and oil began flowing through it in May.

However, the campaign against the Keystone XL pipeline ultimately ended in victory! During the campaign for president in 2020, candidate Joe Biden promised that, if elected, he would rescind the construction permit for the Keystone XL pipeline. On Inauguration Day in January 2021, he made good on his promise. Six months later TC Energy, the fossil-fuel company pushing Keystone XL terminated the project.[19]

Unfortunately, the oil is still flowing at Standing Rock despite court victories. In 2020, a federal judge struck down a key federal permit, and ordered the US Army Corps of Engineers to conduct a comprehensive environmental review. However, the pipeline was allowed to continue operating. In February 2022, the US Supreme Court rejected the pipeline operator's bid to challenge the 2020 ruling, but the oil continues to flow. Although the Biden administration has the power to close the pipeline while the review is being conducted, it has so far chosen not to do so.[20]

The battle continues over the Dakota Access Pipeline, Line 3, and other pillars of the fossil-fuel industry around the world. As Ursula says, you keep going, you keep trying, and there are no stars in the sky proclaiming you're going to be successful. But the exemplary civil resistance campaign waged by the courageous young people of Standing Rock offers a wealth of wisdom and inspiration for climate justice educators and their students.

Chapter 6 will tell more stories of young people fighting for climate justice and share their ideas for how educators can support students to become effective activists.

CHAPTER 6

Support Students to Act for Climate Justice

ARTE ROMERO Y CARVER entered high school feeling disheartened about life in general, and what she learned there about the climate crisis only made her feel worse. But she found her way to climate activism.

Arte grew up in Santa Fe, New Mexico. She's twenty years old and now lives in Saint Louis attending Washington University. She is Chicana Nortena. Her father is white, and her mother is Chicana. They divorced when Arte was two or three, and she says she bounced back and forth between her parents. Both parents were living below the poverty line, but she got to know their extended families and noticed that cousins on her father's side were generally doing well academically and considering college, while cousins on her mother's side were dealing with drug addiction, homelessness, and incarceration. "When I entered high school," she says, "I didn't have a complex class analysis, but I had this experience of inequality. I felt deeply cynical and hopeless and deadened by my lived education."

She joined a debate club. Her introduction to the climate crisis was reading a policy paper from the National Centre for Climate Restoration that described the dire consequences of climate change for human life and civilization. "So, I had my childhood mixed background, which gave me primary examples of inequality," she recalls, "and my high school had me read a paper that related to inequality in the sense that climate change was going to kill everyone. I didn't want to do anything. I didn't think I *could* do anything. I felt essentially useless. The most I could do was offer cynical takes in the government class I was taking."

Then, in the summer of 2019, toward the end of her sophomore year, a friend invited her to come to a city council meeting and speak in favor of a resolution supporting the Green New Deal. "I have no idea why I went," she says. "I think maybe I was just bored and had nothing else to do on a Friday night." She gave a short speech and heard other young people give comments, all making the same point: "We're afraid! We need to do something!"

She met some of the young people after the meeting. They invited her to come to their office. "At that moment," she says, "I realized I can't do this alone, I alone don't stand a chance against these forces. But now I'm not alone! I accepted their invitation. That's how it started."

Arte was fortunate to meet a group of young people who rescued her from despair and cynicism. But she deserved much more from her school. The climate crisis calls on educators to support students in acting for climate justice. Young people are naturally action oriented. They have made major contributions to many social movements throughout history, including the civil rights movement, the movement to end apartheid in South Africa, and the movement to end the nuclear arms race. Currently, they are providing powerful, creative, and highly visible leadership for climate justice, as demonstrated by Fridays for Future, the Sunrise Movement, and the Standing Rock campaign. Action is an antidote to despair, and research shows that taking action mitigates the negative physical and psychological impacts of traumatic events. As educators, we need to support and celebrate our students' participation in the movement.

In this chapter you will hear more from Arte and meet Peter, Olivia, and Sara, who, like Arte, explain how they became climate activists. They share their experiences and accomplishments in the climate movement, discuss their school experiences—positive and negative—and offer their wisdom about how educators can best fulfill their responsibilities to students in this time of climate crisis.

After hearing from the four young people, you will learn how Bayard Faithfull, whose work was introduced in previous chapters, achieved "educational nirvana" as he and his students worked together in the thrilling lead-up to the September 20, 2019, climate march in New York City.

PIVOTAL MOMENTS IN THE TURN TOWARD CLIMATE ACTIVISM

Why and how do young people make the shift to activism—and what role can schools play in supporting them? Peter Sallinger, Olivia Wohlgemuth, and Sara Poon tell their stories.

Peter Sallinger

Peter Sallinger grew up in Portland, Oregon, surrounded by natural beauty, a couple of hours from the Pacific Ocean and an hour from the Cascade Mountains. His father is a wildlife conservationist, and his mother is a former park naturalist who does nature programming with elementary school students. He attended Sunnyside Environmental School in Portland, a K–8 public school that educates students to love and understand the natural world. Says Peter, "Sunnyside connected us with nature and also helped us understand climate change and environmental degradation."

As part of the school's curriculum, eighth graders worked in small groups that met throughout the year to plan and carry out an action project on an issue of their choice. When Peter was in seventh grade, he had witnessed one of these groups testify before city officials on climate-related concerns. "This was a time when it was unusual for young people to testify," Peter recalls. "I watched the testimony and was inspired. When it was my turn in eighth grade, I joined a group focusing on climate change. We, too, testified before city officials, and they listened to us! That's when I realized I could have agency in the climate movement. That started me working for the next seven years of my life on climate issues."

Olivia Wohlgemuth

Olivia Wohlgemuth became involved in climate organizing after she heard Greta Thunberg speak and was inspired by her call for youth action. Recalls Olivia, "Greta and lots of people my age around the world were saying that we had the power to influence how the public and the government were thinking about the climate crisis. That was really empowering for me."

She decided to recruit students from her large New York City public high school (Fiorello H. LaGuardia High School of Music & Art and Performing Arts) to participate in a student climate march on March 15, 2019. "I went around talking with students and teachers and explaining why we were walking out. And beyond my wildest dreams, a third to a half of the students joined the walkout—about a thousand kids! It was incredible to see how much the students really cared and how they were just waiting for an opportunity to get involved." Olivia helped organize participation in other climate strikes that year, including the big one on September 20.

"That walkout on March 15 was a real turning point for me," Oliva says. "I've always known climate change was a dire issue. I was making personal changes and encouraging people around me to make personal changes—like composting and using less plastic. It all seemed so futile, such an uphill climb. My organizing is something I can do on a larger scale. It's what I believe in, and I can find community—people to do it with."

Sara Poon

Sara Poon's first experience learning about climate change was during her sophomore year at the Bronx High School of Science in New York City, when she got involved with a student club called the League for Environmental and Animal Protection (LEAP). Says Sara, "I learned about pollution and how harmful the agricultural industry has been for animals and how greatly the industry has impacted the climate and the Earth. It really frustrated me."

The club was also involved with Fridays for Future and organized a climate strike at the school that brought students from Bronx Science to rally in Manhattan. "Since then," Sara says, "I've found myself working with organizations and attending events—like with the Climate Museum and the Climate and Resilience Education Task Force (CRETF).

"The frustration drove me to tackle this issue," she says.

> At the same time, I was meeting people from climate organizations that showed me a different side, which was hope. Both these things—hope and frustration about how hurt the Earth is becoming—motivated me to get more people involved. I just kept on speaking to other people to have them understand the situation and how to voice their thoughts on climate change. Organizing just comes naturally to me, especially since I'm comfortable to know I'm not the only one who feels this way and there are many people out there dedicating themselves to this movement.

Reflecting on how she was drawn to caring about the environment in the first place, Sara says that her perspective on nature was shaped by being from a low-income, first-generation immigrant household. She experienced different types of pollution firsthand in her low-income community. Growing up, she never went camping and rarely went to the beach. It was this lack of experience with nature—or what is commonly thought of as nature—that motivated her to get involved in the climate movement. "People who live close to fields and woods are working to protect what they already have," she explains. "Organizers from urban areas like me, who haven't grown up with nature in our backyards, want to give what we've lacked to ourselves and future generations. It's our lack of contact with nature that drives us to work for climate justice. People who have nature in their environment, and those of us who don't, are both emotional about losing it to climate change, but in different ways. We may have different perspectives, different backstories, but we're all united to tackle this issue."

A common thread runs through these stories. Arte, Peter, Olivia, and Sara turned toward climate activism when they connected with other young people and realized that they could make a difference.

The schools Peter and Sara attended actively encouraged their civic engagement. Olivia's school, while not actively supporting her involvement, was a place where nearly three thousand students were coming together daily, and the administration did not prevent her from using that fertile ground to organize her walkout.

Schools are well positioned to help students connect with each other, learn the skills of democratic participation, and find meaning in work to create a better world. But, as Arte's experience suggests, schools can end up doing just the opposite, if they don't balance apocalyptic information with opportunities for engagement and community.

EXPERIENCES WITH THE CLIMATE MOVEMENT

What can the experiences of these four young people tell us about how schools can prepare young people for effective civic participation?

Arte Romero y Carver

All through her years in high school, Arte continued to work with the friends she made at the city council meeting. Eventually, they called themselves Youth United for Climate Crisis Action (YUCCA). She is proud of their accomplishments, which include mobilizing thousands of people to take part in the climate strike and rally at the Santa Fe State Capital Building. YUCCA also staged a protest inside the governor's office calling for abolition of fracking, declaration of a climate emergency, a just transition of the economy away from fossil fuels, and investment in community solar. "Our older white allies decided to join the sit-in," recalls Arte. "The police came and arrested our white allies but not us. It was a polite and respectful arrest due to the age and status of the white people." In another action YUCCA erected a "guillotine" in front of the State House to demonstrate how the state's inaction on climate change was killing people. The guillotine's rope was attached to a block of ice. As the ice melted, the blade of the guillotine dropped lower and lower.

Although the protesters didn't get a meeting with the governor, they met with the head of the governor's climate change task force. "We took charge of the meeting," Arte says. "We opened with a land acknowledgment, and then interrogated him. We got some good, if depressing, information about how much nonaction the task force was taking. I was proud of being able to run this meeting and to talk as if I wasn't a child, and I was proud of myself and my comrades for disrupting that meeting so politely and so effectively. Eventually, we got some results: we helped get a solar bill passed by the legislature."

She reflects that some of her most hopeful experiences in the movement have not been in the protests: "I'm in college now and I've stepped back in a big way. I'm no longer an active member of YUCCA, but others have taken over responsibilities I've left behind. I'm proud of them. They're probably doing a better job than I did. A beautiful part of a movement is that you're replaceable in it. That's awesome!"

In Saint Louis, she is looking for a path to continue her activism for climate justice. "I've met people in the social-justice struggles there," she says.

> They're intelligent and caring. But when I bring up the climate crisis, it's a nonstarter. They see the political struggle around climate change as a hobby for wealthy white people. They find it bizarre that I could connect climate change with racial justice. I don't fault them because there is such a huge disconnect because of how people perceive climate change and how people perceive racial justice. You can grow up in a situation of extreme environmental racism—for example, asthma from air pollution that makes you susceptible to COVID—but you're not necessarily aware of it because it's slow murder.
>
> Then you have an environmental movement that has too often characterized climate change as a threat to the Earth, as opposed to a threat to human lives. I have a lot of sympathy for Greta Thunberg, I think she's done some good and hard things and I commend her bravery. I imagine that she would be wonderful to have a conversation with. That said, I think it's dangerous that she has become the prominent figurehead of the global environmental movement, a northern European girl who took a boat across the sea to speak at the climate march in New York City. I know people just as young as she is who are protesting. When she's the symbol of the global climate movement and you don't see water protectors in the media and you're told the problem with climate change is that it hurts polar bears, I can understand why my new friends aren't drawn to the climate movement.

Arte is passionate about bridging the gap between the climate and social justice movements. She explains:

> We need to help people see that climate change is racial violence. It's murder/suicide caused by white supremacy unabated. We need to abolish fossil fuels because of the slow violence they're bringing, and we need to liberate people from the violence they're experiencing daily from poverty, hunger, lack of health care, and police violence. If you're going to be evicted in a few weeks, and I'm asking you to be interested in the climate crisis, I need to be able to offer you and your children something tangible—like food, a good job and income, high-quality day care, and universal health care. Our movement must bring climate and justice together.

Regarding the future, Arte says, "I wandered around Santa Fe until I found a way to be useful, and now that I'm in college I'm looking for the same thing—a place to be useful."

Peter

After Sunnyside, Peter attended what he characterizes as a "normal, majority-white, upper-middle-class public high school," which offered hardly anything related to climate justice. As a result, he worked outside of school with a variety of organizations to influence city climate policy.

His greatest accomplishment, and the one he's proudest of, is his successful effort alongside other youth to establish the Portland Youth Climate Council. Says Peter, "Most of my work during my high school years was to establish the Council, gain legitimacy for it, and work with city officials to bring a youth perspective into the halls of power."

An example of his work with the Youth Council is a campaign to electrify city buses. The council decided to bring together youth groups for a summit on electrification. It turned out that some of these groups had been working for a long time to get free transit for youth. "We realized that we couldn't just push through electrification without working with these groups to make sure their policy agenda got met, too," Peter recalls. "It's challenging to accomplish climate justice on the ground, but extremely important and rewarding. The Youth Council is mostly white, as is Portland, because of a lot of racism in the past. Redlining has pushed people of color to the edges of the city. That made it somewhat harder to get youth of color to come all the way downtown to a meeting. There was certainly a learning curve when it came to issues of inequity. It's easy to talk about but requires a real commitment on the ground as well."

City council members and government officials have praised Peter and his youthful colleagues and have commended them for showing up. "But I'd rather they would listen to what we have to say and act!" Peter says.

> I want to tell them, "Yes, you've passed free transportation for students, but it's on a 'one-year-at-a-time' basis. So, we have to keep coming back year after year to advocate for it. When we show up and you say you're impressed, it gets old because you have the power to do the right thing so that we don't have to keep coming back!"

What excites Peter most about the climate movement is the agency youth have seized in the last few years.

> Youth are a powerful force on the world stage, for sure, and it's great that all those protests around the world are getting lots of attention. But those protests also have local contingents that are pushing their local community leaders to change policy at the local level. I'm proud that I'm leaving behind a vehicle for students to express their opinions on environmental issues. When I was in eighth grade, I didn't have that vehicle. Every city and state government should have a Youth Council.

> Lots of youth don't realize that there are steps beyond marching and social media. They don't know that they can take the power they've built through the march to City Hall. This is no fault of their own. They haven't been taught that by our society, by their parents, by our schools. They haven't been taught that they have the power to effect change.

Peter's main focus has shifted. At the time of this interview he was a sophomore at Carleton College in Northfield, Minnesota, ready to declare his major in political science on the international relations track. He hopes to pursue a career in diplomacy and international relations. He currently works as an adviser to his college on green transportation.

Olivia

Olivia says that her understanding of effective tactics has evolved since she worked to organize her school to participate in the climate strike. She has come to see the need for direct action, "using your body and your organizing to directly intercept and disrupt systems." Accordingly, she and her best friend started Extinction Rebellion Youth New York (XRYNYC) in October 2019. In February 2020, right before the pandemic began, they staged a guerrilla fashion show, featuring sustainable "trashion" outfits and demanding that the fashion industry mitigate its role in the climate crisis.

She graduated from high school in June 2020 and stepped back from leadership of XRYNYC, as the members' ages generally spanned grades 8 to 12. That summer, she joined in the protests for racial justice following George Floyd's murder. With some fellow organizers from XRYNYC, she coordinated a youth mutual-aid and protest-safety network to support the protesters. During a gap year (2020–2021), she organized with the Climate and Resilience Education Task Force (CRETF) in New York City to support youth in advocating for the passage of climate education legislation in the New York State Senate. She also worked as an organizer for a progressive candidate running for mayor in the primaries.

At the end of May 2021, Olivia took a break from organizing for the first time in over two years. She writes:

> Quite frankly, I was disillusioned by the stunning lack of substantive or noticeable change that had occurred because of my organizing. I had helped mobilize hundreds of thousands of students to strike for the climate, and I had joined in striking weekly myself for a year. I had organized direct action with XRYNYC, I had advocated for legislation, I had protested in the streets for racial justice every day for a whole summer, and I had spent sixty hours a week organizing for a grassroots mayoral candidate who ultimately proved unable to follow through on the radical ideas I'd been drawn to. I was exhausted and burnt out, and sick of the empty promises and praises that youth organizers are given by our leaders and public.

She acknowledges:

> I'm still recovering from that burnout. Climate organizing has never left my mind or intentions. I plan to engage with it again, very soon. However, I need to do it in a way that's intentional. After having organized in so many modes and pursued so many tactics that have been inadequate or flawed, I am still looking for something that makes me hopeful again about the productivity and usefulness of the energy I'm expending.
>
> I still believe in the power of youth organizing, of climate education, and of people power, and I still think these things represent the only path we have to stop the climate crisis. It's the fight of our lives and for our lives. We won't stop before we see the

changes we're demanding, because we have no other choice. It's optimism within pessimism. It feels so dire and that's the reason we're going to persist no matter what. That raw and uninhibited energy is what motivates me and gives me hope. I find it really exciting.

But I'm proud of myself for recognizing when to step back and take the space I need, because when I go back into the world of climate organizing, I can be more intentional, focused, and energetic in the work I do.

I'm a freshman in college, and I haven't decided on a major. Whatever I pick, I'm going to do it with a concentration in education. My plan after college is to become a teacher, either with elementary school students or teaching theater. Organizing will be part of my life throughout my future, even if it's not what I do as a profession. I'm considering majoring in theater or environmental studies. At LaGuardia, I was a theater major, and performing arts continue to be a very important part of my life. It's one of my favorite ways to build community.

Sara

Working with the Green Team (a student club started by three teachers at her school), Sara helped develop and complete a major project: a Google document tool kit for teachers and students in grades K–12 (see the appendix). It's interdisciplinary and hands-on, sorted by subject and grade level. Explains Sara, "As students we were able to identify what type of information would be most easily digested and interesting to people. It's for people who are having a hard time figuring out where they want to start in educating about the topic. It has reached an entire network of teachers in the New York City Schools and beyond. The influence we had was a great success." Sara and her teacher Matthew Sarker are members of CRETF, which brings together educators and students from schools throughout New York City for regular meetings throughout the year. CRETF has been instrumental in publicizing and distributing the tool kit.

"COVID was a challenge," observes Sara.

> But I think a lot of climate organizations went above and beyond to keep the movement going and making it a virtual platform. I attended lots of climate summits and workshops on Zoom. Even though we were physically separated, and we couldn't rally or interact in person, we were so resilient to connect so many people to the movement. Zoom and social media gave some people a voice that they might not have had before.
>
> The climate movement has gotten a lot of attention. And that was what we intended for it. And a lot of politicians are trying to cater to us and our motivation as youth. I think my generation really wants to salvage, if that's the right word, what we have left, in politics as well as in conservation. I'm excited to see what we can do when we become professionals in the field, which is very soon.

Sara is now specializing in environmental studies as a biology major at Stony Brook University. "The reason I'm so passionate about the topic," she says, "is that there are so many things to talk about. There are so many subjects to tackle and conversations to have and different perspectives. I think that's really fun."

In these stories, we see not only the power of mass climate-strike demonstrations to inspire and mobilize lots of people but also the importance of organizations that enable activists to continue the work when the excitement is over. Through YUCCA, Arte stayed involved, as the group collaborated with other organizations to develop specific demands and orchestrate direct action campaigns to advocate for them. Peter established the Portland Youth Climate Council to mobilize youth to influence the city's environmental policy making. Olivia and her friend founded XRYNYC. She coordinated a youth mutual-aid network for racial-justice protesters, supported youth groups in advocating for climate education legislation, and organized for a mayoral primary campaign. The Green Team engaged Sara and her friends in the ongoing project of producing and distributing the tool kit. Each of these initiatives is based on a different strategy for advancing change; all are useful in building community, maintaining hope, strengthening knowledge, and making a difference.

To organize mass protests, build cohesive organizations, and forge collaborative partnerships, student activists need social and emotional skills, such as listening, assertiveness, problem solving, conflict resolution, and racial and cultural sensitivity. They need skills in writing, public speaking, and thinking strategically and creatively about challenges that arise, possible solutions, and levers for change. As Peter and Sara confirm, schools can make important contributions to youth activism by helping students develop these skills. They can do so without taking sides on partisan political issues. But like Arte and Olivia, too many young activists have had to develop these skills on their own.

SCHOOL EXPERIENCES, POSITIVE AND NEGATIVE

How did schools support, or fail to support, these young people in becoming climate activists? What can we learn from their experiences?

Arte

Arte found little support for her climate justice activism in high school or college. Earlier, she explained how reading a policy paper about the climate crisis had left her feeling powerless and useless. She took an Advanced Placement (AP) environmental-science course in high school after she'd been doing climate organizing for a year but tuned it out.

> We spent way too much time on how climate change was happening. There were essentially no policy recommendations, and we didn't talk at all about climate justice or the relationships between white supremacy, capitalism, colonialism, land, and climate change.
>
> There's an attempt to talk about climate justice in the college course I'm taking now, but I find that people are afraid to say the words white supremacy, and I don't think that we can talk about climate change in the US, if we aren't able to say those words. I also have a problem with the term Anthropocene to refer to the geological epoch we're in with humans in charge. "Look at what humans have done!" people say, "This is what humans do when they're in charge." No! It's what European colonialism does when it's in charge. Colonialism is based on a distinct racist ideology that justifies the exploitation of Indigenous people, the seizing of their land, and the destruction of the environment. This ideology has been dominant for only a small part of human history.

Peter

"My K–8 school was a case study in what educators should be doing," asserts Peter. "Sunnyside was probably unlike any school in the country in the amount of civic engagement students experienced, the support we received to find our voice, and the knowledge we acquired. Going into eighth grade, I had been learning about the environment from kindergarten on. I had the facts in my back pocket. I felt confident enough to speak in public. I'd been learning about environmental issues and protest movements."

He'd also been exposed to a variety of perspectives on climate issues. When some older students at Sunnyside learned that ranchers in eastern Oregon were killing wolves to protect their livestock, they became incensed. When the students testified against this practice, the ranchers were not pleased. They complained to the Portland school district, charging that the teachers at Sunnyside were indoctrinating their students. The teachers submitted their lesson plan to prove they had not been indoctrinating students. But following the conflict, the school partnered with the 4H Program and the ranchers to create a multiyear exchange program in which Sunnyside students, including Peter, spent a week with rancher families and students from rancher families spent a week with Sunnyside families. While still opposed to the killing of the wolves, students came to understand the ranchers' point of view.

"My learning about the environment in school mostly ended after eighth grade," says Peter.

> I took an AP environmental science class, but coming from a school like Sunnyside, I found the level of discussion to be lacking. I helped form a climate club but felt it should really be the responsibility of the teachers to further students' education about the climate.
>
> Yet I continued to work on climate all the time I was in high school. That just goes to show that if students have a strong science-based education in elementary and middle school—one that shows them they have the power to effect change—they will go on to become politically engaged high schoolers and politically engaged college students. Generally, other students who attended Sunnyside tend to be like me. They may not have worked on these issues to the same extent that I have, but they are tuned in, engaged, and know what they're talking about. It started early. We went and played in the forest and rubbed mud all over our faces. That was important. I give a lot of credit to the teachers at Sunnyside for where I am today.

Olivia

Olivia's experience in high school was mixed. "I took bio/life science," she says.

> No mention of climate change. I took earth science. No mention of climate change. There was nothing in the core curriculum about climate change.
>
> I took an AP environmental science class. We learned from a textbook, and the curriculum was structured to prepare us for the AP exam. It consisted of learning modules aimed at preparing us to write short responses or answer multiple choice questions. The focus was the science of climate and climate change. We studied the biosphere and ecosystems to understand how they're being disrupted by climate change. There was just one short unit on the social implications of climate change. It was an elective class that students weren't required to take. A class that teaches for a test diminishes a student's sense that the information is relevant for the real world and for your life. It rewires your brain to think of what you're learning as important only to pass a test.

On the positive side, LaGuardia High School allowed Olivia to publicize the climate strikes and recruit students and teachers to participate. The school also allowed students to participate in the various strikes and protest marches without taking punitive measures. Also, for the September 2019 climate strike, Olivia prepared a slide presentation to explain why students were doing the protest. She convinced a dean to send it out to all the social studies teachers and ask them to show it to their classes. "It wasn't super successful," she says, "Maybe two or three of them did."

But a couple of teachers invited her to come to their classes to share her knowledge and tell students about the protest. Reflects Olivia, "For a teacher to reach out and say, 'I think what you're doing is important for my students to know about'—that's one of the most powerful things an educator can do. It might seem like a bare minimum, but you would be surprised by how few teachers are willing to do it. Just feeling that support, feeling listened to, and feeling that my teachers think the work I'm doing is important enough to bring into their classrooms—that's one of the most helpful things that a teacher ever did."

Sara

Sara says that her school did not offer any classes on climate change. She learned about the climate crisis from student clubs, LEAP (described earlier) and the Green Team, and from the teachers who sponsored them.

"Three teachers came together to start the Green Team," recalls Sara.

> They kind of ran it, but not really. What they really wanted was to get out of the way and let the students do what they wanted to do with the support of the teachers as advisers. They had most of the resources and the information, which was then provided to the students. But I think the most significant thing they did was to support us, not guiding every move we made, but leading and not leading, being more of an adviser than someone to tell us what to do the way a teacher would. We weren't doing assignments. We were doing projects we wanted to do around the school based on problems we saw that were important to address. We need to have more teachers willing to have these kinds of conversations with their students.
>
> My teacher Matthew Sarker was involved with lots of organizations. He was always in the loop about different events, different workshops all over the city that his students could attend. And he emailed his students links to different workshops. He was one of the first three teachers who started the Green Team at my school. And the first sustainability coordinator, whose name was Edward Wren, sparked my want to organize. He had conversations with me all the time between dismissal and club meetings. We would

just talk about the climate movement and climate change in general, and then what we wanted for the school.

I know that it was very exhausting for Mr. Sarker after Mr. Wren left our school. With just one teacher thinking about how to engage students in doing something like this, it's almost impossible. It's a big time commitment. It's very exhausting. It's also very stressful to want to do all these things, but not have the resources or administrative support to do them. Matthew needed more support from his colleagues at the school. To motivate your students to get into climate organizing or support students for what they want to do, you need to have conversations, open conversations, and be willing to expand to people who aren't already in the community. A lot of networking is involved.

These stories offer many takeaways. Following are a few of mine:

- The climate crisis is not only a topic for science classes. Students must explore the root causes of the crisis, including its history, politics, and economics, and educators must have the courage to allow white supremacy into the conversation.
- The grades from preK to 8 are critical in providing a foundation for climate justice education, as Peter's experience demonstrates.
- Because snobbery, arrogance, and judgmental attitudes can undermine efforts to build a movement that unites climate and justice, listening to the perspectives of others is an essential skill for climate organizers—and one worth cultivating in school, as Sunnyside did.
- I was struck by the poignancy of Olivia's saying how much it meant to her when a couple of teachers asked her to present to their classes. She felt supported, listened to, and validated for

her climate organizing. Although it was a small gesture, it was one that only a few of her teachers were willing to make.

- Sara captures the challenge that teacher mentors face in balancing student autonomy with support and guidance.
- Sara's story demonstrates how important a student climate club can be, as well as how stressful it can be for a teacher to sponsor a club in addition to managing all their other responsibilities. Teachers absolutely need support from the administration, including fewer classes to teach.

ADVICE FOR EDUCATORS

We can distill the experience of these four students into key points for educators.

Educate to Unite the Movements for Climate and Justice

Arte's experience shows how critical it is to connect movements for climate and justice. As she asserts, "There's such a disconnect in people's minds between the movement to save the environment and the movement for social justice. We need to bridge that gap. That's the main thing I ask of educators."

Alas, we have a long way to go to achieve this. To the extent that the high schools our four young people attended are representative (and I think it's fair to say that they are), climate education, if offered at all, is an elective course narrowly focused on the science of climate change and geared to prepare students to pass the AP environmental science test.

Arte proposes a helpful step in the right direction: "Listen to your students! If your classroom is in any way diverse, there will be students who have lived experience with some aspect of climate justice. Crowd-source truth by drawing out your students' lived experience."

Olivia agrees with Arte that education is key to overcoming the disconnect between the movements for climate and justice. She says:

> Climate education is an essential building block because there are widespread misconceptions about what's driving climate change and what we can do to solve it. There are so many proposals, like electric cars, people going vegetarian, or technological innovation. These Band-Aid solutions reflect a dangerous misunderstanding of the situation we're in. What's really driving climate change are systemic racism and capitalism—and by capitalism, I mean putting profit over people and seeing things like food as a commodity rather than a source of nourishment for people. We need to be honest with ourselves, with our community, and with the public about the issues actually at play here and use that understanding to motivate people into action that goes beyond individual choices and embraces collective community care and intervention to create the world we want to see.

Working with the Portland Youth Climate Council, Peter demonstrated how to bring climate and justice together when he united the student campaign for electrification of city buses with the campaign for free transit, led by low-income students of color who, because of racism, tend to live on the outskirts of town.

Make Climate Education Continuous for Grades preK–12

Lacking contact with nature as she was growing up, Sara calls on schools to nurture a loving relationship with nature from a young age. She would doubtless have enjoyed attending the K–8 Sunnyside Environmental School. Peter says his school-based climate education ended for all intents and purposes after eighth grade. At his high school in Portland, he might have appreciated participating in something like Sara's Green Team. These two youth climate activists are strong advocates for making climate education part of the core curriculum for grades preK to 12.

Olivia adds, "There's always a way that the climate crisis connects to the subject that you're teaching. Find those connections and dedicate some lessons to them. Since we don't have a climate-education mandate, it needs to start with teachers taking the initiative to do it in their classrooms. That's how we're most realistically going to see that shift."

Support Student Activism

In Peter's view, the top priority for climate education is to show students how to effect change. "I think youth know what's going on. They're pretty tuned in to social media. They know that climate change is real. Thanks to Sunnyside, I already knew a lot about how to make a difference, but the students around me in high school didn't necessarily have that information. I would have loved to have had teachers who taught us about policy-making processes at a local level. That's not a partisan political thing. It's about how you effect change in this country."

Strongly agreeing with Peter, Olivia calls on educators to combine teaching about climate change with ways for students to engage and get plugged in to the movement. "Teaching the climate crisis without teaching action can actually be harmful," she says. "It's important for young people to feel empowered and get the resources and support to get involved."

Peter suggests that educators encourage students to be active in their own way. "Not all the students in your classes are going to respond in the same way," he says. "Some might choose to do nothing. Some might choose to continue posting on social media because that's how most students respond to social issues right now. Some will join the marches, which have had enormous impact. But talking from my background, I believe if we can get youth to believe that they can talk with an elected official and that person will listen to them, if we can support them in affecting policy, not just in Portland but around the country, it will have a major impact."

Olivia agrees with Peter, but she would add that educators introduce students to a range of options for getting involved, including nonviolent direct action, which she experienced through her work with XRYNYC and Black Lives Matter (BLM), and electoral work, which, in her case, involved working for a candidate in a mayoral primary.

She adds a final plea to educators: "Know your students. If one of them takes the initiative to act for climate justice or expresses interest in doing so, please ask them how you can support them."

Make Climate Education Interdisciplinary and Project Based

Olivia would start by getting rid of all AP tests, especially those for courses in climate and the environment. She would make climate education part of the core curriculum, and she would make it project based. "By project based," she explains, "I mean projects that have a real-time impact on the world around us. Since climate justice is so topical and relevant to the real world and our lives, there's no excuse for keeping the learning inside the classroom."

"Why can't we visit a community garden?" she asks. "Why can't we learn about urban agriculture? Why can't we have a place-based education when the concepts we're learning about are relevant to our daily lives? We should connect with local organizations, local organizers, and local projects that are implementing the things we're learning about."

She took part in a program outside of school during spring break called NY2X. "We spent the whole spring break visiting farms around the city and spending a day with the leaders or farmers there," she explains.

> They were excited to talk with students. We volunteered there and learned about their operation. It was one of the most incredible educational experiences I had in the city.
>
> The future of climate education is more field trips! We had no field trips in my high school. I had friends who kept volunteering

> on a farm for the next two years after making that spring-break visit. The power of that is so real and it means so much more than reading a textbook or seeing a video.

Mentor a Student Climate Justice Club at Your School

Sara's teacher Matthew Sarker provides a good model, as does Bayard Faithfull, whose work as a mentor for student activists is described next. Just keep Sara's cautionary point in mind: it takes time and energy to mentor a club. Convince your administration of its importance and of their responsibility to give you the time and resources to do it.

EDUCATIONAL NIRVANA: REFLECTIONS FROM BAYARD FAITHFULL

What can we learn from Bayard's many years of teaching for climate justice?

"Over the years I taught the Global Environmental Politics course for seniors at Beacon, the conversation changed," observes Bayard.

> For the first five years, it was about climate change as a future threat—something that was going to affect our grandchildren. Beginning around 2018, students began to see climate change as a crisis that would affect their survival on the planet.
>
> The students also began to realize that the climate crisis is going to affect poor people around the world more than anybody else. And so, the class and the climate club shifted, going from "green is nice, we hug trees" to "this is an existential issue that involves race, it involves class, it involves colonialism." A sea change occurred. Greta Thunberg has been an exemplar of how young people have come to see the environmental movement and the role of young people within it.
>
> Much of the literature about the climate crisis is apocalyptic. At the beginning of the course, I would always say that a lot

of our reading is going to lead to depression and frustration and anger, and the job here is not to make you crawl into a hole and feel depressed. The job is to summon up righteous anger that the powerful have made these decisions and are willing to give away your future for short-term profits. That's something you should be angry about.

So, we would go from depression to "We can change this, and we have to change this. If we don't change this, we're really screwed." The climate club and the class helped to explain to other kids as well that this wasn't about recycling newspapers. It wasn't about being nice. It was about our collective survival on the planet, with the poor people of the world in line to suffer most. The depression part is real. It's something that teachers working with students on climate need to think about and frame again and again, not as an ending point but as an invitation to activism. This was a constant conversation in the class.

I believe that serious activism—whether it's the civil rights movement or the movement to end the Vietnam War—involves living on that line of fear and terror, not letting it engulf you, but turning it into indignation and willingness to fight for justice. You need both. Unless the issue hits close to home, it's hard to put in the energy and commitment required to build a movement. As climate educators, we need to help students look at reality deeply while offering multiple paths forward.

My high point in teaching about environmentalism was in the fall of 2019. It was so exciting because we were talking about the climate crisis in class and, at the same time, kids in the environmental club and my Global Environmental Politics class were building toward the September 20 climate march. Kids were saying, "There's this meeting tomorrow night" or "there's this protest about the pipeline on Sunday, let's all get out there." It wasn't me suggesting what they might do. They were taking the initiative.

They were wearing t-shirts they'd made that had environmental slogans on them. They were joining students from other schools protesting at the UN every Friday. They were participating in a network of students from schools across the city who met weekly at the Ethical Culture Society to push things forward and prepare for next steps. They were educating themselves in the skills of movement building: How do we use the media? How do we use art to make powerful messages? How do we address race, class, and gender as we work to save the environment?

To me, it's educational nirvana when you're helping kids understand reality in greater depth and they've already grasped enough to commit time and energy to act—to pull their friends in and put it on social media and make it a cool thing to do. A snowball effect occurred. Part of it was good organizing on the part of the students. Part of it was feeling the energy for the movement across the country and the world and wanting to be part of it.

The excitement spread to teachers and students throughout the school and led to a teach-in on the day of the march. Bayard explains:

Another teacher and I organized the day, but it wouldn't have happened without the enthusiasm of the students. They had been organizing all summer long. They were already going full speed ahead when school opened in September. Once our teachers saw hundreds of kids strongly motivated and interested in the climate crisis, they hopped on board. On that day we had thirty-three different workshops. It didn't matter what grade the kids were in. They could sign up for workshops ahead of time and the expectation was that after the workshops they would go to the climate march.

Teachers used their disciplinary focus to discuss aspects of the climate crisis. Several English teachers did wonderful things, inviting kids to write about the climate crisis, sharing hopes and fears and expressing utopian visions. Science teachers taught some of the basic science. A teacher who is into coral research and does lots of scuba diving did a workshop on what's happening with the coral reefs. Some physics teachers talked about solar and wind power. Math teachers looked at the cost of environmental damage across the country and climate risk. We had folks doing the politics and looking at strategies AOC [Representative Alexandria Ocasio-Cortez of New York] had proposed. An exciting day! And a model for school-wide climate-justice education, if we could extend it throughout the year.

Reflecting on his years of teaching, Bayard says:

I want students to be more than passive receptacles. Too often we ask kids to take in all this knowledge and we don't ask them to do a lot with it. We ask them to spit it back in a test and spit it back on a paper, but we don't ask them to apply their learning. At a school like Beacon, we ask students to take issues seriously, whether it's the AIDS crisis or racism or climate change. We believe that deep learning takes place when we grasp an issue with our heart and soul and move from purely studying it to trying to help create social change.

It's inspiring to facilitate that and see learners become teachers. The students study. They understand. They take what they need from teachers, and then they go out to educate other people. They're grasping new information because they really want it, not because we're telling them they'll get an A. That's real learning. Not all kids find their purpose in activism. There are lots of paths. My hope is that they take their learning into something that is meaningful.

What I love about Beacon graduates is that many of them are in caring professions where they're practicing social justice at different levels. They are not all full-time activists. That's not a viable path for everybody. But they are in places where they're doing good things.

These high school years are full of exuberance, and that's cause for celebration.

Through the summer and fall of 2019, the youth climate movement was building momentum. On September 20, it reached the whirlwind stage, as an estimated six million young people and adults around the world joined the climate strike.[1] The march was set to be only the beginning. Major follow-ups were being planned for the spring. But this was not to be, for in March 2020, the COVID-19 crisis shut down the schools. The pandemic broke the momentum. It was simply too hard and too risky to mobilize students.

Then another whirlwind engulfed activists, triggered by the murder of George Floyd on May 25, 2020. The Black Lives Matter (BLM) uprising shifted the focus of activists to racial justice. As noted, Olivia spent the summer organizing and protesting for BLM and creating a mutual-aid and protest-support network for protesters. The uprising demonstrated the deep yearning for racial justice in this country. Emerging within a year of each other, these two whirlwinds reveal the deep well of potential support for climate justice and the power that will be generated if we can bring the two movements together.

In the wake of the BLM uprising, as schools were considering how to strengthen their antiracist curricula and engage teachers in antiracist professional learning, the inevitable backlash came. The Republican Party sought an advantage in the upcoming midterm elections by stirring up its base to intimidate educators—already exhausted and disheartened by the challenges of teaching during the pandemic—from addressing racism at all. Meanwhile, our four student activists continued their climate justice work through organizations they created or joined.

Social movements experience both whirlwind periods and movement-building periods in which activists labor through organizations to sustain the work and build toward the next whirlwind. The youth climate movement drew in the four young people featured in this chapter and changed their lives, along with the lives of hundreds of thousands of young people around the world. Like Olivia and Arte, most will need to stand back from time to time to decide where next to focus their time and energy. Some, like Peter and Sara, may steadily move forward on clear paths. One way or another, I expect that Arte, Peter, Olivia, and Sara will be contributing to the climate justice movement for a long time to come. As Olivia says, "What excites me about the climate movement is the relentlessness of it—the determination coming from the principle that we have no choice. It's the fight of our lives and for our lives and we're not going to stop before we see the changes we're demanding."

It's our job as educators to educate and mentor many more young people to join them on that path.

CHAPTER 7

Engage the Whole School—and Beyond

ON TUESDAY, SEPTEMBER 8, 2020, the Almeda wildfire started on the north end of Ashland, a town of twenty thousand people in southeastern Oregon. Forty-mile-an-hour winds drove the fire through the towns of Talent (population 6,500) and Phoenix (population 4,600). In just a few hours, the fire had burned 2,800 structures and killed three people. Some 20 percent of the people in the fire's path were living in poverty, and a large proportion of the structures destroyed were mobile homes and low-income housing for Latinx people and their families who pick grapes and work in hotels.[1]

The Phoenix-Talent School District enrolls some 2,600 students. An estimated 30 percent were directly affected by the disaster. The fire took almost everyone by surprise. Little emergency information was broadcast; people learned of the fire from the smoky skies and Facebook. Evacuation was sudden and chaotic. It was the first day of school, and a principal reported that elementary school students, on Zoom because of the pandemic, witnessed scenes in classmates' homes of frantic parents screaming, "Fire! Fire!" and grabbing their children to flee.

The experience of the Phoenix-Talent School District is unique only in the scale of the disaster. In January 2022 the US Government Accountability Office issued a report on the impacts of weather and climate disasters on schools, finding that "Over half of public-school districts [are] in counties that experienced presidentially declared major disasters from 2017 to 2019." In the years following the report, the country has seen only larger and more widespread climate catastrophes. Wildfires are the problem in the West; floods are the threat in the South.[2]

In this chapter, the principal of Phoenix Elementary School describes how she and her staff responded to the disaster. The chapter also provides portraits of two schools that are models of schoolwide climate justice education. They are Sunnyside Environmental School in Portland, Oregon, which immerses students in the love and study of the natural world, and the Math and Science Exploratory School, a middle school in Brooklyn, New York, which engages all of its students in project-based learning on climate-related themes through its exploration program. The final section of the chapter focuses on school transformation, drawing wisdom from a principal who transformed her school.

RESPONDING TO A CLIMATE-RELATED DISASTER

Shawna Schleif and Phoenix Elementary School

When Shawna Schleif woke up on September 8, 2020, the air felt different. It was warm and unusually gusty. Shawna is the principal of Phoenix Elementary School in Phoenix, Oregon, which then served 370 students in grades K–5, 60 percent of whom were Latinx. Around 10 a.m. she got a phone call from a friend in Ashland who told her that a fire had started there. But Ashland was fifteen miles away; the fire shouldn't affect the drive-through program Shawna had organized for families to pick up Chromebooks for their children.

After working fourteen years as a teacher and administrator in the Phoenix-Talent School District, Shawna had become principal of Phoenix Elementary in September 2019. In March 2020, the COVID-19 pandemic forced educators in the entire district to join educators across the country in reshaping how to do school. Now another year of virtual instruction lay ahead, and the new Chromebooks would help.

With no community alert system in place, Shawna, now in her office, learned by word of mouth that the fire was moving closer to Talent and Phoenix. At noon, she called off the drive-through. She sent her staff home and left herself, grabbing her own two sons who attended the daycare center right across the street from Phoenix Elementary. At 3 p.m. she drove back into Phoenix to pick up a friend's child from that same daycare because her friend was stuck in traffic and couldn't get to her child. She assumed that the gray sky and flakes of soot drifting through the area were coming by the wind from the Ashland fire. By the time she got back home, she learned that a donut shop three blocks from her school was burning. "I had no clue how close and destructive the fire had become," she says.

Shawna and her husband had lived in Talent for eleven years before moving to their current home on seventeen acres of wooded land looking down on Phoenix. In the back of her mind, she had always worried about the safety of her own home, but had never imagined that a fire could rip through the towns of Talent and Phoenix. Although their house seemed safe, the fire was so unpredictable that she and her family decided to flee. They drove twenty-five miles north and stayed with a family that offered to take them in.

Shawna recalls:

> All night I was on Facebook, watching with horror as Talent and Phoenix burned and learning that the trailer parks where many of our families lived were burning as well. A horrendous night! I get

emotional just thinking about it. My colleagues and I were texting and calling each other to find out where we were. There was no rest that night, watching what was happening and contacting people.

The next day we drove down to our house and saw that it was safe. My husband took the boys, and I drove to the Jackson County Expo Center because I knew that's where families were being funneled. I remember being with a family and hearing their story and thinking, "All I can do is be here for you and listen. I don't have anything to offer you except my ear." That's how we began our journey of crisis response.

Within twenty-four hours, Shawna knew where all her fifty staff members were, how they were doing, and what their needs were. One had lost her home. Without access to the databases in their school, they pieced together contact information and began calling families.

"I'm a member of a Facebook group of principals, and I put out a request for advice," recalls Shawna.

"I know some of you have been here before," I wrote. A principal from Paradise, California, site of a recent devastating wildfire, replied, "You're going to get stuff and stuff and lots of stuff and more stuff. You'll need to figure out how to deal with it." She was absolutely right!

As we connected with our families, we tried to support them with resources we had—stuff, water, childcare, health care, or whatever. We set up command centers and distribution centers. Staff self-selected into leadership roles based on their skills and interests.

The biggest need was for emotional support. It was heavy. Nearly 40 percent of our families lost their homes. When you lose your home, you lose much more. A lot of our families didn't have much to begin with. Many are not here legally, but they have

> lived here for decades and built lives they're proud of. Someone might look and see a trailer park and think, disparagingly, it's just a trailer park, but these people had worked hard and were proud of owning their trailer. They had put everything they had into it. Most didn't have insurance and couldn't afford to replace what they had.
>
> The staff were calling families and listening to their stories. I supported the staff by listening to their concerns, accepting their feelings, remaining calm, and urging them to take care of themselves.

After a couple of weeks as crisis responders, Shawna and her staff became social workers. Many of the Phoenix Elementary School families had ended up at the Expo Center. Located in the town of Center Point, about twenty minutes from Phoenix, the Expo Center has plenty of space with seven large buildings and an amphitheater. Concerts, rodeos, horse shows, and the county fair normally take place there. The Red Cross set up shop and later FEMA (the Federal Emergency Management Agency) had trailers in the RV park nearby.

"We rotated staff through, meeting with families, identifying their needs and linking them with resources," recalls Shawna.

> Luckily, the husband of our assistant superintendent works for the county. He helped us utilize the resources of the county, state, and federal governments. We worked with our community partners and neighboring districts. We set up several satellite schools. We distributed clothing, food, and health care as well as educational resources. Our schools have strong partnerships with healthcare programs for students and families, and we helped establish satellite healthcare stations.
>
> Then we entered the third phase: It was time to make school happen. Thanks to heroic work by the fire department, all of

> Phoenix's school buildings were saved. Because of the fire, the state granted the Phoenix-Talent School District permission to return to in-person instruction sooner than other districts. Some of our kids were back in person in November 2020. By January, we were implementing a hybrid model (half a day in-person and half a day virtual). In-person instruction was fully restored in April after spring break.
>
> Just getting the kids to school was a huge challenge because so many were now scattered across a large geographic area. We bussed kids from all over. When you have an event like this and you're in crisis response mode, sometimes your creativity comes from just doing the next right thing. Instead of operating with your bright lights on, you operate with your fog lights on. You just do what lies in front of you, and magical things happen.

Shawna's passions as an educator are social and emotional learning (SEL) and equity. "As I grew up, I endured a lot of adverse childhood experiences," she explains.

> Our family was poor. I was the second youngest of six children. I came to depend on mentors, including teachers. It was natural for me to become a teacher because I wanted to have the impact on young people that my teachers had had on me. But for grades one through four I attended a private Christian school where I felt "othered" because of our family's socioeconomic status. I felt like I didn't belong. As an educator, I want to ensure that everybody has a sense of belonging, no matter what. I also have a natural tendency to see people for their gifts—to honor people for who they are.

"Building trust, strong relationships, and a sense of belonging is the foundation of a good school," says Shawna.

> It carries you forward with any tragedy you might face. We are a school that really values relationships, and we understand that everything hinges on creating connections with each other, our students, and our families. You can do amazing things when that is in place—amazingly hard things. This positive culture was here when I got here. People are here for the right reasons. They're flexible. They work together well. They enjoy working together.
>
> As for the kids, they were super excited to be back. They had also experienced trauma. Our focus was on tending to their social and emotional needs by establishing regular routines and fostering a sense of belonging, and a sense of safety. We had to balance making school safe, supportive, and predictable with pushing them from their comfort zones into their learning zones.

An important area for student learning was developing their social and emotional *skills*. Even before the pandemic, Shawna and her colleagues were seeing increasing numbers of kids exhibiting aggressive behavior. The pandemic and the fire only made it worse. Building a culture of predictability and safety required improving students' skills in understanding and managing their feelings—in a word, regulation. Before the pandemic, the school had established a HUG room and HUG spaces in classrooms. HUG stands for Hello, Update, and Goodbye. Recently, the school has embraced a research-based SEL Program called RULER (Recognizing, Understanding, Labeling, Expressing, and Regulating), developed by the Center for Emotional Intelligence at Yale University. Insights and skills from RULER are now integrated into the HUG program and throughout the school. A student struggling with regulation enters the HUG room (Hello) and, with the help of the HUG teacher, identifies the feelings they're having according to RULER's mood meter, a colorful chart listing the full range of feelings. The student then chooses a "regulation station." Options include playing with sand, drawing, or sitting in a tent to be alone for a while. When the student is ready, the HUG teacher has a conversation with the student. They discuss what happened, including the students' feelings, what triggered them, and what the student might do differently in the future (Update). Then, if all goes well, it's Goodbye—and back to the classroom.

"We teach the kids that we all have feelings," explains Shawna.

> Feelings aren't good or bad; they just are. We can choose what we do when we have a feeling. If we use our emotional brains, we may make a mistake and harm someone. It's best to use our wise brain—involving our prefrontal cortex—to make a smart choice. Our aim is to demystify and de-shame emotions and emotional responses. We believe that kids will do well if they can. We would never expel a kid because they don't know math facts. So why expel a kid for lacking the skills to regulate, communicate effectively, and get their needs met in what we would call a prosocial way? We're educators—we need to teach them. We have found the HUG room helpful. Now joining it with RULER, it works even better. In a district our size we can learn and implement pretty quickly. We try things a lot. When we know better, we do better. That's our motto.

The state of Oregon and the Phoenix-Talent School District have provided critical support for Shawna's efforts to create safe and supportive learning environments and to boost kids' social and emotional skills. Despite the drop in enrollment during the pandemic, the state guaranteed stable funding for at least the next five years. Now, even with the drop in enrollment caused by the fire, Phoenix Elementary still has the same funding and is able to reduce class sizes.

While doing their best to provide a calm, safe, predictable sanctuary for their students, Shawna and her colleagues have found their work lives to be far from calm and predictable over the past two years. "We've experienced change after change after change," says Shawna.

> We'd be doing one thing and new guidelines would come down from the CDC [Centers for Disease Control and Prevention] or the state and we would have to shift, and this happened again and again. We started to detest the word "pivot." Pivot became a bad word in our district!
>
> The pandemic generated continual conflict. We wanted to have the kids back in person, but not everybody came back. They said, "No, it's not safe." Teachers had to adapt by teaching kids in person while Zooming kids in. That stretched us to the limit.
>
> The political climate was a factor as well. During the first year after the fire, people were still revering teachers. As parents managed their kids at home during the pandemic, they stopped taking teachers for granted: "Wow! What amazing work you do!" By the summer after the fire, the attitude began to shift from gratitude to challenging educators—on COVID mitigation strategies, and other polarizing issues. Suddenly, our board meetings became very well attended.
>
> I appreciated that our staff rolled with the ups and downs. There were tears, stress, trauma, and exhaustion, to be sure; and yet, when someone was in a valley, someone was there to lift them up. We supported each other and that saw us through.

Posted on the wall in Shawna's office is the Trauma Stewardship Institute's "Tiny Survival Guide." Shawna has read articles and heard talks by the Institute's leader, Laura van Demoot Lipsky, and likes her ideas. The one-page guide provides thirteen guidelines to prevent trauma from lodging in your body and weighing you down. They include "Protect Your Mornings" (don't go straight to the news); "Be Active in Mind, Body, and Spirit"; and "Laugh."

To avoid storing stress and trauma in the body, Lipsky suggests "metabolizing" them, that is, channeling them into action—anything from taking a walk to having a courageous conversation with someone. "I'm an active person and that resonated with me," observes Shawna. "'Be aware of your addictions' was another one that struck me. I need to curb my addiction to productivity! And laughter has been so freeing to us at Phoenix Elementary. We laugh a lot. You can't do this work unless you can find balance."

As the 2022–23 school year began, Shawna said that the wildfire, "Capital T Trauma," is still present in the hearts and minds of people in her school and her community. "I sometimes struggle to talk about it without crying," she acknowledges. "It's still raw and will be so for a long time. But being vulnerable, being together, and being with the children, we are celebrating our resilience and our continuing efforts to give our kids a great education. This year we seem to be back to something closer to normal. It feels really positive."

Hats off to Shawna, her staff, her students, and their families. May the years ahead be calm, safe, predictable, and productive—with no pivots and lots of laughter!

Following are some of my takeaways from Shawna's story:

- I applaud Shawna's conviction that kids will do well if they can. If they are struggling to understand and manage their feelings, we need to teach them, not punish them.
- Metabolize trauma (and secondary trauma) rather than store it in your body—that is, convert it to energy and action. What an intriguing idea. Yes! Walk, run, exercise, and take action to help people who have experienced trauma and to address the causes of trauma. This is a good practice for young people as well as for

adults. Kids who have experienced trauma need lots of physical activity and opportunities to become helpers and activists in ways appropriate to their ages.

- Kudos to the state of Oregon and the Phoenix-Talent School District for enabling Shawna to reduce class size so that her teachers could better support students' recovery from the double whammy of the pandemic and the fire. All cities and states across the country should follow this example.

What are your takeaways from Shawna's story?

WHOLE-SCHOOL CLIMATE JUSTICE EDUCATION

Jan Zuckerman and Sunnyside Environmental School

From rural, conservative Phoenix and Talent in southeastern Oregon, we turn to Sunnyside Environmental School in progressive Portland, Oregon, the K–8 school Peter Sallinger attended. Sunnyside began as Environmental Middle School, founded in 1995 by Jan Zuckerman and Sarah Taylor. The school is notable for immersing students in nature through a unique multidisciplinary curriculum, for building a vibrant school community with celebration of nature at its core, and for its lasting impact on its students.

"I had taught elementary school for several years," explains Jan, "and I noticed that some of our top students who had always loved to learn felt their creativity and imagination squashed when they went to middle school. Sarah, who at the time was studying to become an administrator, wrote about her ideal school, one that would immerse students in the natural world, giving them the opportunity to notice it, connect with it, play in it, learn about it, love it, and work to protect it."

Building on these ideas, Sarah and Jan wrote a proposal for the school that was accepted by the Portland Public Schools School Board. The rest was up to Jan and Sarah. They found space in a school building that had some empty rooms. They held an open house to introduce the school and recruit students. To their surprise, the auditorium filled to overflowing. Families were hungry for an alternative middle school. The school opened with 120 students, grew to 240, and eventually became a focus option/neighborhood K–8 school in the Sunnyside neighborhood of Portland.

All the classes in the middle school were mixed age, consisting of sixth, seventh, and eighth graders. Students rotated through in-depth explorations of three nature themes that integrated all subject areas: the Year of the River, the Year of the Forest, and the Year of the Mountain. Over their three years in middle school, they experienced all three of these themes. Every class would leave the school one day a week to study out in the field, including one site they would visit regularly throughout the year and get to know.

The middle school curriculum was based on the Scottish Storyline Method, which Jan had embraced when she first started teaching. Developed in Scotland, Storyline uses students' enthusiasm for creating and living in stories to make learning memorable. For example, during the Year of the River, Jan would ask her students to envision a natural setting with a river that they might have visited or seen pictures of. She would ask them, "What is a river? What might *our* river look like? What plants might you see?" Students would work together to create a large frieze or mural of their river. Then Jan would ask, "What animals might visit our river?" Later, once the river ecosystem was created, she would ask, "What people might visit our river? What might these people do there?" Brainstorming, building on their shared knowledge, students would then create characters who would be connected to the river in some way.

She would take the students to Brookside Wetlands, an inner-city wetland with a creek, accessible by city bus. This is the site they would visit at least monthly throughout the year. "First, they would just explore," says Jan. "'Here's a mapping activity. Go out and try to map the area. We'll help you.' Then, 'What do you see? What animals, what plants? Go out and look and then we'll all come back to share what we discovered.' "

Back in the classroom, they often compared what they observed out in the field, with their river, sometimes adding to their frieze of the river and its surroundings.

"We taught them about nature journaling," says Jan. "Each student had a special spot at Brookside Wetland where they would go to journal, to record what they were seeing and hearing, thinking or feeling, to sketch, or maybe just to lie down, close their eyes, and listen, and then come back to share what they had experienced. I had parent volunteers and we spread out to make sure kids weren't jumping in the creek. There were strict rules about safety."

Jan would often invite someone from the Bureau of Environmental Services or other experts in the field to come and teach students about the native species and their roles in the ecosystem and about invasive species. The students might do service work, like pulling invasive species or collecting water samples to monitor levels of oxygen and pH in the creek and the pond. "One year we saw a bunch of bullfrogs and realized they were non-native frogs," recalls Jan. "So, we did a whole study of native amphibians as our science inquiry. During the winter, even in rain and snow, we'd drag students out to the Brookside Wetland and it would be wet and cold and we'd come back and have hot chocolate."

In the classroom Jan would introduce an incident that would affect the health of the ecosystem the class had envisioned and represented in the frieze. "I might introduce an issue like pollution or invasive species or wildlife dying out," explains Jan. "It depended on what our staff wanted to teach, what was going on in the world, and what the kids were interested in. We would teach the kids about the topic by weaving it into the storyline. The students' characters would see the problems through their perspectives and figure out ways to work together to solve the problems. The beauty of Storyline is it's so creative and uses imagination, and you get to become someone that you're not."

In addition to Brookside Wetlands, they also visited a dam and a fish hatchery and went to the Willamette River, which is a Superfund cleanup site, to learn about its history and the efforts to restore it. They studied the rivers of the United States, including the histories of those rivers from the time of the first Indigenous people to the present. Students would choose a river to study in addition to what they were learning from their visits to the nearby Willamette. They would learn about the features of a river, including the eddies, curves, rapids, and waterfalls, and write stories of their lives as though they were a river.

The school went beyond immersion in the natural world. "As an environmental school, we knew we had to address environmental issues," says Jan.

> We had a teach-in on the climate crisis and invited Dr. Riki Ott, marine toxicologist and oil-spill expert, to be our keynote speaker. We said, "We don't want you to show those pictures of climate chaos and scare the living daylights out of the kids." But she started off right away with all these gruesome photos. She just went right in, and you could hear a pin drop. And we just looked at each other. Then she said, "What an opportunity we have! We're alive at this very time in history to get to do something about this." She just flipped the whole thing upside down and the energy was, Yeeeeeees!—and then we went right into the workshops. It turned out to be an incredibly powerful and empowering teach-in.

In addition to the environment-stewardship opportunities integrated into their fieldwork and Storyline activities, Jan and her colleagues developed a service-learning program. Sixth graders were required to choose a close-to-home project that would make a practical difference. Seventh graders volunteered with an organization and learned about its work and presented a speech to their peers to teach them about the organization and their experience volunteering there. Eighth graders had to organize themselves into "cohorts," each of which would learn about a social or environmental justice issue that they cared deeply about and develop a project to address it. They had to do research, decide on an action they wanted to take, carry it out, and educate their classmates and the community in the process. School faculty and parents mentored the students in their service projects.

Jan mentored the climate-change cohort in which Peter Sallinger participated as an eighth grader. After Peter graduated from Sunnyside, she continued to mentor him and other young people as they worked to establish the Portland Youth Climate Council. "When I reflect on my experience as a mentor, the first thing that comes to mind is a sense of humor," says Jan.

> I feel that a lot of the time I was just fumbling around. A teacher I once teamed with had a big sign in our classroom that said, "Real Learning Is Messy." That sums it up!
>
> When Riki Ott said, "What an opportunity we have, to be alive at this time!" It really shifted my way of thinking. Mentoring is not just about what I can create for the students, but what am I doing? It's not only about supporting the students but doing it with the students and supporting them in that way. As an adult, I'm alive at this critical time, too. My responsibility is to act and get other adults to do the work they should be doing. It's also about learning what the youth want to do, and then finding resources in the community to support them and provide opportunities for their voices to be heard. That's my job as a mentor.

From its beginning, Sunnyside Environmental School integrated nature; Storyline; stewardship; inquiry; service learning; activism; mentoring; and, at its heart, celebration. Jan explains:

> We began the year with an all-middle-school campout, rotating students through basic ecology classes, ending each night with a big celebratory campfire. At school we began most days with a morning meeting to sing and learn together. We always held a big harvest festival in the fall and a big festival in December. Depending on that year's theme, it would be either the River Festival, the Forest Festival, or the Pangaea Festival. (Pangaea is a time in geological history when our continents were connected in one large land mass. We chose that name because the Year of the Mountain involved in-depth study of geology.) Parents and members of the community would come, and we'd open our classrooms to showcase the culmination of the Storyline and all that we had learned. We'd have food and singing and dancing. We were all learning together and our learning was joyful and fun—that's the culture we tried to create.

They succeeded!

"Dozens and dozens of our graduates are now working for the environment, including ones we could have never imagined doing so," says Jan. "Kids who were the biggest troublemakers now have their own organic farms. They've gone into forestry and all sorts of environmental careers. 'You do that!?!' I exclaim when I hear what they're up to. One went to Costa Rica and spent hundreds of hours helping to identify, categorize, and organize native cloud-forest plants, which a university keeps in temperature-regulated rooms. I never would have guessed it in a million years."

Which ideas, activities, or practices of Sunnyside Environmental School could you adapt for your own school? Perhaps a slice of nature that your students might get to know, accessible by a short walk or public bus ride? Occasions for a celebration? Ways to integrate art? Ways to involve students in making a difference?

Deanna D'Onofrio and Will Dych and the Math and Science Exploratory School

This middle school has found a way to offer students subject-area classes and multidisciplinary project-based learning—and to do justice to both. Furthermore, the school focuses its Exploration curriculum for all three grades primarily on climate justice, because the school's leadership and faculty recognize the urgency of educating students for climate justice and the need for a multidisciplinary, project-based approach to do that most effectively. Educators for climate justice would do well to embrace this model. See if you agree.

Founded more than twenty years ago, the Math and Science Exploratory School is a public middle school in Brooklyn, New York. Deanna D'Onofrio and Will Dych team-teach sixth graders. As the school's name suggests, the founding vision was to engage students in interdisciplinary, project-based learning. Students have their regular classes in math, science, and language arts. All students also participate in the school's Exploration program, which engages them in in-depth studies of important topics that cut across academic disciplines. Exploration is not an add-on or an extracurricular activity, but rather it sits at the heart of the school's mission. All 540 students in the school have "Exploration" for two periods and one double period per week throughout the school year. Currently, many of the themes in the Exploration program have to do with the environment and climate change. Sixth graders spend the year exploring food and water. The themes for seventh grade are art for social change and green infrastructure and design. Eighth graders study the United Nations Sustainable Development Goals and design solutions for reaching them.

Deanna and Will helped design the Exploration department in its current form and have taught exploration full time for eight years. When I interviewed them, it was March 2022, and they and their students had been exploring food and food justice since September.

The first module of the unit was food and culture. Students learned about the Lenape, the native people who were the original inhabitants of what is now New York City and the surrounding areas. They learned about the food the Lenape people ate and the sustainable practices they followed to live in harmony with nature.

Next, they explored African American food culture with the help of an exhibit prepared by the Museum of Food and Drink (MoFAD) in Brooklyn, New York. The Museum created a Legacy Quilt of African American "food heroes." The Museum's exhibits, including the Legacy Quilt, are viewable online, and the Museum invited the public to create and submit quilt patches for inclusion.[3] Deanna and Will engaged their students in doing research and creating construction-paper quilt patches of African American food heroes. The result was a beautiful quilt of some 180 unique and colorful patches, which went up in a magnificent display in a school hallway. Some of the students' patches were submitted to the Museum and added to its online Legacy Quilt.

As a culminating activity for this first module, Deanna and Will invited students to share a recipe for a dish enjoyed by their family. It didn't have to be related to their culture. Students created illustrated versions of their recipes, which were gathered into a digital cookbook. The fall weather was still good enough for parents to join their children for a shared meal, featuring samples of their favorite recipes, in the school's courtyard.

The second module involved hands-on observation of germinating seeds. "We got very science-y," Deanna says. "Students learned about the plants' life cycles and how plants make food. We gave them four seeds each and asked them to find seeds around their homes as well. Students put the seeds in small sealable, reusable plastic bags with some water for them to germinate. They kept plant journals and tracked plant growth."

Adds Will, "They practiced science skills: careful observation, recording their observations, measuring growth, making predictions and inferences. Success was not based on whether the seeds germinated. I explained that scientists can learn whether or not things turn out as they hoped or predicted."

The students followed the plant life cycle from seed to germination, to growth, to harvest. They also set up an indoor food garden, using upcycled berry containers and grow lights, to grow microgreens. After a couple of weeks, they had a "tasting" of their microgreens and recorded their findings—for example, arugula was "bland, but grassy." Reflects Deanna, "The kids had so much fun, connecting with the natural world in such a simple way."

The third module was food justice. They began by studying the current food system in the United States. Deanna and Will introduced students to the links in the food-supply chain: planting, growing, harvesting, packaging, refrigerating, transporting, displaying in the stores, selling and buying, cooking, and eating. They prepared a set of posters, each naming a link in the food chain. They distributed the posters to students and asked them to stand in a line to put the links in the chain in order.

Then, they introduced the concept of sustainability, beginning with a word-web activity: Will wrote "sustainability" in the middle of a piece of chart paper and charted the students' free associations with the word. After discussion and a quick check with *Britannica Kids*, they came up with a definition of sustainability as humans interacting with the environment to ensure resources for future generations. They showed the students the film *Climate Change 101* by Bill Nye[4] and followed with a brainstorming session: What are some sustainable things we already do? Kids came up with ideas like eating vegetarian or biking. Deanna and Will invited the students to create a piece of art to express their answer to the question, What is sustainability?

"It was wide open," explains Deanna. "They could represent why we need sustainability or how we can achieve it. Their art showed everything from smokestacks to scenes of nature to someone riding a bicycle. They expressed the concept in many creative ways."

Then they took another look at our current food system. With students again standing in line with posters of the food chain, Will asked, "Given what we've learned about the plant life cycle and sustainability, how can we make our food system more sustainable? For example, what steps can we eliminate from the food supply chain?" The students identified the costs to the consumer and the environment of plastic packaging and transporting food long distances from farm to stores. Deanna and Will went on to engage students in case studies of sustainable alternatives to our current system, including farmers markets and Brooklyn Grange, which owns and operates three large-scale rooftop farms in Brooklyn and Queens, designs and builds green spaces, and promotes sustainable living.

Students learned about the challenges our food system faces in getting healthy food to all people. Students read a hard-hitting, two-part photo article in the *New York Times* magazine from which they learned that one in eight US households faces food insecurity and fourteen million children need immediate food assistance. Although food insecurity has been exacerbated by the pandemic, for most of these people the instability will persist after the pandemic.[5]

Digging deeper into food insecurity, students learned about the underlying causes, including food deserts and food apartheid, unemployment, low wages, unstable housing, rising medical costs, and unreliable transportation. They learned that the term "food desert" refers to low-income communities, often communities of color, that lack access to healthy and affordable food, especially fresh fruits and vegetables. Will explained that food justice leaders are now encouraging people to use the term "food apartheid" instead of food desert. Their aim is to highlight the racist policies that limit access to healthy food and to promote community-driven solutions and systems change.[6]

The unit culminated with Food Justice Action Projects. In preparation, students learned about local efforts to address food insecurity, including CHiPS (Community Help in Park Slope), which runs a soup kitchen, food pantry, and shelter and support services for new and expecting mothers; the global Fight for $15 campaign to raise the minimum wage for low-wage workers, including farm workers, to fifteen dollars per hour; and CUCS (Center for Urban Community Services), a local group that provides housing, food, medical care, job training, and other support services for homeless people or those at risk of homelessness.

For their project, students could advocate, volunteer, raise money, make personal changes, or do acts of environmental stewardship. They had to document their project by providing its title, a summary, and two pieces of evidence to prove they worked on the project (e.g., a copy of a flyer they used to publicize their bake sale and a photo of themselves doing the sale). They also had to submit a final reflection on the following questions: How did your project make a positive impact on food justice or the natural environment? How has your thinking or behavior changed as a result of planning and carrying out this project? What is something important you learned? Finally, what's your "glow," something you're proud of, and what's your "grow," something you might improve if you do something like this again?

In 2021, while still facing the challenges of pandemic and hybrid teaching, 180 sixth graders participated and posted the documentation of their projects in Padlet, a new cloud-based software that provides virtual bulletin boards ("padlets") to post student work on a particular assignment. The platform was an ideal way to share students' achievements with parents in an online expo. In 2022, students were able to share their photos, flyers, and other documentation with each other in person.

Beneath a colorful photo of Anya and Maria selling baked goods to a customer, Anya wrote, "Maria and I had a bake sale and donated $300 to CHiPS." Jude created a poster titled "Sustainable Food," which showed two hands, one of a white person and one of a person of color, holding up a globe representing the Earth divided into four sections. Each section featured a different color and included brief explanations of four key concepts: local, accessible, healthy, and no waste. The side of the poster featured a head-and-shoulder photo of Jude wearing glasses, a sweatshirt, and a baseball cap on backward. Amelia created a "Food Workers Art Piece," which spelled out FIGHT in colorful, individually designed, eye-grabbing letters; below FIGHT, she wrote "$15" in vibrant purple. In addition to sharing that her hand started to hurt from creating the letters, she wrote that the project had increased her understanding of how little food workers earn. Noah wrote, "For my food-justice action project I raised $2,330 for CUCS to help get people off the streets and in a safer place. I first made a flyer asking for donations and then I sent it out all around my neighborhood, to the school community, and to my family." He included a link to the flyer.

Deanna and Will love being part of the Exploration team. "We're passionate and proud of what we're doing," Deanna says. "It's fun to see all the creative things kids come up with in their projects. We're able to teach our values—to find ethical expression in our work. Our teaching is an expression of who we are."

Deanna has been an activist since fifth grade, when she wrote letters to the superintendent of her school district on Long Island to protest the disposable utensils in the cafeteria. "Even back then I was passionate and idealistic," she says. "That's why I love working with kids this age. We get in there with them, and they get it. They know what's right. They know what's fair. And they want to do something about it."

For Will, it was awe at natural wonders on camping trips to the southwestern United States that sparked his enthusiasm for environmental education. "Bryce Canyon, Grand Canyon—it was eye opening," he says. "I was inspired by the incredible beauty of the natural world and wanted to do all I could to protect it."

Reflecting on their work, Deanna says, "We try to find that balance between showing the kids the truth, but not breaking their hearts. We infuse our hard lessons with hope and empowerment. We don't want them to think it's so big that there's nothing they can do. Part of how I cope with the climate crisis is by educating my students about the situation and making sure they understand that they have the power to make a difference."

One thing I admire about Deanna's and Will's work is the way they integrate art into their curricula. The quilt patches of African American food heroes, the art pieces representing students' understanding of sustainability, and the padlets documenting their action projects gave students the opportunity to reflect on their learning, integrate it into their lives, and communicate it to others in powerful, creative ways. I agree with Deanna that it's lots of fun to see what the kids can come up with when given the chance.

I also appreciate the model the school has created for providing both subject-based learning and a rich multidisciplinary, project-based exploratory curriculum focused on climate justice. What do you think? Would such a model work for your school?

GETTING FROM HERE TO THERE

Roberta Davenport and the Art of School Transformation

You may well be thinking that it's great to learn about schools that are all in for climate justice education, but how do you move your school in that direction, especially with all that's going on in the world right now?

Over the years, my organization, Morningside Center, has worked with many principals who transformed their schools. We were honored to contribute to their achievements. One such principal was Roberta Davenport, who from 2003 to 2015 served as leader of the Daniel Hale Williams School for Students preK to 5, more commonly referred to as Public School 307 (P.S. 307). I share her story for the inspiration and wisdom it offers about the art of school transformation.

One of ten children, Roberta grew up in Farragut Houses, a low-income housing project in an industrial section of Brooklyn. Her father was a Korean War veteran who worked for thirty-five years as a pipefitter in the nearby Brooklyn Naval Shipyard. Her mother was a homemaker. Says Roberta, "Ours was a tight-knit community with strong family traditions, close ties with neighbors, and a strong relationship with a nearby Catholic church and its affiliated community center." As a young person, Roberta volunteered at the community center, doing a variety of activities with young people and seldom venturing outside her neighborhood. She attended Catholic school through eighth grade and then the public Bay Ridge High School from which she graduated in the mid-sixties. With federal funds from President Lyndon Johnson's Great Society program, the community center awarded Roberta and other young people from the neighborhood "Community Leadership Scholarships" to attend Marymount Manhattan College, a college for young women on the Upper East Side of Manhattan. "We helped to integrate Marymount," Roberta says.

Upon graduating with a major in studio arts and a minor in education, Roberta taught in a day-care center "with leaders who were highly professional and gave me a great foundation in teaching and child development." While serving in a variety of teaching and leadership positions in the New York City public schools over the next two decades, she earned a master's degree in educational technology from Teachers College, Columbia University, and later a master's degree in educational leadership from the Principals Institute of Bank Street College of Education. She assumed the principalship of P.S. 307 in 2003.

P.S. 307 is across the street from the Farragut Houses. It was built after Roberta had grown up, but her three younger siblings attended the school, and her mother worked there as a school aide. "What a sweet and wonderful gift," she says, "to have the opportunity to give back to the community that had helped shape my character and given me so much support!"

As a new principal, Roberta didn't expect her first year to be easy. But she was soon to learn the full extent of what she was in for. Within her first month, a group of eight students broke into the school on a weekend, enjoyed some takeout Chinese food, and then wreaked destruction throughout the building. "For the kids to express in such a raw way how they felt about the school—it was eye-opening," she says. "In a way, it was a blessing. I didn't have to guess what was going on in the school and what I needed to do. It was right there in my face!"

She had already experienced another unwelcome surprise. She recalls, "We brought the kids into the auditorium for me to introduce myself. I asked that the lights be turned on and was informed that the lights were on, but only three of thirty or more were working. 'What message does that give to the students about how much they are valued?' I thought to myself."

The school was so far from her vision of what a school should be that she wasn't sure where to begin. "A school should belong to the children," she says. "It should be a special place just for them. Like the community that supported me, a school should be all the adults working together to build a place worthy of the children. I was determined to shift the characterization of our students from 'these horrible kids' to these wonderful kids, full of promise. We needed to show them we valued them. They weren't 'bad.' They were showing us what they needed."

Her first step was to listen to the students. "What kind of school do you want?" she asked them. "What would make you want to come to school?" After taking in their thoughts, she told them her hopes for them and for the school and opened up a conversation. It seemed that no one had previously offered a vision of what a school could be that aimed to address their expressed needs.

She asked the staff for their ideas, shared what she was hearing from the kids, and presented her perspective. Together they decided to develop a Code of Conduct aimed at ensuring everyone's safety, a top priority for students and staff alike. It laid out clear expectations for social behavior in school and stated that all had to take responsibility for living the code. Roberta introduced the Code of Conduct to students in the now well-lit auditorium and joined teachers in discussing it with students in their classrooms.

A group of teachers, parents, and administrators also created a Student Declaration, as follows:

I am a P.S. 307 scholar.
I am expected to leave a lasting legacy by always striving for excellence.
Every day I am an active, enthusiastic, and responsible learner.
I work hard and make smart choices.
I am respectful of
myself
my school
my community.
I am inspired to contribute generously to the wellbeing of my school.

"The Student Declaration became a living document for our students," says Roberta, "They studied it. They recited it in unison at the start of all activities and events. They strove to live up to the ideals embedded within it. We began each day and all whole-school gatherings with the Declaration."

As these measures produced improvements in student behavior, order, and safety, Roberta turned her attention to addressing the social and emotional competency of students and staff on a deeper level. "We won't have a successful school," she told staff and parents, "until all our students feel a sense of value in themselves and learn to manage their feelings and behavior."

She wanted to go deep, using an instructional approach to teach social and emotional skills, understanding that it would serve students throughout their lives. She knew that the school would need help to do this, and she knew that to galvanize the staff she needed to engage them in choosing an appropriate partner. She had heard good things about Morningside Center and saw that the organization was sponsoring a Saturday conference. She recruited a group of interested staff and paid for them to attend.

They enjoyed it, but were skeptical: Sounds good, they said, but what does it look like in practice? Will it work with our children? Roberta arranged for the staff team to visit P.S. 24, a school in Brooklyn serving Latinx and Black students, which was implementing Morningside Center's programs schoolwide. The teachers loved what they saw. With Roberta called away for a family emergency, the teacher leadership group ran the faculty conference in which the staff decided to implement The 4Rs (Reading, Writing, Respect, and Resolution), Morningside Center's grade-specific, interactive preK–5 program integrating SEL and language arts. In her budget, Roberta found the funding for The 4Rs curriculum materials and the services of a Morningside Center staff developer, Javier Diaz, for training and classroom coaching of the teachers. Monday became 4Rs day. All the teachers gave a 4Rs lesson on Mondays throughout the school year, and Javier was there to support them.

SEL instruction brought Roberta's vision for the school to a new level. Students began using social and emotional skills in their daily interactions with peers and teachers. Teachers noticed an increase in students' caring and cooperative behavior. Roberta noticed improvements in teachers' interactions with students and with each other as well.

Of course, some teachers were not on board with this shift in the school's direction. They left, affording the opportunity for Roberta and her faculty to hire new teachers strongly aligned with the evolving vision.

What about the parents? "When I started out at P.S. 307, I believed that the school should reflect the values of the community," offers Roberta.

> Along the way, I decided to flip that. I worked to get the community to reflect the values of the school. It wasn't about disrespecting the community. It was about recognizing need. The parents wanted a great school for their kids, but they didn't know what that meant, what that would look like. We were creating a school that students were eager to come to. I wanted parents to enjoy coming to our school as well. We transformed our auditorium into a place where parents came often, not to be talked at or preached at, but to experience the talents and gifts of their children. Inspired by what their children were achieving, they would ask, "How can I help?" We carved out real ways for them to get involved. It developed organically.
>
> We also forged strong bonds with parents by the protocol we followed when we had an issue with a child. We would appreciate the parent for coming in, present the issue without judgment, and say we wanted to partner with the parent(s) to help the child succeed. We'd listen to their personal stories and ideas for how to move forward, share our thinking, and work out a plan. The tone was, "Let's bring our heads and hearts together to help the child."

Roberta's vision continued to evolve. Once the school established a culture that valued children, the priority was to provide multiple paths for student achievement. That meant enriching the curriculum and continuing to develop productive partnerships. To foster student leadership, Javier Diaz and interested teachers built on the ongoing schoolwide 4Rs instruction to train and coach students to be mediators, available at lunch and recess and by referral to solve disputes among their peers.

"We launched a developmentally driven Early Childhood Academy," says Roberta.

> We took our preK, kindergarten, and first grades and created a school within a school, because so many of our kids were coming in with developmental delays. The goal was to prepare them for second grade. We identified teachers who understood developmental milestones and had effective strategies for helping kids achieve them. We had a psychologist and speech and hearing services. We had focused parent meetings on nutrition. The 4Rs program was critical in boosting the social and emotional skills of the children and their parents. We brought in an autism spectrum disorder program that became a flagship for the city. We believed in serving the special needs of all our students. We didn't deny anybody.

Partnering with arts organizations, P.S. 307 created a strong arts program, including violin, keyboard, choir, visual arts, and ballet. Exposure to the world became important because too many students seemed to know little about it beyond their neighborhood. "We had kids who were scared to walk across the Brooklyn Bridge because they thought it would collapse," Roberta recalls. "I took a group of students to a Barnes and Noble store, and they were amazed: 'You mean the only thing they sell in this store is books?' In the children's section, they took books that interested them off the shelves and sat down and read and looked at the pictures, surrounded by books. We didn't leave until each of them had chosen three books to take home with them."

Where did the funds come from for these partnerships? Roberta is charismatic and energetic, to be sure. But she could not have brought in these resources if people had not fallen in love with the school as soon as they walked through the door. They loved Roberta. They loved the beauty of the building with children's art, other creative expressions, academic work, and artifacts on the walls and in the hallways. They loved the proud, intelligent young people who took them on a tour around the school. They loved what they saw in classrooms. "I never wanted people to tell me our kids were cute," says Roberta, "I wanted people to say that they were smart, thoughtful, caring, intelligent, and happy to be students at P.S. 307."

The crowning recognition of P.S. 307's achievement came when the New York City Department of Education awarded the school a $2 million grant to establish the Daniel Hale Williams Magnet School for STEM Studies. Daniel Hale Williams was an African American surgeon who in 1893 performed the first successful open-heart surgery. He opened Provident Hospital in Chicago, the first medical facility to have an interracial staff. Williams later became chief surgeon of the Freedmen's Hospital in Washington, D.C., which provided care for formerly enslaved African Americans. He would be proud, I think, that such a wonderful school bears his name.

Reflecting on Roberta's adventures at P.S. 307, I am struck that she began by listening to her students—really listening. Her questions were good ones: What kind of school do you want? What would make you want to come to school? How can our school best support you during this challenging time? She listened and she shared her thoughts, giving students the message that she valued them as partners in shaping the school. She took in what they said and then, integrating their thoughts and concerns with her ideas, articulated a vision that students could get behind because they had helped create it. In light of the mental health and other challenges our young people are facing these days, school leaders would do well to devote substantial time to listen and converse with students and explicitly integrate students' thinking into the ongoing process of envisioning and shaping their schools.

Do you agree? What are your reflections on Roberta's story? What are your take-aways from the work of Shawna, Jan, Deanna, and Will? What are some next steps you can take to enhance your school's work in educating for climate justice?

CHAPTER 8

Go Forth with Heart, Joy, and a Fighting Spirit

"The Summer Day"
by Mary Oliver

Who made the world?
Who made the swan, and the black bear?
Who made the grasshopper?
This grasshopper, I mean-
the one who has flung herself out of the grass,
the one who is eating sugar out of my hand,
who is moving her jaws back and forth instead of up and down-
who is gazing around with her enormous and complicated eyes.
Now she lifts her pale forearms and thoroughly washes her face.
Now she snaps her wings open, and floats away.
I don't know exactly what a prayer is.
I do know how to pay attention, how to fall down
into the grass, how to kneel down in the grass,
how to be idle and blessed, how to stroll through the fields,
which is what I have been doing all day.
Tell me, what else should I have done?
Doesn't everything die at last, and too soon?
Tell me, what is it you plan to do
with your one wild and precious life?[1]

I LOVE MARY OLIVER'S poem because it speaks to me of the wonder of life on Earth, a precious gift we too often take for granted. I am moved that it does so through close, loving observation of a humble grasshopper. We learn that the poet knows how to pay attention and to be idle and blessed, having spent the day strolling through the fields. Which leads us to the question at the end of the poem: What do you plan to do with your one wild and precious life?

For sure, we should take time to stroll through the fields, as Mary Oliver does. And, oh, how nice it would be to spend some time idle and blessed. But for our day job, in our calling as educators, what shall we do? I hope you will join me in stating loudly and clearly, "I'm going to teach—and organize—for climate justice!" Of course, that's not the only thing I hope for us. I want us to take good care of ourselves and have joyous, loving relationships with our students and colleagues. I want us to feel the satisfaction of fulfilling our calling as educators and contributing to the Great Turning. I want us to discover new strengths, make new friends, and have fun on this greatest adventure of our lives.

In this book, I have presented a vision of education to address the needs of our young people now and in the future and to prepare them to make a positive contribution to the world they are growing into. A vibrant, powerful climate justice movement is essential for creating a future worthy of our children. Radical, transformative climate justice education is essential to the success of that movement.

Currently, climate justice education as envisioned here takes place only in a relatively small number of schools and classrooms. If several thousand educators read this book and are inspired to bring top-quality climate justice education to their students, that will be wonderful. But we don't have the luxury of settling for that. Our goal must be to bring radical, transformative climate justice education to every classroom and school in the country.

"Good luck with that!" you may say. Public schools are underfunded, hamstrung by standardized tests, facing staffing shortages amid a student mental health crisis, and dealing with laws passed by Republican-controlled state legislatures aimed at preventing teachers from addressing racial and gender equity in their classrooms. Embrace climate justice education? You must be kidding!

I don't underestimate the challenges. But, as I argue, the conditions in public schools are largely the result of government policies that can be changed. Schools are places with tremendous strategic potential for climate justice education, and teachers are organizing to fight back against two decades of government policies that have undermined the public schools and teaching as a calling.

What if educators passionate for climate justice join their colleagues to organize a movement to wrest public education away from the budget cutters and market-driven "reformers" and work with students, parents, and community members to create public schools that serve students' needs; teach the values and skills of democracy; promote social justice; and provide the respect, autonomy, and support teachers need to thrive?

What if those climate justice educators inspire their colleagues and spark a movement that during the next fifteen years spreads radical, transformative climate justice education widely to public preK–12 schools throughout the country?

What if all the educators, children, and young people in those schools and classes feel welcome as members of beloved communities, develop strong social and emotional skills, stand up for justice in their schools and communities, learn to understand and love nature, gain deep understanding of the climate crisis, practice active hope, embrace positive visions for the future, and act to make the world more just and sustainable with strong support from adult allies?

What if, while in school and throughout their adult lives, millions of these people, educated from a young age in climate justice and active hope, flood into the climate justice movement and make a decisive contribution that not only enables humanity to avoid the worst but also puts us well on the path to embracing new systems for the economy, energy, and food that have humanity living within the Earth's finite resources while sharing them fairly?

This could happen. This needs to happen. If we can make it happen, it won't be the first time an impossible dream has come true.

This chapter has three sections: "A Path Forward" makes the case for the strategic importance of schools in advancing the climate justice movement; and it proposes an audacious strategy for spreading high-quality climate justice education wide and deep and for revitalizing schools as places for adults and young people to build strong supportive relationships, have fun, learn, celebrate, and practice active hope. The strategy draws on lessons learned from the "teacher insurgency" in the United States during 2018 and 2019 and from the educational work of the Landless Workers Movement in Brazil.

"Story from the Classroom" features Jasmine Locke, who teaches for liberation in her "Lit and Comp" classes for ninth and eleventh graders and is taking leadership in her school, as proposed in "A Path Forward."

"Go Forth!" sends you off to change the world.

A PATH FORWARD

Strategic Importance of Schools for the Climate Movement

Public schools are the obvious places to educate for climate justice. Ninety percent or 50.8 million young people attend public schools and work closely with adults whose job (and, for many, their calling) is to prepare students to thrive, now and in the future.[2] With their whole lives before them, our students have the biggest stake in a positive future. They deserve to be fully informed (in ways appropriate to their ages, of course) about the calamity that's coming their way, to know that millions of adults are working hard to mitigate its impact, and to feel that their teachers care and are trying to prepare them to deal with it as best they can.

Young people spend huge amounts of time in school and school-related activities. If used well, that time gives them ample opportunity to study topics in depth, take field trips, have discussions with peers, share feelings, and receive mentoring from adults. Where else can this happen, if not in school?

In schools, large numbers of young people come together daily in one place. This provides opportunities for them to meet with like-minded peers and form clubs. It facilitates mobilization for a movement event like the September 20, 2019, march or an uprising like the nationwide wave of protests that erupted after the murder of George Floyd.

Of course, these strategic advantages of schools as places to educate, organize, and mobilize young people for climate justice are the reasons why fossil-fuel interests, and the politicians they fund, do their best to ensure that the public schools remain overwhelmed, neutral, and silent. They must not succeed. We must fiercely contest their efforts to keep the public schools in line as a pillar holding up the status quo.

However, as Leo Casey explains in *The Teacher Insurgency: A Strategic and Organizing Perspective*, we must acknowledge that the first two decades of the twenty-first century have been tough for democratic public education. Influenced by educational "reformers" committed to imposing their free-market ideology on education, George W. Bush launched his No Child Left Behind (NCLB) program in 2001, which deflected attention from the inequities baked into the public education system through class and racial segregation and blamed public schools and educators for the poor levels of achievement of low-income students of color. Claiming the mantle of the civil rights movement, NCLB instituted a regimen of standardized tests aimed at addressing inequities by holding teachers accountable and punishing schools and teachers whose students didn't perform well on the tests. In addition to creating this top-down testing system, NCLB promoted "school choice." By providing other options for parents and students, vouchers and charter schools would introduce free-market competition as a stick to prod public schools to improve.[3]

Public education suffered another huge blow from the Great Recession of 2008. While banks that created the financial crisis were bailed out, funds for public schools were slashed. A few numbers are telling. From 2008 to 2018, K–12 enrollments in the United States increased 1.5 million, but school employment was down 170,000 positions. By 2018, teacher salaries had declined by 4.5 percent since before the 2008 recession.

By spring of 2018, postrecession austerity policies had left the public schools with oversized classes, outdated textbooks, crumbling school buildings, elimination of arts and physical education, and cutting of reduced health care and social services.

Unfortunately, the Obama administration continued these top-down technocratic free-market-inspired "reforms" of the G. W. Bush era with its Race to the Top Program (RTTT). With states facing sharp declines in tax revenues, RTTT offered states incentives to adopt new standardized test systems for school accountability, teacher evaluation, and student promotion and to enact policies to expand vouchers and charter schools, which draw funds away from public schools.

Donald Trump continued in this vein by appointing as Secretary for Education, Betsy DeVos, a strong advocate for charter schools. But the technocratic, free-market-inspired reform movement was already losing its credibility. For all the time and money wasted in preparing students for the tests and administering them, the huge amount of data collected showed that NCLB and RTTT produced virtually no improvement in student outcomes. Research on charter schools showed the same.

Meanwhile, a huge gap was opening up between what teachers expect and deserve from their profession and the daily reality they and their students experience. Again, a couple of numbers speak volumes: 44 percent of first-year teachers leave the profession within five years. The annual attrition rate for public school teachers in the United States is double that of teachers in other industrial countries.[4]

Some left-wing academics have argued that the role of public schools in a capitalist society is to hold in place the existing systems of inequity. The past two decades certainly support this thesis. But history past and present provides ample evidence that, as Italian political philosopher Antonio Gramsci argued, public schools are ambiguous institutions. Public schools can also offer opportunities to organize resistance.

During the past two decades, I have helped lead positive developments in public education that support Gramsci's point. Social and emotional learning (SEL) grew into a nationwide movement during this period. At its best, SEL is a strategy for transforming schools, as Roberta Davenport demonstrated at Public School 307 and Morningside Center has demonstrated through its work with hundreds of schools during the past three decades.

Despite its unfortunate RTTT program, the Obama administration did at least one good thing for public education and our students. It reviewed school discipline data; saw that Black, Latinx, and LGBTQ students were disproportionately targeted for punitive discipline, including suspensions; and connected the dots to show that this was creating a school-to-prison pipeline and contributing to the plague of mass incarceration. It urged schools to move away from so-called zero-tolerance discipline policies and use other ways to improve student behavior, including SEL, restorative practices, implicit-bias training, and racial equity programs. With federal funds and local funds, Morningside Center has worked with many schools to implement these programs during the past fifteen years.

Despite oppressive conditions, many teachers find ways to maintain their integrity and autonomy. The stories of teachers featured in this book demonstrate the creativity and persistence of educators who are passionate to maintain the integrity of their profession, address the true needs of their students, and fulfill their responsibility to educate for democracy and climate justice. We have seen how teachers can assert autonomy and agency in making creative use of required curricula to address climate justice. We also have seen how some schools have banded together to win waivers from standardized testing in exchange for using performance-based methods of assessment. It's no accident that some of the outstanding examples of climate justice featured in this book come from such schools.

However, the challenges for public schools continue. When the murder of George Floyd sparked the Black Lives Matter uprising around the country, many educators rightly saw the uprising as a racial reckoning for our country and an opportunity to educate faculty and students. As they began planning to expand existing programs or introduce new ones, the Republicans organized a backlash against such programs. This demonstrates that the right is all too aware of the potential of the public schools to subvert their white supremacist agenda.

It's clear: the public schools have potential as a space for radical, transformative climate justice education. We need to help them realize that potential. The teacher strikes of 2018–2019, as described and analyzed by Leo Casey in *The Teacher Insurgency*, provide inspiration and insight for how we might do just that.

The Teacher Insurgency

On March 6, 2018, an extraordinary event took place. The Republican-controlled legislature of West Virginia passed a law granting teachers, education workers, and public service workers a

5 percent pay raise, ending a two-week teachers strike. In West Virginia, the state legislature decides salaries and health coverage for teachers across the state. Incensed by the Republican governor's proposal of a 1 percent pay hike and cuts in teachers' health coverage, teachers in four counties in the southern part of the state, former strongholds of the United Mine Workers Union, staged a one-day walkout in protest. Teachers in several other counties followed suit. Soon teachers and union officials from across the state were talking with each other about what to do next. More counties had one-day strikes. The three national affiliates of the unions provided organizational support. On February 22, the entire educational workforce of West Virginia went on strike and began demonstrating in the state capital. The slogan for the strike was "55 Strong," to call attention to the fact that the strike had the support of teachers and educational workers in all 55 West Virginia counties. The strike took everyone by surprise, even those who organized it. Strikes by public employees were illegal in West Virginia, which made the strike an act of civil disobedience.

Inspired by West Virginia, teachers struck in other states as well, including Oklahoma, Kentucky, Arizona, and North Carolina. Following West Virginia's model, these were not only strikes for increased pay and health benefits but also protests against the underfunding of public schools and other public services. The emphasis was on solidarity with all education workers, not only teachers, as well as with other public service workers.[5]

Strikes continued into 2019, including four in large cities: Los Angeles, Oakland, Denver, and Chicago. As in West Virginia, organizers went beyond demands for increases in pay and health coverage. For example, five years before their strike in 2019, the Los Angeles teachers' union began a process of community engagement that resulted in Reclaim Our Schools Los Angeles (ROSLA), a coalition of four organizations. Together they hammered out a set of demands they called

"The Platform for the Common Good," which included small class sizes, more counselors and mental health services for students, and fewer standardized tests. As the time for the strike approached, other community organizations joined to support the strike. As a result of all this work with the community, the strike received massive support from the community and won major common-good demands as well as increases in teacher compensation.[6]

Casey argues that the teacher insurgency models a strategy for standing up to the attacks on public education and creating the public schools our young people need and deserve. The key is teachers organizing to develop the power to win the funding and create the conditions for great teaching to flourish—teaching that truly meets the needs of our twenty-first-century students.

Casey distinguishes between organizing and mobilizing. Mobilizing is corralling large numbers of people for a demonstration or a one-off event. These days, mobilizing occurs primarily through social media. Organizing involves in-depth conversations with friends and strangers, exploring open-ended questions, and doing lots of listening. The aim of organizing is to understand the issues on people's minds and why those issues are important to them. In this way, the organizer builds strong relationships and learns what demands for change are likely to resonate with the most people. Mobilizing complements organizing; it's essential. But organizing builds solidarity and strength in the face of adversity.[7]

The organizing needs to extend beyond the school and engage the community in helping to shape the campaign, as the Los Angeles teachers' union did in creating ROSLA. Furthermore, teachers, their unions, and their allies must be ready to use a full range of tactics to advance their cause, including strikes, of course, but also direct action, negotiation, advocacy, and electoral work.[8]

Casey also argues that teachers organizing teachers is most effective when rooted in an understanding of teacher identity—what he calls the collective "we" of teachers. He describes four dimensions of what it means to be a teacher, calling them "discourses" to acknowledge that they are fluid, sometimes contested, and can mean different things to different people. They are teaching as nurturance, teaching as profession, teaching as labor and craft, and teaching as democratic work. These dimensions make sense to me. They are what I was expecting and looking forward to when I became a teacher—and what I found at the East Harlem Block Schools, the parent-controlled storefront school where I worked as teacher-director for seven years. Casey devotes a chapter to each of these discourses—chapters well worth reading. Suffice it to say here that a major cause of burnout and attrition among public school teachers is the gap between what people hope for when choosing the vocation and the working conditions that make it hard to nurture students, do democratic work, develop their craft, exercise professional autonomy, and pay their bills.[9]

Take nurturance as an example. If there's one dimension of a teachers' responsibility we can all agree on, it is to nurture and care for our students. Teachers do care, for sure. But, as Casey argues, the school system needs to support teachers' individual ethic of care with "a politics of care"—that is, the systems and resources that make caring possible in a school, including adequate staffing so that class sizes can be viable and student mental health services so that teachers are not overwhelmed by needs they can't fulfill. What a great conversation to have in a school! What a terrific issue to organize around![10]

Those of us committed to expanding climate justice education in the public schools must make common cause with teachers and their unions as they fight to make public schools hospitable to great teaching. For only in schools hospitable to great teaching can transformational climate justice education flourish.

More inspiration for a viable path forward comes from the Landless Workers Movement in Brazil.

The Landless Workers Movement

The Landless Workers Movement (known in Portuguese as the *Movimento dos Trabalhadores Rurais Sem Terra*, or MST) emerged in Brazil in the mid-eighties around the time the military, which had ruled the country since 1964, gave up power and democracy was restored. MST launched a program of audacious land occupation in which impoverished farmers took over unused estates in the southern part of Brazil and turned them into cooperative farms. Legal justification for these land reform efforts came from a provision in the 1988 constitution that called for transformation of abandoned land to serve a public good. By 2020, MST had 1.5 million members and had established two thousand permanent settlements with some 340,000 families. MST also maintains more than 120 community health clinics and provides food to people in need through sixty-six food processing facilities.[11]

Most relevant to our concerns in this book, MST has developed an innovative program of radical schooling for Brazilian children, youth, and adults. In 2018, the movement was operating two thousand schools with thousands of teachers aligned with MST's radical pedagogy educating some 250,000 students—this despite many of the schools being funded and administered by state and local governments. Employing the teaching practices of Paulo Freire, the curriculum engages students in studying agrarian reform, social-justice movements, and the principles of agroecology, the model of sustainable agriculture that rejects agribusiness.

How can this occur in a country where land is highly concentrated in a few hands? A 2016 Oxfam study found that 1 percent of the farms in Brazil occupy 44 percent of the arable land. Of the 180.5 million acres of crop land, 84 percent is devoted to agribusiness—large plots of land growing soy, corn, and sugar cane with extensive use of fertilizer and pesticides. When this land concentration took place, beginning in the sixties, many peasants were forced off their land. As the country moved toward democracy in the eighties, peasants saw an opportunity to organize. MST's success in occupying unproductive land evoked an extremely hostile reaction from large plantation owners, state authorities, and mainstream media. Violence was a major challenge for MST in the eighties and nineties, as military police and hired guns sent by plantation owners murdered MST leaders.[12]

The key point for climate justice educators is this: MST's agenda went beyond democratizing access to land. They also wanted their members and the public to embrace a way of seeing the world that was very different from that of agribusiness interests. They wanted their members to be proud of their peasant heritage and identity and to put priority on community well-being, soil quality, and biodiversity rather than on making profits. With wealthy business interests exerting strong influence over state authorities, they knew they could not count on state-funded schools to foster the radical shift in social and political consciousness at the heart of their movement.

The trick was knowing how to intervene and introduce reforms without being co-opted—without their efforts ending up serving to maintain the inequitable social, political, and economic systems MST was working to change. They found a way. The key has been to keep their movement engaged in implementing and governing the reforms—and always at the ready to use movement tools of protest and direct action to maintain the integrity of the reforms.

MST has a clear and strong organizational infrastructure. The 1.5 million members are the peasants who work on the farms and live in the local settlements. Each settlement has a *nucleo* (nucleus), a decision-making body of ten to twenty people who put in time above and beyond their daily work on the farms. Each nucleus elects one of their own to serve a two-year term on a representative body that makes decisions and resolves conflicts for a group of local settlements. There are representative regional and national decision-making bodies as well.

The schools MST has created have decision-making bodies as well. Called *instancias*, they consist of teachers, administrators, and community members, some of whom double as organizers accountable to the movement. In her excellent book about MST's educational program, Rebecca Tarlau calls this strategy "contentious co-governance."[13] It works especially well in states that are left-leaning, but it has worked well in right-leaning states with weak educational systems as well as in other states in between left and right. Governmental officials have been willing to live with MST's left politics when MST has been able to provide services the state otherwise would not be able to provide.

MST's creative work in schools run and administered by the government has brought hundreds of thousands of young people and women into the movement. It has enabled movement members to earn diplomas and degrees. It has afforded opportunities for movement educators to model, or "prefigure," their vision for the future in the here and now of state-run schools—to create "model utopias," if you will.

Contentious co-governance is not easy. It's radically different from winning approval for reform. It is bringing a cohesive social movement into a state institution as part of a larger strategy for social change. Movement activists, some of whom are educators, forge collegial relationships as they negotiate with school officials and teachers to introduce and carry out reforms. But if an issue arises that can't be resolved by negotiation, they may go into the streets to protest. Co-governance, prefiguration, negotiation, and direct action go together. Tension and conflict are built into the collaboration and require ongoing conversation.

Now, informed and inspired by the 2018–2019 teacher insurgency and MST's remarkable radical education model, we can chart a path forward for climate justice educators.

Strategy for Spreading High-Quality Climate Justice Education

It starts with you: an educator modeling radical, transformative teaching for climate justice or one inspired and ready to do so. You develop your teaching to provide a living example of high-quality climate justice education, and you decide to become an organizer for climate justice as well. Every school is different, of course, but the following sketch illustrates how your organizing might unfold.

You reach out to colleagues, beginning with those likely to be most sympathetic, and share your passion for climate justice education and an overview of your current work. You invite them to ask questions, share their experiences, and express their concerns. You invite them to observe your teaching and give you feedback. You do a lot of listening.

As opportunities arise, you broach the topic with colleagues beyond your trusted circle, opening conversations. Again, you listen well to understand what issues are on people's minds and why those issues are important to them.

You extend an open invitation to faculty to participate in a study group, using *Teach for Climate Justice* as a starting place for discussion. You make your intentions clear. You are organizing to develop a group of colleagues who are strongly committed to expanding and deepening the teaching of climate justice in the school as part of a larger goal: to help the school better serve the needs of students and teachers. You are completely transparent with the administration and the teachers' union about what you are doing and why—and you invite them to join the study group.

Over time, a group of teachers and administrators emerges who are interested in exploring the topic in an ongoing way. Good, open-ended conversations continue about vision, challenges, curricula, and classroom experiences. You encourage colleagues to bring climate justice education into their teaching. Working together to develop knowledge, pedagogy, and teaching skills, the group becomes a professional learning community.

With approval from the administration, you invite students to meet to explore setting up a student climate club. With a colleague to join you in mentoring the group, you listen as the students share their feelings about the climate crisis: what they know, what they want to learn, and what they might like to do.

You share the climate justice education work you're doing with parents and members of the community. Again, this effort is about having great conversations: "Here's what we're doing. What do you think?" Stay nonjudgmental. Tease out the issues on parents' minds and their reasons for being concerned about those issues. Listen. Frame teaching for climate justice as addressing students' needs, preparing them for the world they are living in and growing into.

Arrange ways for students to share what they're learning or doing directly with other students and adults in the school community through gallery walks, auditorium presentations, and celebrations. Students might be engaged in climate-related projects, such as organizing aid for a school or community hit by a climate disaster.

Express your support for additional counseling and mental health services and for a schoolwide social and emotional learning (SEL) program to help the school become a beloved community as a foundation for climate justice.

Gradually, garner support for schoolwide implementation of climate justice education, with teachers having time to work together to plan it. They can draw on resources listed in *Teach for Climate Justice* and their own creativity, knowing that it will always be a dynamic work in progress. As traction develops at the school, garner support and push for districtwide implementation.

Become active in the union, sharing what you've learned from your conversations with colleagues, students, and parents about the issues on people's minds and the reasons people find those issues important.

Form an *instancia* group consisting of teachers, administrators, students, parents, and community members, closely allied with the union or working alongside it to stand in solidarity for a great school that truly meets the needs of students and families, including climate justice education.

Joining with the union, the administration, students, parents, and the community, develop a platform for the common good, along the lines of the 2019 teachers' strike in Los Angeles. Call for significant increases in funding for public schools, smaller class sizes, culturally responsive SEL programs, more guidance and mental health services, other demands of special relevance to the school community, climate justice education, and no more "teaching to the test."

Take action to bring about the needed changes using a variety of tactics, including meetings with government officials, protests, direct action, electoral work, strikes, and mutual aid. Make the school the hub of a community fighting for climate justice.

Public schools can be pillars holding up the status quo. But they don't have to be. We need to contest the ongoing efforts of fossil-fuel interests and racist, authoritarian demagogues to keep the climate crisis and racial injustice off the agenda of the public schools. We need to dissolve the pillar into a hotbed of transformation. It is perfectly appropriate for public schools to be centers for climate justice organizing, because the climate justice movement, like great public education in general, is about our children's future. It's not about window dressing like mandating a climate unit in the science curriculum. Borrowing from MST's playbook, it's about the climate justice movement entering the public schools as part of a larger strategy to usher in a sea change in public consciousness and economic and political systems. MST recognized the potential for state-sponsored schooling to serve their movement. Against the odds, MST's leaders seized on a sliver of opportunity that opened up in their country to do so. If they can do it in Brazil, we can do it here.

Yes, it will be daunting for educators, already overwhelmed, to become organizers in addition to everything else we're called to do. But that's the price we pay for being so strategically well positioned to help achieve the Great Turning. Climate justice educators are key players in the climate justice movement. We represent the movement that needs to stay close at hand to keep the public schools focused on ensuring a positive future for our young people. We do our part by teaching and organizing.

That said, the timing is right for the next section of the chapter. You will meet a teacher who is teaching and organizing for liberation—and having a great time doing it!

STORY FROM THE CLASSROOM

Jasmine Locke is teaching for liberation and taking leadership to transform her school, doing the kind of organizing envisioned in the path forward sketched out in this chapter.

Jasmine Locke

Westview High School in Beaverton, Oregon, serves students of color and white students in roughly equal numbers. Jasmine believes that the school is doing a good job of addressing the needs of both sections of the town. But it hasn't always been that way. Jasmine grew up in Beaverton and had all her K–12 schooling there. "I felt ostracized," she recalls. "I struggled with my mixed identity and didn't have my first Black teacher until high school." When asked what she wanted to be when she grew up, she always said, "I want to be a teacher." But as an undergraduate in a teacher preparation program at Boise State University, she was placed as a student teacher in a fourth-grade class that just didn't feel right.

"I don't think education is for me," she told her adviser. He asked her why she had wanted to go into education in the first place, and she told him about her experience as a K–12 student in Beaverton. He helped her see that her problem was not with education, but with what was going on in that fourth-grade classroom.

"I realized that my grounding as an educator would be to fight for the students," she recalls. "I would fight for marginalized people like myself so they wouldn't have to go through what I went through. I would help students find their voice, find their joys, find their passions, and then support them in using their voices to disrupt for what they care about. That led me to the communities I've sought out in my teaching career and the colleagues that I want to partner with and collaborate with."

She's happy at Westview. "These are my people: radical educators, liberators, abolitionists," she says. "We're working to be a community school with an emerging philosophy that centers equity, restorative practices, and social and emotional learning."

It hasn't been easy. The 2021–22 school year was her first year at Westview. Before joining the faculty at Westview, she had taught American history for five years at Stoller Middle School in Beaverton. "The shift from middle school to high school was challenging," she acknowledges.

> The conversations are much deeper than what I'd experienced with my middle schoolers. But students' needs have expanded way more than I expected. Our kids carry so much through those front doors every day. They are tired, worn down, stressed, and overwhelmed, because the level of production shifted from virtual learning last year to back in person with a full schedule. And so many upsetting things are going on in the world: Buffalo, Uvalde, the January 6 hearings, the war in Ukraine, the continuing pandemic, inflation.
>
> I was forced to ask myself, "How is my professional practice lining up with being an ally to the students in what they're going

through?" I worked hard to fight habits of urgency and perfectionism and strict timeframes and schedules, and I did so in a transparent way with my students. I took them with me on the journey. And hard as it's been, this has been one of my most rewarding years of teaching. I feel very connected with my kids. I feel very connected to my school community. I feel very affirmed. I think that was because I let go of a lot of fear and put all my trust in my students.

But it's exhausting! I continually remind myself that rest is resistance, joy is resistance, and my existence as a Black female is resistance. My very presence changes the game for folks. When I'm feeling tired and overwhelmed, I'm just honest with my kids. I say, "I'm feeling overwhelmed, you guys. What happened in Texas is bringing up a lot for me. And these are some of the top five emotions that I'm feeling. I am trying to be present with you in this space. But my mind and my body feel elsewhere. I'm trying to do my best. But Ms. Locke is not fully present today."

I open myself up to them and remind myself that that, too, is resistance. To show up every day, especially with joy, that's resistance. I try just to smile. I'm thinking to myself, "Don't let them win. If we get down and tired, the system's winning." Our students need folks who are willing to show them what open and vulnerable processing looks like. Otherwise, we're gonna embody the oppression and send more students through a machine to become capitalist robots. This year I've had students saying, "Ms. Locke, you're the first teacher I've had who feels like an actual human outside of their role."

I try to create a learning community, as opposed to schooling. Together we make community agreements. The aim is a safe learning space that centers joy, where we are comfortable enough to take risks. Sitting and receiving is not learning.

Class periods start with a check-in, sometimes a circle, sometimes a journal prompt. Then at the end of the day, we pause to

> consider one thing that's brought us joy today or one thing we're grateful for. Or, if we can't think of anything that brought us joy, what's something we can do to bring joy to someone else? Because bringing joy to others can bring joy to us.

Jasmine has an open-door policy. During lunch, students can come in and sit down in a chair next to her desk to say they'd like a personal check-in. "We all need it," Jasmine says. "The students are starting to ask me if I could use a check-in!"

Jasmine bases her curriculum on Dr. Gholdy Muhammad's Historically Responsive Literacy Model. Explains Jasmine, "The framework is inspired and informed by Black Literary Societies organized by 'free' Black people during the nineteenth century in such northern cities as Boston, New York, and Philadelphia. Its units are identity, skills, intellect, and criticality, infused with joy. I see a lot of myself in Gholdy. Like members of the Black Literacy Societies, we begin by exploring our identities, culture, and race, and read and write our voices into disruption for the protection, liberation, and celebration of all."[14]

All eleventh graders focus on narrative and argument writing in their Lit and Comp classes. Jasmine's students spent the first semester on narrative writing. It fit well with Gholdy Muhammad's first two units on identity and skills: Who am I? What experiences have I had? What do I care about? What are my passions? Do I agree with the identities that have been cast upon me by others, society, and myself? And what part of my identity do I have flexibility in? Can I grow in that area?

"We had a lot of fun with the narrative unit," she observes.

> The students explored a question I put out to them: What's your aesthetic? What are the music, colors, writing, speaking, films, clothes, TV shows, dancing, and sports that appeal to you? What

> brings you joy? The unit on aesthetics made the students aware of what they're wearing, saying, listening to, interacting with. It deepened their awareness of their identity and led to exploring how our individual identity connects to collective identities, like my family, my community, my race, my gender, my country.
>
> That tied into skills. If we're grounded in who we are, what we believe in, and what we care about, what are the skills that are going to amplify our voices? We used mentor texts, including memoirs, autobiographies, poetry, slam poetry, and fiction, *The House on Mango Street*. I showed them how to read a text and notice examples of the writer's craft and use what they learned to revise and improve their stories.

In the second semester, Jasmine's students take on argument and activism. "Find something that connects with your identity—with something you really care about," she tells the students. "Then let's get our background knowledge ('intellect,' in Gholdy's terms). Now let's explore the discussion people are having about the topic. What do we want to say? What change would we like to see ('criticality')? How are we going to say it?"

As a class, they chose to focus on the justice system. Their mentor video was *13th*, the award-winning 2016 documentary film about the Thirteenth Amendment to the US Constitution, which abolished involuntary servitude, except as a punishment for conviction of a crime. The film argues that slavery was continued after the Civil War by criminalizing behavior that allows police to arrest disproportionately high numbers of Black people, leading to mass incarceration, which affects mostly people of color. The class did an ethos/pathos/logos analysis of the documentary. The mentor text for the unit was *Just Mercy: A Story of Justice and Redemption* by Bryan Stevenson, which tells a moving true story of redemption and calls for an end to mass incarceration.[15]

For their argument paper, Jasmine gave students the choice to do a deeper dive into the justice system or to focus on a specific aspect of the justice system. Students chose from a range of topics, including the death penalty, parole, sexual assault, mental health services for inmates, education for inmates, abortion, and the Second Amendment.

Jasmine also engaged her eleventh graders in what she called a multigenre project. They could do this project on the justice system, the topic they had chosen for their argument piece, or a third topic they wanted to make a statement about. The students' exploration of aesthetics in the first semester was tied in as they considered the genres they wanted to use for their project.

One of the students did her project on *Roe v. Wade* and abortion. A talented artist, she created a beautiful portrait of a young woman with a red band over her mouth. Under the portrait she wrote, "Treat us equally instead of sequels to the man's story." It came with a poem she had been working on called "Silenced."

"In our end-of-year conference," Jessica recalls, "the student said she had shown the painting to her mother. 'I can't put the red band over her mouth,' she told her mother. 'It's gonna ruin it!' Her mother said, 'It's gonna change it, for sure. It's gonna elevate it from being an art piece to being an art piece that makes a statement.' She put the red band over the young woman's mouth, and was happy she did."

Jasmine is looking forward to the "gallery walk" her Lit and Comp classes will do to admire their classmates' multigenre projects.

In addition to teaching for liberation in her Lit and Comp classes, Jasmine has been taking leadership in her school. The topic is caring, which she addressed in her master's thesis. "I explored the tenets of white supremacist culture and how they show up in our educational settings," she explains.

> I argued that organizational care is a powerful way to disrupt white supremacist culture in schools. The discipline disparities between

> white and Black students are due to Black students feeling they're not cared about and don't belong. So, they drop out. How do we get all our kids in instead of out? One way is to show all our folks we care—students and staff. We need to care for our staff so that they can care for our students. I challenged my administration to introduce organizational care routines, structures, and sustainable practices for next year. Burnout is so real. Can you imagine if all teachers could honestly say, "I love my job, I love being here"? Education would be in a whole different place. One way we can directly disrupt and combat burnout is to show we care.

But building a culture of caring in a school is complicated. It requires conversations about how we can care for each other. "Food and coffee are love to me," says Jasmine. "If you give me a little snack like that, I feel cared for. But maybe my colleague down the hall doesn't like coffee. So, we have to be grounded in how we like to be cared for and how we show care for others."

With that in mind, Jasmine organized a "community care week," which included teachers sharing information about their favorite drink and receiving the drink from a random staff member along with the staff member's favorite quote. "It was a big hit," says Jasmine, "and now we have all the information at hand when it's somebody's birthday."

She also decided to take on the discipline disparities. "I had been hearing from students about too many instances of harm occurring," Jasmine says, "and I was experiencing some myself." She made a presentation to a meeting of the Race and Ethnic Studies class, which the school offers to juniors and seniors. She shared the last three years of school discipline data, which show students of color disproportionately involved in discipline incidents. She suggested that one form of organizational care for disrupting the disproportionality could be "implicit bias reporting and supporting." With a safe way to report instances of harm, the school community could better understand the nature and scope of the problem and stop the harmful behavior that was making groups of students feel unwelcome and uncared for. Jasmine engaged students from the class in creating a reporting form students or staff could use to report unintentional slights or "microaggressions," not for punitive purposes but for healing the harm and increasing awareness.

Some of the students from the class decided to set up a student group to see the project through. They formed Student Advocates for Equity (SAFE). Through ongoing consultation with teachers and union representatives and feedback from the school's equity accountability team, they completed the form for use in the 2022–23 school year.

For SAFE, this is just the first step. The students see their role as supporting students and faculty when reports come in. They met with the administrator for equity and inclusion at the district office to ask that SAFE members be trained in restorative practices so that they can be part of the facilitation team for meetings aimed at healing harm. They surveyed graduating seniors to get their perspectives. They are planning community-building events in the coming school year for staff and students. SAFE members will also host "lunch bunch tables" where kids can sit if they don't have friends to sit with. "SAFE is committed to tackling bias, racism, and all the phobias and -isms in our school setting," says Jasmine.

Good adult mentor that she is, Jasmine tells the students every meeting, "Y'all, I'm here to get out of the way. Tell me what the obstacles are, what are the questions, and I will go and run and ask. But y'all, just focus on what you need. Do that and I will do the lift."

It is a pleasure to follow the adventures of a teacher who has truly found her vocation. Jasmine obviously loves creating a learning community for her students and engaging them in learning for liberation. The love and joy she shares so generously come back to her in life-sustaining connections with her inner self, her students, and her colleagues. She has found the place where her deep gladness meets her students' great hunger. Jasmine is living what Parker Palmer calls "the undivided life"—a life of integrity in which inner life and outer life are one.[16] To the extent that we as educators can close the gap between what we know our students need and what we are able to give, we lay the foundation for resilience.

I love Jasmine's opening and closing rituals and her open door. I love her sharing feelings and vulnerability while showing up with joy. I love how she has turned "Lit and Comp" into a dynamic curriculum to explore identity, skills, intellect, and action for social justice. While living the undivided life herself, Jasmine has created a curriculum that encourages her students to find their joy, their passion, and their deep gladness and base their work for liberation upon it.

I feel awe and admiration for teachers like Jasmine who show up for their students day after day, welcoming their feelings, concerns, and questions about the perplexing and upsetting events unfolding in today's world. How important it is for young people to have a safe space to process these events! How important it is for young people to have the steady presence of an adult who is there for them in all her joy, honesty, integrity, and vulnerability!

Jasmine shows that fighting back can be a resilience strategy. She finds her leadership for organizational caring deeply satisfying. Yes, it's a demanding project requiring additional work. But it offers the promise of transforming her school into a place where all belong, thus righting the wrongs she suffered as a student. Rather than continuing to witness harm being done, it enables her to close even more the gap between what her students need and what she can give them.

Will SAFE's lunch bunch initiative help more students feel that they belong? Will the implicit bias reporting and supporting prove successful in moving the school toward a culture of caring and inclusion? These are works in progress. Jasmine and the students are sparking great conversations about the politics of caring in their school. They are building relationships and organizing support for improvements aimed at enabling the school to better serve the needs of students, faculty, and families. This is just the beginning.

Through her innovative teaching and organizing for liberation, Jasmine shows what is possible for the justice part of climate justice education. What about the climate part? I opened the book with Jasmine's observation that the climate crisis is weighing on her students and causing them to lose trust in adults. My hope for Jasmine and her students at Westview is that the science and social studies teachers at her school step up, if they haven't already, to address the climate crisis, joining her in creating a multidisciplinary project-based, exploratory curriculum for the school on climate justice.

GO FORTH!

I am grateful to the twenty-five educators and students I met by Zoom and interviewed for this book. It is an honor to share their ideas, stories, and enthusiasm here. I hope I have done justice to their heroic work. My intention has been to expand educators' awareness of what is necessary and what is possible in educating for climate justice. May their stories inspire thousands upon thousands of educators to come on board!

Teaching radical, transformative climate justice is an adventure. Hard times and huge challenges lie ahead. Sometimes we'll feel elated, sometimes we'll feel despair, and sometimes we'll just be trying to put one foot in front of the other. But with the ultimate outcome not yet decided, we have a chance to turn things around. Inspired by our love for nature, our love for life, and our love for our students, we take that chance—and embrace adventure.

I embrace the idea of hope as something we practice rather than something we have. We envision what we *hope for*, discern how we can best contribute to realizing what we hope for, and get to work. Passionate about our vocation of nurturing young people, we build community, foster learning, and promote democracy, deriving our sustenance from the love and joy of educating a generation of courageous, intelligent, wise, nonviolent fighters for climate justice.

I expect to join with others to establish an online center where radical climate justice educators from across the country and around the world can continue the conversations and sharing of ideas and resources inspired by this book (see the appendix, Climate Justice Resources for Educators).

Take good care of yourself. Do what you need to do to stay in touch with your inner self—your goodness, your love, your gladness, and the sources of your inspiration. Take walks in the woods and fields. Read poetry. Listen to your favorite music. With a trusted partner, cry, laugh, yawn, shake, and rage when you need to and support others in doing the same.

When you get tired, rest.

Go forth—with heart, joy, and a fighting spirit!

APPENDIX

Climate Justice Resources for Educators

CURRICULAR RESOURCES

Bigelow, Bill, and Tim Swinehart. *A People's Curriculum for the Earth: Teaching Climate Change and Environmental Crisis*. Milwaukee, WI: Rethinking Schools, 2014.

"Clean Network." Climate Literacy and Energy Awareness Network. Last modified June 28, 2022. https://cleanet.org/clean/community/index.html.

"Climate Action Simulation." Climate Interactive. Accessed December 27, 2022. https://www.climateinteractive.org/climate-action-simulation/.

"Climate Change Education and Climate Justice." North American Association for Environmental Education. Accessed December 27, 2022. https://naaee.org/programs/climate-change-education.

"Climate Change Education Module." Resources for Educators. NYC Environmental Protection. Accessed December 27, 2022. https://www1.nyc.gov/site/dep/environment/climate-change-education-module.page.

"Climate Change Resources for Educators and Students." US Environmental Protection Agency. Updated October 6, 2022. https://www.epa.gov/climate-change/climate-change-resources-educators-and-students.

C Roads Project. https://www.climateinteractive.org/c-roads/.

"Explore Renewable Energy." KidWind. Accessed December 27, 2022. https://www.kidwind.org/.

"For Educators." NASA Global Climate Change. Updated December 16, 2022. https://climate.nasa.gov/for-educators/.

"Global Environmental Politics." Bayard's Website, The Beacon School. Accessed December 27, 2022. https://sites.google.com/beaconschool.org/faithfull/global-environmental-politics.

"Green Design Lab." Solar One. Accessed December 27, 2022. https://www.solar1.org/green-design-lab/.

"Making the Green New Deal a Reality." The Beacon School. February 2019. https://drive.google.com/file/d/1NhbjQxXsfVAlS9ye2S57x_eddoXyTnjN/view.

Reiss, Richard. "Energetic: Teaching the Future." City Atlas, February 21, 2020. https://newyork.thecityatlas.org/lifestyle/we-turned-the-future-of-new-york-city-into-a-board-game/.

Rethinking Schools. Accessed December 27, 2022. https://rethinkingschools.org/.

Subject to Climate. Accessed December 27, 2022. https://subjecttoclimate.org/.

Sustainability Challenge. Accessed December 27, 2022. https://drive.google.com/file/d/1gCvCEPsIZMFn0zWalndQSx3LWnc4q4pN/view.

"Teachable Moment Lessons." Morningside Center for Teaching Social Responsibility. Accessed December 27, 2022. http://www.teachablemoment.org/.

ThoughtBox. Accessed December 27, 2022. https://www.thoughtboxeducation.com/.

Zinn Education Project. Accessed December 27, 2022. https://www.zinnedproject.org/.

RESOURCES ALIGNED WITH CHAPTERS OF *TEACH FOR CLIMATE JUSTICE*

Chapter 1

Bryk, Anthony S., Louis M. Gomez, Alicia Grunow, and Paul G. Le Mahieu. *Learning to Improve: How America's Schools Can Get Better at Getting Better*. Cambridge, MA: Harvard Education Press, 2015.

Collaborative for Academic, Social, and Emotional Learning (CASEL). Accessed December 27, 2022. https://casel.org/.

Hammond, Zaretta. *Culturally Responsive Teaching and the Brain: Promoting Authentic Engagement and Rigor Among Culturally and Linguistically Diverse Students*. Thousand Oaks, CA: Corwin, 2015.

Kendi, Ibram X. *How to Be an Antiracist*. New York: One World, 2019.

Love, Bettina L. *We Want to Do More Than Just Survive: Abolitionist Teaching and the Pursuit of Educational Freedom*. Boston, MA: Beacon, 2019.

Morningside Center for Teaching Social Responsibility. Accessed December 27, 2022. https://www.morningsidecenter.org/.

Muhammad, Gholdy. *Cultivating Genius: An Equity Framework for Culturally and Historically Responsive Literacy*. New York: Scholastic, 2020.

Ray, Sarah Jaquette. *A Field Guide to Climate Anxiety: How to Keep Your Cool on a Warming Planet*. Oakland: University of California Press, 2020.

A Resource for Equitable Classroom Practices, 2010. Rockville, MD: Equity Initiatives Unit of Montgomery County Public Schools, 2010.

Singleton, Glenn E. *Courageous Conversations About Race: A Field Guide for Achieving Equity in Schools*. Thousand Oaks, CA: Corwin, 2005.

———. *More Courageous Conversations About Race*. Thousand Oaks, CA: Corwin, 2013.

Chapter 2

Carson, Rachel. *The Sense of Wonder: A Celebration of Nature for Parents and Children*. New York: HarperCollins, 1965.

———. *Silent Spring*. Boston: Houghton Mifflin, 1962.

Kimmerer, Robin Wall. *Braiding Sweet Grass: Indigenous Wisdom, Scientific Knowledge and the Teachings of Plants*. Minneapolis, MN: Milkweed, 2013.

Orr, David W. *Earth and Mind: On Education, Environment, and the Human Prospect*, 10th anniversary ed. Washington, DC: Island, 2004.

Park, Linda Sue. *A Long Walk to Water: Based on a True Story*. Boston: Houghton Mifflin, 2011.

Powers, Richard. *The Overstory*. London: Random House, 2018.

Chapter 3

Attenborough, David. *A Life on Our Planet: My Witness Statement and a Vision for the Future*. New York: Grand Central, 2020.

Butler, Octavia E. *Parable of the Sower*. New York: Four Walls Eight Windows, 1993.

"Climate Change Library." Literary Hub. Accessed December 27, 2022. https://lithub.com/story-type/climate-change-library/.

Climate and Resilience Education Task Force in NYC. *CRETF ClimEd Survey 2021*. June 11, 2021. https://static1.squarespace.com/static/6001a539f8f42f6c20a08362/t/61d7371b336fc71c4a409186/1641494299699/CRETF+ClimEd+Survey+2021.pdf.

Eisenstein, Charles. *Climate: A New Story*. Berkeley, CA: North Atlantic, 2018.

Hawken, Paul, ed. *Drawdown: The Most Comprehensive Plan Ever Proposed to Reverse Global Warming*. Vancouver, BC: Langara College, 2017.

Intergovernmental Science-Policy Platform on Biodiversity and Ecosystem Services. *Global Assessment Report on Biodiversity and Ecosystem Services of the Intergovernmental Science-Policy Platform on Biodiversity and Ecosystem Services*, eds. Eduardo Brondizio, Josef Settele, Sandra Díaz, and Hien T. Ngo. Bonn, Germany: IPBES Secretariat, 2019. https://ipbes.net/global-assessment.

———. "Key Messages." In *Summary for Policymakers of the Global Assessment Report on Biodiversity and Ecosystem Services*, eds. S. Díaz, J. Settele, E. S. Brondízio, H. T. Ngo, M. Guèze, J. Agard, A. Arneth, P. Balvanera, K. A. Brauman, S. H. M. Butchart, K. M. A. Chan, L. A. Garibaldi, K. Ichii, J. Liu, S. M. Subramanian, G. F. Midgley, P. Miloslavich, Z. Molnár, D. Obura, A. Pfaff, S. Polasky, A. Purvis, J. Razzaque, B. Reyers, R. Roy Chowdhury, Y. J. Shin, I. J. Visseren-Hamakers, K. J. Willis, and C. N. Zayas, 12–14. Bonn, Germany: IPBES Secretariat, 2019. https://zenodo.org/record/3553579#.YuwPY3bMLb0.

Intergovernmental Panel on Climate Change. "Summary for Policymakers." In *Climate Change 2021: The Physical Science Basis. Contribution of Working Group I to the Sixth Assessment Report of the Intergovernmental Panel on Climate Change*, eds. V. Masson-Delmotte, P. Zhai, A. Pirani, S. L. Connors, C. Péan, S. Berger, N. Caud, Y. Chen, L. Goldfarb, M. I. Gomis, M. Huang, K. Leitzell, E. Lonnoy, J. B. R. Matthews, T. K. Maycock, T. Waterfield, O. Yelekçi, R. Yu, and B. Zho, 3–32. Cambridge: Cambridge University Press, 2021. https://www.ipcc.ch/report/ar6/wg1/downloads/report/IPCC_AR6_WGI_SPM.pdf.

Kenner, Robert, dir. *Food, Inc.* Magnolia Pictures, 2009.

Klein, Naomi. *On Fire: The (Burning) Case for a Green New Deal.* New York: Simon & Schuster, 2019.

———. *This Changes Everything: Capitalism vs. the Climate.* New York: Simon & Schuster, 2014.

McKibben, Bill. *Eaarth: Making a Life on a Tough New Planet.* New York: Times Books, 2010.

———. *Falter: Has the Human Game Begun to Play Itself Out?* New York: Henry Holt, 2019.

Next Generation Science Standards. https://www.nextgenscience.org/.

Nye, Bill. It's Not Magic, It's Science. Accessed December 27, 2022. https://www.billnye.com.

Pollan, Michael. *The Omnivore's Dilemma: A Natural History of Four Meals.* New York: Penguin, 2006.

Quinn, Daniel. *Ishmael: An Adventure of the Mind and Spirit.* New York: Bantam, 1992.

Shiva, Vandana. *Soil Not Oil: Environmental Justice in a Time of Climate Crisis.* Cambridge, MA: South End, 2008.

Wallace-Wells, David. *The Uninhabitable Earth: Life After Warming.* New York: Tim Duggan, 2020.

"What Is the ACE Framework?" Coalition for Climate Education Policy. North American Association for Environmental Education. https://www.climateedpolicy.org/resources/what-ace-framework.

"Who Will Feed Us?" ETC Group. June 18, 2020. https://etcgroup.org/whowillfeedus.

Chapter 4

Brown, Adrienne M. *Emergent Strategy: Shaping Change, Changing Worlds.* Chico, CA: AK Press, 2021.

———. *Holding Change: The Way of Emergent Strategy Facilitation and Mediation.* Chico, CA: AK Press, 2021.

Brown, Lester. *Plan B 4.0: Mobilizing to Save Civilization.* New York: W.W. Norton, 2009.

"Climate Solutions 101." Project Drawdown. Accessed December 27, 2022. https://drawdown.org/climate-solutions-101.

Cooperative Climate Futures. Accessed December 27, 2022. https://ccfutures.co/.

Hawken, Paul, ed. *Drawdown: The Most Comprehensive Plan Ever Proposed to Reverse Global Warming*. Vancouver, BC: Langara College, 2017.

Johnson, Ayana Elizabeth, and Katharine K. Wilkinson, eds. *All We Can Save: Truth, Courage, and Solutions for the Climate Crisis*. New York: One World, 2021.

Macy, Joanna, and Chris Johnstone. *Active Hope: How to Face the Mess We're in Without Going Crazy*. Novato, CA: New World Library, 2012.

Mitchell, Sherri. *Sacred Instructions: Indigenous Wisdom for Living Spirit-Based Change*. Berkeley, CA: North Atlantic, 2018.

"Movement Generation Justice and Ecology Project." Just Transition Zine. Accessed August 12, 2022. https://movementgeneration.org/justtransition/.

Chapter 5

"American Experience: Freedom Riders." Season 23, Episode 11. Public Broadcasting Service. February 6, 2012. https://www.pbs.org/video/american-experience-freedom-riders/.

Chenoweth, Erica, and Maria J. Stephan. *Why Civil Resistance Works: The Strategic Logic of Nonviolent Conflict*. New York: Columbia University Press, 2013.

Elbein, Saul. "The Youth Group That Launched a Movement at Standing Rock." *New York Times Magazine*. January 31, 2017. https://www.nytimes.com/2017/01/31/magazine/the-youth-group-that-launched-a-movement-at-standing-rock.html.

Engler, Mark, and Paul Engler. *This Is an Uprising: How Nonviolent Revolt Is Shaping the Twenty-First Century*. Oakville, ON: Bold Type, 2016.

Gasch, Renee, and Julia Reticker-Flynn. "Youth Activist Toolkit." Advocates for Youth. April 2019. https://advocatesforyouth.org/wp-content/uploads/2019/04/Youth-Activist-Toolkit.pdf.

Haga, Kazu. *Healing Resistance: A Radically Different Response to Harm*. Berkeley, CA: Parallax, 2020.

Indigenous Environmental Network (IEN). https://ienearth.org.

Moore-Backman, Chris. *The Gandhian Iceberg: A Nonviolence Manifesto for the Age of the Great Turning*. Reno, NV: Be the Change Project, 2016.

Moyer, Bill. *Doing Democracy: The MAP Model for Organizing Social Movements*. Gabriola Island, BC: New Society, 2001.

Our Climate. Accessed December 27, 2022. https://ourclimate.us.

Simon, Evan. "Meet the Youths at the Heart of the Standing Rock Protests Against the Dakota Access Pipeline." *ABC News*. February 25, 2017. https://abcnews.go.com/US/meet-youth-heart-standing-rock-protests-dakota-access/story?id=45719115.

Theoharis, Jeanne, and Brandy Colbert. *The Rebellious Life of Mrs. Rosa Parks*. Boston, MA: Beacon, 2021.

"US Indigenous Studies: Standing Rock Syllabus." Holman Library, Green River College. Accessed December 27, 2022. https://libguides.greenriver.edu/c.php?g=409498&p=4055813.

Wolfe-Rocca, Ursula. "Teaching Climate Disobedience: Using the Film *Necessity* in the Classroom." Zinn Education Project. Accessed December 27, 2022. https://www.zinnedproject.org/materials/necessity-lesson.

Zinn Education Project. "Teaching SNCC: The Organization at the Heart of the Civil Rights Revolution." https://www.zinnedproject.org/materials/teaching-sncc.

Chapter 6

ACE: Action for the Climate Emergency. Accessed December 27, 2022. https://acespace.org/.

Climate Generation. Accessed December 27, 2022. https://www.climategen.org/.

Metzger-Carter, Nancy. Sonoma Academy. Accessed December 27, 2022. https://www.sonomaacademy.org/nancy-metzger-carter.

Student and Educator Climate Resource Toolkit. Climate and Resilience Education Task Force Youth Steering Committee, 2021. https://docs.google.com/document/d/18ij35jrR-Q8vY1dK_hAuhO0XViH5XwhZjMqMEVFpyVw/edit.

Chapter 7

"Centering Racial Equity." Morningside Center for Teaching Social Responsibility. Accessed December 27, 2022. https://www.morningsidecenter.org/centering-racial-equity.

"Legacy Quilt of African American Food Heroes." Museum of Food and Drink (MoFAD). Brooklyn, NY. https://www.mofad.org/the-legacy-quilt.

Nye, Bill. *Climate Change 101 with Bill Nye*. National Geographic, 2015. https://www.youtube.com/watch?v=EtW2rrLHs08.

TEL: Transformational Educational Leadership. Accessed December 27, 2022. https://www.teleadership.org/.

Chapter 8

Casey, Leo. *The Teacher Insurgency: A Strategic and Organizing Perspective*. Cambridge, MA: Harvard Education Press, 2020.

Oliver, Mary. *Devotions: The Selected Poems of Mary Oliver*. New York: Penguin, 2017.

Roderick, Tom. "Teach Climate Justice: Tools for Teaching and Organizing." www.teachclimatejustice.org.

Tarlau, Rebecca. *Occupying Schools, Occupying Land: How the Landless Workers Movement Transformed Brazilian Education*. New York: Oxford University Press, 2019.

SELF CARE

The Awen Center. Accessed December 27, 2022. http://www.TheAwenCenter.org/.

Intrator, Sam A., and Megan Scribner, eds. *Leading from Within: Poetry That Sustains the Courage to Lead*. San Francisco, CA: Jossey-Bass, 2007.

———, eds. *Teaching with Fire: Poetry That Sustains the Courage to Teach*. San Francisco, CA: Jossey-Bass, 2003.

———, eds. *Teaching with Heart: Poetry That Speaks to the Courage to Teach*. San Francisco, CA: Jossey-Bass, 2014.

Lantieri, Linda, ed. *Schools with Spirit: Nurturing the Inner Lives of Children and Teachers*. Boston, MA: Beacon, 2002.

Palmer, Parker J. *A Hidden Wholeness: The Journey Toward an Undivided Life, Welcoming the Soul and Weaving Community in a Wounded World*. San Francisco, CA: Jossey-Bass, 2008.

———. *Let Your Life Speak: Listening to the Voice of Vocation*. San Francisco, CA: Jossey-Bass, 1999.

Palmer, Parker J., and Megan Scribner. *The Courage to Teach Guide for Reflection and Renewal*. San Francisco, CA: Jossey-Bass, 2017.

CLIMATE EDUCATION POLICY

"Action for Climate Empowerment." United Nations Framework Convention on Climate Change. Accessed December 27, 2022. https://unfccc.int/topics/education-youth/the-big-picture/what-is-action-for-climate-empowerment.

Climate Resilience Education Task Force (CRETF). https://www.cretf.org/.

Environmental Education Advisory Council of New York City. *EEAC Newsletter*, Summer 2018. https://eeac-nyc.org/files/newsletters/EEACnewsletter201808.pdf.

US Congress. House. *Supporting the Teaching of Climate Change in Schools.* HR 29. 117th Congress. Introduced in House January 11, 2021. https://www.congress.gov/117/bills/hres29/BILLS-117hres29ih.pdf.

NOTES

INTRODUCTION

1. Joanna Macy and Chris Johnstone, *Active Hope: How to Face the Mess We're in Without Going Crazy* (Novato, CA: New World Library, 2012).
2. World Bank data, https://databankfiles.worldbank.org/data/download/GDP.pdf.
3. Noah Kirsch, "The 3 Richest Americans Hold More Wealth Than Bottom 50% of the Country, Study Finds," *Forbes*, November 9, 2017, https://www.forbes.com/sites/noahkirsch/2017/11/09/the-3-richest-americans-hold-more-wealth-than-bottom-50-of-country-study-finds/?sh=347054e43cf8.
4. Parker Palmer, *A Hidden Wholeness: The Journey Toward an Undivided Life* (San Francisco, CA: Jossey-Bass, 2004), 3.
5. Macy and Johnstone, *Active Hope*, 3.

CHAPTER 1

1. Madeline Will, "Teens Are Struggling with Climate Anxiety. Schools Haven't Caught Up Yet," Ed Week, December 7, 2022.
2. Peggy Ray et al., *Resolving Conflict Creatively: A Teaching Guide for Grades Kindergarten Through Six* (New York: Morningside Center for Teaching Social Responsibility, 1993, 1996, 2007).
3. Glenn Singleton, *Courageous Conversations about Race: A Field Guide to Achieving Equity in Schools and Beyond* (Thousand Oaks, CA: Corwin, 2021).
4. Beth Strano, "Invitation to Brave Space," available on the Internet.
5. Michelle Alexander, *The New Jim Crow: Mass Incarceration in the Age of Color Blindness* (New York: New Press, 2012).

6. Andre Perry, "Column: The Educational Value of a Black Teacher," Hechinger Report, May 26, 2020, https://hechingerreport.org/the-educational-value-of-a-black-teacher/.
7. Katherine Schaeffer, "America's Public School Teachers Are Far Less Racially and Ethnically Diverse Than Their Students," Pew Research Center, December 10, 2021, https://www.pewresearch.org/fact-tank/2021/12/10/americas-public-school-teachers-are-far-less-racially-and-ethnically-diverse-than-their-students/.
8. Zaretta Hammond, *Culturally Responsive Teaching and the Brain: Promoting Authentic Engagement and Rigor Among Culturally and Linguistically Diverse Students* (Thousand Oaks, CA: Corwin, 2015).
9. *A Resource for Equitable Classroom Practices, 2010* (Rockville, MD: Equity Initiatives Unit of Montgomery County Public Schools, 2010).
10. Anthony S. Bryk et al., *Learning to Improve: How America's Schools Can Get Better at Getting Better* (Cambridge, MA: Harvard Education Press, 2015).
11. Fred Rogers and Barry Head, *Mister Rogers Talks with Parents* (Milwaukee, WI: Hal Leonard, 1983).
12. Audre Lorde, *A Burst of Light: And Other Essays* (Mineola, NY: Ixis, 2017). An unabridged replication of the work initially published by Firebrand Books, 1988.

CHAPTER 2

1. Joanna Macy and Chris Johnstone, *Active Hope: How to Face the Mess We're in Without Going Crazy* (Novato, CA: New World Library, 2012).
2. Rachel Carson, *Silent Spring* (New York: Houghton-Mifflin, 1962).
3. Robin Wall Kimmerer, *Braiding Sweetgrass: Indigenous Wisdom, Scientific Knowledge and the Teachings of Plants* (Minneapolis, MN: Milkweed, 2013).
4. Brian Doyle, "Joyas Voladoras," *American Scholar*, Autumn 2004; Heather Swan, "Victor," *About Place Journal* 4, no. 4; and W. H. Auden, "Musée des Beaux Arts," in *Another Time* (London: Faber & Faber, 1940).
5. Rachel Carson, *The Sense of Wonder: A Celebration of Nature for Parents and Children* (New York: HarperCollins, 1995), 45, 88.
6. Carson, *Silent Spring*, 45.
7. David W. Orr, *Earth and Mind: On Education, Environment, and the Human Prospect*, 10th anniversary ed. (Washington, DC: Island, 2004), 147.

8. Chris Van Allsburg, *Just a Dream* (New York: HarperCollins, 1990).
9. Orr, *Earth and Mind*, 131–53.
10. "Global Issues: Water," United Nations, accessed December 27, 2022, https://www.un.org/en/global-issues/water.
11. Linda Sue Park, *A Long Walk to Water: Based on a True Story* (Boston: Houghton Mifflin, 2011).

CHAPTER 3

1. Intergovernmental Panel on Climate Change, "Summary for Policymakers," in *Climate Change 2021, the Physical Science Basis, Contribution of Working Group I to the Sixth Assessment Report of the Intergovernmental Panel on Climate Change*, ed. V. Masson-Delmotte et al. (Cambridge: Cambridge University Press, 2021), 3–32.
2. Intergovernmental Science-Policy Platform on Biodiversity and Ecosystem Services (IPBES), *Global Assessment Report on Biodiversity and Ecosystem Services of the Intergovernmental Science-Policy Platform on Biodiversity and Ecosystem Services*, ed. Eduardo Brondizio et al. (Bonn, Germany: IPBES Secretaries, 2019).
3. IPBES, *Global Assessment Report*.
4. David Attenborough, *A Life on Our Planet: My Witness Statement and a Vision for the Future* (New York: Grand Central, 2020), 109–11.
5. Attenborough, *A Life on Our Planet*, 112–21.
6. Intergovernmental Science-Policy Platform on Biodiversity and Ecosystem Services, "Key Messages," in *Summary for Policymakers of the Global Assessment Report on Biodiversity and Ecosystem Services*, ed. S. Díaz et al. (Bonn, Germany: IPBES Secretariat), 12–14.
7. Bill McKibben, *Falter: Has the Human Game Begun to Play Itself Out?* (New York, Henry Holt, 2019), 89.
8. McKibben, *Falter*, 74.
9. McKibben, *Falter*, 76.
10. McKibben, *Falter*, 86.
11. Mark Bittman, "How to Feed the World," editorial, *New York Times*, October 14, 2013, https://www.nytimes.com/2013/10/15/opinion/how-to-feed-the-world.html.
12. Octavia E. Butler, *Parable of the Sower* (New York and London: Grand Central, 2000).
13. Butler, *Parable of the Sower*, 17.

14. Xochitl Bentley, "Adjusting to Uncertainty: Systems Thinking with Octavia Butler," Moving Writers, January 4, 2021, https://movingwriters.org/2021/01/04, 4.
15. Daniel Quinn, *Ishmael: An Adventure of the Mind and Spirit* (New York: Bantam, 1992).
16. Quinn, *Ishmael*, 25.
17. Rainforest Action Network, November 25, 2021, https://www.ran.org/.
18. Nancy Harris and David Gibbs, "Forests Absorb Twice as Much Carbon as They Emit Each Year," World Resources Institute, January 21, 2021, https://www.wri.org/insights/forests-absorb-twice-much-carbon-they-emit-each-year.
19. Gabrielle Gurley, "The COP26 Parting Shot? Wait Until Next Year," *American Prospect*, November 18, 2021, https://prospect.org/environment/the-cop26-parting-shot-wait-until-next-year.
20. Stephen Castle and Megan Specia, "COP26 Protestors Back an Array of Causes, Connected by Climate Change," *New York Times*, November 8, 2021, https://www.nytimes.com/2021/11/06/world/europe/cop-climate-protests.html.
21. Cary Funk and Brian Kennedy, "How Americans See Climate Change and the Environment in Seven Charts," *Pew Research Center*, April 23, 2020, https://www.pewresearch.org/fact-tank/2020/04/21/how-americans-see-climate-change-and-the-environment-in-7-charts.
22. Damian Carrington, "Cop26: Polling Data Is Overwhelming—People Want Leaders to Act," *The Guardian*, November 21, 2021, https://www.theguardian.com/environment/2021/nov/01/cop26-polling-data-is-overwhelming-people-want-leaders-to-act.
23. Paul Hawken, ed., *Drawdown: The Most Comprehensive Plan Ever Proposed to Reverse Global Warming* (New York: Penguin, 2017), 3.
24. Lisa Friedman, "How to Hand Out Billions in Climate Subsidies? Podesta Aims to Tread Very Carefully," *New York Times*, December 15, 2022.
25. Sarah Kaplan, "COP27 Leaves World on Dangerous Warming Path Despite Historic Climate Fund," Washington Post, November 20, 2022.
26. Kaplan, "COP27 Leaves World on Dangerous Warming Path."
27. Kaplan, "COP27 Leaves World on Dangerous Warming Path."
28. Bill McKibben, "From Climate Exhortation to Climate Execution," *The New Yorker*, December 27, 2022.

29. Cora Engelbrecht, "Coke Is a Sponsor of the Climate Summit in Egypt, Some Activists Aren't Happy," *New York Times*, November 7, 2022, https://www.nytimes.com/2022/11/07/climate/coca-cola-sponsor-cop27-climate-egypt.html.
30. Kaplan, "COP27 Leaves World on Dangerous Warming Path."
31. Hiroko Tabuchi, "Inside Saudi Arabia's Strategy to Keep the World Hooked on Oil," *New York Times*, November 21, 2022.

CHAPTER 4

1. Joanna Macy and Chris Johnstone, *Active Hope: How to Face the Mess We're in Without Going Crazy* (Novato, CA: New World Library, 2012), 26–33.
2. Macy and Johnstone, *Active Hope*, 13–26.
3. Macy and Johnstone, *Active Hope*, 35.
4. Frederick Buechner, *Wishful Thinking: A Seeker's ABC* (New York: Harper Collins, 1993).
5. David Attenborough, *A Life on Our Planet: My Witness Statement and a Vision for the Future* (New York: Grand Central, 2020), 126.
6. Attenborough, *A Life on Our Planet*, 133–35.
7. Rhiana Gunn-Wright, "A Green New Deal for All of Us," in *All We Can Save: Truth, Courage, and Solutions for the Climate Crisis*, ed. Ayana Elizabeth Johnson and Katharine K. Wilkinson (New York: One World, 2021), 92–102.
8. Paul Hawken, ed., *Drawdown: The Most Comprehensive Plan Ever Proposed to Reverse Global Warming* (New York: Penguin, 2017), 2–3.
9. Sean Sweeney, *Another Energy Is Possible*, Vol. 44.2, Publication Series Ecology (Berlin, Germany: Heinrich Boll, 2018), 12.
10. Sweeney, *Another Energy*, 5–36.
11. Attenborough, *A Life on Our Planet*, 159–61.
12. Cooperative Climate Futures, https://ccfutures.co/.
13. East New York Farms, https://ucceny.org/enyf/.
14. Hawken, *Drawdown*, 46–47.
15. Hawken, *Drawdown*, 54–55.
16. Hawken, *Drawdown*, 54–55.
17. Attenborough, *A Life on Our Planet*, 170.
18. Hawken, *Drawdown*, 39.
19. Hawken, *Drawdown*, 39–40.

20. Hawken, *Drawdown*, 81.
21. Hawken, *Drawdown*, 82.
22. Hawken, *Drawdown*, 81.
23. Hawken, *Drawdown*, 81.
24. Hawken, *Drawdown*, 78–79.
25. Hawken, *Drawdown*, 78.
26. Ayana Elizabeth Johnson and Katharine K. Wilkinson, ed., *All We Can Save: Truth, Courage, and Solutions for the Climate Crisis* (New York: One World, 2021).
27. Linda Sue Park, *A Long Walk to Water: Based on a True Story* (Boston: Houghton Mifflin, 2011).
28. Attenborough, *A Life on Our Planet*, 147.
29. Attenborough, *A Life on Our Planet*, 147–58.
30. Attenborough, *A Life on Our Planet*, 204–7.
31. Attenborough, *A Life on Our Planet*, 207–8.
32. Sherri Mitchell, "Indigenous Prophecy and Mother Earth," in *All We Can Save: Truth, Courage, and Solutions for the Climate Crisis*, ed. Ayana Elizabeth Johnson and Katharine K. Wilkinson (New York: One World, 2021), 16–28.
33. Robin Wall Kimmerer, *Braiding Sweetgrass: Indigenous Wisdom, Scientific Knowledge, and the Teachings of Plants* (Minneapolis, MN: Milkweed, 2013), 105–17.
34. Kimmerer, *Braiding Sweetgrass*, x.
35. Kimmerer, *Braiding Sweetgrass*, 183.
36. Seamus Heaney, "The Cure at Troy" (Excerpt), in *Leading from Within*, ed. Sam M. Intrator and Megan Scribner (San Francisco, CA: Jossey-Bass, 2007), 146.

CHAPTER 5

1. "Get on the Bus: The Freedom Riders of 1961," Fresh Air, January 12, 2006, https://www.npr.org/2006/01/12/5149667/get-on-the-bus-the-freedom-riders-of-1961.
2. *Freedom Riders: Threatened, Attacked, Jailed*, directed by Stanley Nelson (PBS American Experience Films, 2011).
3. Mark Engler and Paul Engler, *This Is an Uprising: How Nonviolent Revolt Is Shaping the Twenty-First Century* (New York: Nation Books, 2016), 14–17, 90–92.

4. Erica Chenoweth and Maria J. Stephan, *Why Civil Resistance Works: The Strategic Logic of Nonviolent Conflict* (New York: Columbia University Press, 2013).
5. Engler and Engler, *This Is an Uprising*, 107–11.
6. Bill Moyer, *Doing Democracy: The MAP Model for Organizing Social Movements* (Gabriola Island, BC: New Society, 2001).
7. Engler and Engler, *This Is an Uprising*, 179–96.
8. John Rieder, *Martin Luther King, Jr's Letter from Birmingham Jail and the Struggle That Changed a Nation* (New York: Bloomsbury, 2014).
9. Engler and Engler, *This Is an Uprising*, 197–223.
10. Engler and Engler, *This Is an Uprising*, 205.
11. Elizabeth Kolbert, "Poles Apart," *The New Yorker*, January 3 and 10, 2022, 72.
12. Chenoweth and Stephan, *Why Civil Resistance Works*.
13. Roger Hallam, "Now We Know Conventional Campaigning Won't Prevent Our Extinction," *The Guardian*, May 1, 2019, https://www.theguardian.com/commentisfree/2019/may/01/extinction-rebellion-non-violent-civil-disobedience.
14. Ursula Wolfe-Rocca, "Teaching Climate Disobedience: Using the Film *Necessity* in the Classroom," Zinn Education Project, zinnedproject.org.
15. Saul Elbein, "The Youth Group That Launched a Movement at Standing Rock," *New York Times Magazine*, January 31, 2017, https://www.nytimes.com/2017/01/31/magazine/the-youth-group-that-launched-a-movement-at-standing-rock.html.
16. Elbein, "The Youth Group That Launched a Movement at Standing Rock."
17. Evan Simon, "Meet the Youths at the Heart of the Standing Rock Protests Against the Dakota Access Pipeline," *ABC News*, February 25, 2017, https://abcnews.go.com/US/meet-youth-heart-standing-rock-protests-dakota-access/story?id=45719115.
18. Elbein, "The Youth Group That Launched a Movement at Standing Rock."
19. Coral Davenport, "The Keystone XL Pipeline Project Has Been Terminated," *New York Times*, June 9, 2021.
20. Acee Agoyo, "Fate of Dakota Access Pipeline Lies in Biden's Hands," Indianz.com, February 22, 2022.

CHAPTER 6

1. Matthew Taylor, Jonathan Watts, and John Bartlett, "Climate Crisis: 6 Million People Join Latest Wave of Protest," *The Guardian*, US Edition, September 27, 2019, https://www.theguardian.com/environment/2019/sep/27/climate-crisis-6-million-people-join-latest-wave-of-worldwide-protests.

CHAPTER 7

1. Nisha Burton, "A Hurricane with Fire," accessed December 27, 2022, https://nishaburton.com/a-hurricane-with-fire/.
2. Andrea Stanley, "How Extreme Weather Has Created a Disaster for School Infrastructure," *Washington Post*, April 13, 2022, https://www.washingtonpost.com/magazine/2022/04/13/climate-school-migration/.
3. "Legacy Quilt of African American Food Heroes," Museum of Food and Drink (MoFAD), Brooklyn, New York, https://www.mofad.org/the-legacy-quilt.
4. Bill Nye, *Climate Change 101 with Bill Nye*, National Geographic, 2015, https://www.youtube.com/watch?v=EtW2rrLHs08.
5. Adrian Nicole LeBlanc, Photos by Brenda Ann Kenneally, "America at Hunger's Edge," *New York Times*, September 4, 2022, https://www.nytimes.com/interactive/2020/09/02/magazine/food-insecurity-hunger-us.html; and Adrian Nicole LeBlanc, "How Hunger Persists in a Rich Society Like America," *New York Times*, September 2, 2022, https://www.nytimes.com/2020/09/02/magazine/food-security-united-states.html.
6. Nina Sevilla, "Food Apartheid: Racialized Access to Healthy Affordable Food," National Resources Defense Council, April 2, 2021, https://www.nrdc.org/experts/nina-sevilla/food-apartheid-racialized-access-healthy-affordable-food.

CHAPTER 8

1. Mary Oliver, "The Summer Day," *Devotions: The Selected Poems of Mary Oliver* (New York: Penguin, 2017), 316. Reprinted by the permission of The Charlotte Sheedy Literary Agency as agent for the author. Copyright © Mary Oliver 1990 with permission of Bill Reichblum.

2. Maya Riser-Kositsky, "Education Statistics: Facts About American Schools," *Ed Week*, January 3, 2019, https://www.edweek.org/leadership/education-statistics-facts-about-american-schools/2019/01.
3. Leo Casey, *The Teacher Insurgency: A Strategic and Organizing Perspective* (Cambridge, MA: Harvard Education Press, 2020), 19–28.
4. Casey, *The Teacher Insurgency*, 19–28.
5. Casey, *The Teacher Insurgency*, 2–6.
6. Casey, *The Teacher Insurgency*, 124–26.
7. Casey, *The Teacher Insurgency*, 49–65.
8. Casey, *The Teacher Insurgency*, 109–26.
9. Casey, *The Teacher Insurgency*, 129–41.
10. Casey, *The Teacher Insurgency*, 143–51.
11. Mark Engler and Paul Engler, "Interview with Rebecca Tarlau: How Movements Can Maintain Their Radical Vision While Winning Practical Reforms," *Waging Nonviolence*, April 12, 2022, https://wagingnonviolence.org/2022/04.
12. Rafael Forsetto, "Brazil's Landless Workers Persist Through Agroecology," *Civil Eats*, September 30, 2020, https://civileats.com/2020/09/30/brazils-landless-workers-persist-through-agroecology/.
13. Rebecca Tarlau, *Occupying Schools, Occupying Land: How the Landless Workers Movement Transformed Brazilian Education* (Oxford: Oxford University Press, 2019), 7–13.
14. Gholdy Muhammad, "Introduction," in *Cultivating Genius: An Equity Framework for Culturally and Historically Responsive Literacy* (New York: Scholastic, 2020), 8–18.
15. Bryan Stevenson, *Just Mercy: A Story of Justice and Redemption* (New York: Spiegel and Grau, 2004).
16. Parker J. Palmer, *A Hidden Wholeness: The Journey Toward the Undivided Life* (San Francisco, CA: Jossey-Bass, 2004).

ACKNOWLEDGMENTS

Writing *Teach For Climate Justice* has been an adventure. One of the best things about adventures is the people who join in to become part of the story. I welcome the opportunity to thank them here.

First and foremost are the twenty-five educators and student activists whose work is featured in the book. They are school leaders Jan Zuckerman, Roberta Davenport, and Shawna Schleif; and they are teachers Bayard Faithfull, Beth Mowry, Cheryl Grau, Cynthia (Cindy) Vitale, Deanna D'Onofrio, Donnie Rotkin, Erick Espin, Genesis Abreu, Jared Fox, Jasmine Locke, Jessica Sudy, Lesley Younge, Liat Olenick, Megan Wellford, Sarah Outterson-Murphy, Sophie Schwadron, Ursula Wolfe-Rocca, William Dych, and Xochitl Bentley. Thank you for exemplifying the best in climate justice education; for nurturing understanding, agency, and hope in your students; and for taking the time to share your experiences, insights, and wisdom with me.

Thank you, Artemisio (Arte) Romero y Carver, Olivia Wohlgemuth, Peter Sallinger, and Sara Poon, for sharing your activist adventures and reflecting on the ways schools supported or failed to support your work. Your experiences and insights have much to offer educators interested in nurturing young fighters for climate justice. I am honored to include you and your work in the book.

Three Morningside Center staff developers are also featured in the book. Shout-outs to Daniel Coles and Marieke van Woerkom for demonstrating the power of social and emotional learning (SEL) and restorative practices; and to the late Emma Gonzalez for showing how to develop young student leaders through peer mediation and peace-helper programs and diversity panels.

I owe a special debt of gratitude to my editors at Harvard Education Press. In the book's introduction, I explain how my decision to write the book grew out of conversations with Nancy Walser, then acquisitions editor at the press. Through more than a year of back and forth, she helped me shape the book and win a contract. When Nancy retired, Jayne Fargnoli became my editor. We worked together for about six months until Shannon Davis came on board. As she turned my project over to Shannon, Jayne gave me a piece of parting advice: "Do not wander!" "Right on!" I thought. I knew wandering would be a temptation because the topic was so huge. However, I also recalled a line from J. R. R. Tolkien's *Lord of the Rings*: "Not all who wander are lost." I hope I struck a good balance between wandering and staying focused. I'm sure the process was frustrating for Shannon, who remained patient and supportive throughout, even as I missed every deadline we set for chapter after chapter. Although I believe this flexibility was essential for my writing process, I'm grateful that at a certain point Shannon, Jayne, and the board of the press finally gave me a hard deadline. Otherwise, I might still be working on the book.

Laura McClure, my dear friend, longtime colleague, and director of communications for Morningside Center, volunteered to serve as my editorial consultant. Laura reviewed early drafts of all the chapters (and often later drafts as well) and shared her thoughts and suggestions. Making adjustments as necessary, I could then go forward knowing I was on the right track. Thanks so much, Laura!

I deeply appreciate the small group of donors whose contributions enabled me to hire other assistance I needed. They are Carol Beebe and her late husband Walter Beebe, my dear friend Fritz Kleinhans,

Matt Damon, the David and Barbara B. Hirschhorn Foundation, and the Puffin Foundation.

The funds enabled me to hire a research assistant and a copyeditor and to engage a service to transcribe some forty hour-long recorded interviews. Thank you so much! Thanks also to my longtime friends Gary Ferdman and Linda Lantieri, who provided invaluable advice and leads.

Thanks to Morningside Center and Cassie Schwerner, my successor as executive director, for agreeing to be fiscal sponsor for my project. Thank you, Katrena Denard and Cecilia Wu, for keeping track of the funds and paying the invoices.

Isabel Avina served as my research assistant throughout the process of writing the book. Like me, they are strongly committed to radical, transformative climate justice education. Drawing on their extensive knowledge of the field, Isabel introduced me to people, organizations, and ideas I otherwise would not have found. They identified and interviewed the youth climate activists profiled in the book and connected me with several educators whose stories significantly shaped the book. Isabel introduced me to Cooperative Climate Futures, whose research on "The Hub" sharpened my critiques of false solutions for the climate crisis and deepened my thinking about the best ways to achieve a just and sustainable future. Isabel greatly strengthened the "Resources for Educators" section in the appendix. They shared ideas and feedback throughout that enriched my vision for climate justice education. These are huge contributions. Thank you so much, Isabel!

Karen Backstein copyedited all the chapters, eliminating grammatical errors, tightening sentences and paragraphs, and raising cogent questions about content as well. Thank you, Karen. It was a pleasure to work with you.

Kim Armstrong provided expert research and editorial assistance in preparing the "Resources for Educators." Thank you, Kim. A pleasure to work with you, too!

New York City Transcriptions provided accurate and timely transcriptions of the recordings of my interviews. Thank you, Etta Barmann, for coordinating these services. I was so happy to work with people rather than a robot!

Meena Srinivasan and Linda Lantieri of Transformative Educational Leadership (TEL) invited me to be keynote speaker at TEL's annual conference at the Omega Institute in 2021. The topic: "Teach for Climate Justice." What an honor and an opportunity! I enjoyed it, and the experience moved my work forward. Thank you, Meena and Linda!

Mimi Bluestone invited me to moderate a panel on "Parenting in a Time of Climate Crisis," attended by eighty people at Brooklyn's Central Library. Later she invited me and my colleague Marieke van Woerkom to conduct a Zoom workshop for activists with 350.org on "Active Hope: Emotional Resilience in the Face of Climate Crisis," also at Brooklyn's Central Library. Both presentations were well-received and useful in developing my thinking for the book. Thank you, Mimi!

If I gave out lifetime achievement awards, my first two would be to Bill Bigelow, curriculum editor for Rethinking Schools and codirector of the Zinn Education Project and Deborah Menkart, executive director of Teaching for Change and codirector of the Zinn Education Project. Thank you, Bill and Deborah, for all the groundbreaking work you have done throughout your careers and for advising me on *Teach for Climate Justice* and connecting me with two of the educators featured in the book.

Emily Fano works as northeast staff person for the National Wildlife Federation. One of her projects is to coordinate the Climate and Resilience Education Task Force (CRETF), which brings together climate educators and students throughout New York City and beyond to share resources, advocate for climate justice education, and update each other on latest developments. CRETF provided a great way for me to meet people (including Isabel) and follow what's happening in my hometown. Emily, thank you for establishing the task force and working so assiduously to lead it.

I'm grateful to the authors of the books on climate justice that I have found most useful. I know firsthand how challenging it is to write a book, and I appreciate the hard work of these writers and editors and the knowledge, insight, and inspiration they have given me. Thank you, Ayana Elizabeth Johnson and Katharine K. Wilkinson, Bill Bigelow and Tim Swinehart, Bill McKibben, Chris Johnstone and Joanna Macy, David Attenborough, Leo Casey, Mark and Paul Engler, Naomi Klein, Paul Hawken, Rebecca Tarlau, and Robin Wall Kimmerer!

I have three listening partners whom I meet with regularly to share equal time, twenty-five to forty-five minutes each. No discussion, no fixing; just listening actively and welcoming feelings. Thank you, Dorothy Stoneman, John Bell, and Mike Bucci! You help me laugh and cry when I need to.

Finally, I thank my oak-tree partner of more than forty years. Maxine Phillips. You are the love of my life and my anchor. You fill our home with warmth, generosity, and love. Thank you for applying your superb skills as an editor to proofing and editing the final manuscript of this book. Thank you for your patience as I have wrestled with this project for what must have felt like forever. An *extra big hug* for you!

ABOUT THE AUTHOR

Tom Roderick is an educator, activist, and writer based in New York City. For thirty-six years Tom Roderick served as founding executive director of Morningside Center for Teaching Social Responsibility, a national leader in the field of social and emotional learning (SEL) and a leading provider of SEL services in the New York City public schools. During his tenure, Tom founded an array of top-quality SEL programs, including the Resolving Conflict Creatively Program (RCCP), with Linda Lantieri, and The 4Rs (Reading, Writing, Respect, and Resolution), with his wife Maxine Phillips. Major scientific studies of The 4Rs and the RCCP found that these programs foster children's social and emotional development and academic progress and improve the climate for learning. Tom has a bachelor's degree in history from Yale University and a master's degree and honorary doctorate from Bank Street College of Education. He is the author of *A School of Our Own: Parents, Power, and Community at the East Harlem Block Schools* (Teachers College Press, 2001). In May 2018, the Collaborative for Academic, Social, and Emotional Learning (CASEL) awarded Tom its Mary Utne O'Brien Award for Excellence in Expanding Evidence-Based Practice of Social and Emotional Learning. Since retiring from Morningside Center on January 1, 2019, Tom has been at work on *Teach for Climate Justice: A Vision for Transforming Education*, scheduled for publication in spring 2023.

INDEX